JUnit in Action

JUnit in Action

VINCENT MASSOL

with TED HUSTED

MANNING

Greenwich
(74° w. long.)

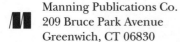

Manning Publications Co.   Copyeditor: Tiffany Taylor
209 Bruce Park Avenue   Typesetter: Tony Roberts
Greenwich, CT 06830   Cover designer: Leslie Haimes

ISBN 1-930110-99-5

Printed in the United States of America

   4 5 6 7 8 9 10 – VHG – 06

contents

preface xiii
acknowledgments xv
about this book xvii
about the authors xxi
about the title xxii
about the cover illustration xxiii

PART 1   JUNIT DISTILLED 1

1   *JUnit jumpstart*   *3*

1.1   Proving it works   *4*

1.2   Starting from scratch   *6*

1.3   Understanding unit testing frameworks   *10*

1.4   Setting up JUnit   *11*

1.5   Testing with JUnit   *13*

1.6   Summary   *16*

2   *Exploring JUnit*   *17*

2.1   Exploring core JUnit   *18*

2.2 Launching tests with test runners *20*

    Selecting a test runner 20 ▪ *Defining your own test runner 21*

2.3 Composing tests with TestSuite *21*

    Running the automatic suite 22 ▪ *Rolling your own test suite 23*

2.4 Collecting parameters with TestResult *25*

2.5 Observing results with TestListener *27*

2.6 Working with TestCase *28*

    Managing resources with a fixture 29
    Creating unit test methods 30

2.7 Stepping through TestCalculator *32*

    Creating a TestSuite 33 ▪ *Creating a TestResult 35*
    Executing the test methods 36
    Reviewing the full JUnit life cycle 37

2.8 Summary *38*

3 *Sampling JUnit 39*

3.1 Introducing the controller component *40*

    Designing the interfaces 41 ▪ *Implementing the base classes 43*

3.2 Let's test it! *45*

    Testing the DefaultController 46 ▪ *Adding a handler 46*
    Processing a request 50 ▪ *Improving testProcessRequest 54*

3.3 Testing exception-handling *55*

    Simulating exceptional conditions 56
    Testing for exceptions 60

3.4 Setting up a project for testing *62*

3.5 Summary *64*

4 *Examining software tests 65*

4.1 The need for unit tests *66*

    Allowing greater test coverage 67 ▪ *Enabling teamwork 67*
    Preventing regression and limiting debugging 67 ▪ *Enabling*
    refactoring 68 ▪ *Improving implementation design 69*
    Serving as developer documentation 69 ▪ *Having fun 70*

4.2 Different kinds of tests *71*

    The four flavors of software tests 71
    The three flavors of unit tests 75

4.3   Determining how good tests are   77

Measuring test coverage   78 ▪ *Generating test coverage reports   79*
Testing interactions   81

4.4   Test-Driven Development   *81*

Tweaking the cycle   81 ▪ *The TDD two-step   83*

4.5   Testing in the development cycle   *84*

4.6   Summary   *87*

5   ***Automating JUnit   88***

5.1   A day in the life   *89*

5.2   Running tests from Ant   *90*

Ant, indispensable Ant   91 ▪ *Ant targets, projects, properties, and
tasks   92* ▪ *The javac task   94* ▪ *The JUnit task   96* ▪ *Putting
Ant to the task   97* ▪ *Pretty printing with JUnitReport   98*
Automatically finding the tests to run   100

5.3   Running tests from Maven   *102*

Maven the goal-seeker   102 ▪ *Configuring Maven for a
project   104* ▪ *Executing JUnit tests with Maven   109*
Handling dependent jars with Maven   109

5.4   Running tests from Eclipse   *112*

Creating an Eclipse project   112
Running JUnit tests in Eclipse   114

5.5   Summary   *116*

PART 2   TESTING STRATEGIES 117

6   ***Coarse-grained testing with stubs   119***

6.1   Introducing stubs   *120*

6.2   Practicing on an HTTP connection sample   *121*

Choosing a stubbing solution   124
Using Jetty as an embedded server   125

6.3   Stubbing the web server's resources   *126*

Setting up the first stub test   126 ▪ *Testing for failure
conditions   132* ▪ *Reviewing the first stub test   133*

6.4 Stubbing the connection   *134*

Producing a custom URL protocol handler   134 ▪ *Creating a JDK HttpURLConnection stub   136* ▪ *Running the test   137*

6.5 Summary   *138*

7 Testing in isolation with mock objects   *139*

7.1 Introducing mock objects   *140*

7.2 Mock tasting: a simple example   *141*

7.3 Using mock objects as a refactoring technique   *146*

Easy refactoring   147 ▪ *Allowing more flexible code   148*

7.4 Practicing on an HTTP connection sample   *150*

Defining the mock object   150 ▪ *Testing a sample method   151*
Try #1: easy method refactoring technique   152
Try #2: refactoring by using a class factory   155

7.5 Using mocks as Trojan horses   *159*

7.6 Deciding when to use mock objects   *163*

7.7 Summary   *164*

8 In-container testing with Cactus   *165*

8.1 The problem with unit-testing components   *166*

8.2 Testing components using mock objects   *167*

Testing the servlet sample using EasyMock   168
Pros and cons of using mock objects to test components   170

8.3 What are integration unit tests?   *172*

8.4 Introducing Cactus   *173*

8.5 Testing components using Cactus   *173*

Running Cactus tests   174 ▪ *Executing the tests using Cactus/Jetty integration   174* ▪ *Drawbacks of in-container testing   178*

8.6 How Cactus works   *179*

Executing client-side and server-side steps   180
Stepping through a test   180

8.7 Summary   *182*

PART 3   TESTING COMPONENTS.................................. 185

9   *Unit-testing servlets and filters*   187

9.1   Presenting the Administration application   *188*

9.2   Writing servlet tests with Cactus   *189*

Designing the first test   190 ▪ *Using Maven to run Cactus tests   192* ▪ *Finishing the Cactus servlet tests   198*

9.3   Testing servlets with mock objects   *204*

Writing a test using DynaMocks and DynaBeans   205 Finishing the DynaMock tests   206

9.4   Writing filter tests with Cactus   *208*

Testing the filter with a SELECT query   209 Testing the filter for other query types   210 Running the Cactus filter tests with Maven   212

9.5   When to use Cactus, and when to use mock objects   *213*

9.6   Summary   *214*

10   *Unit-testing JSPs and taglibs*   215

10.1   Revisiting the Administration application   *216*

10.2   What is JSP unit testing?   *217*

10.3   Unit-testing a JSP in isolation with Cactus   *217*

Executing a JSP with SQL results data   218 ▪ *Writing the Cactus test   219* ▪ *Executing Cactus JSP tests with Maven   222*

10.4   Unit-testing taglibs with Cactus   *224*

Defining a custom tag   225 ▪ *Testing the custom tag   227 Unit-testing tags with a body   228 Unit-testing collaboration tags   233*

10.5   Unit-testing taglibs with mock objects   *233*

Introducing MockMaker and installing its Eclipse plugin   234 Using MockMaker to generate mocks from classes   234

10.6   When to use mock objects and when to use Cactus   *237*

10.7   Summary   *237*

11   *Unit-testing database applications*   239

11.1   Introduction to unit-testing databases   *240*

11.2   Testing business logic in isolation from the database   *242*

    Implementing a database access layer interface   243 ▪ Setting up a mock database interface layer   244
    Mocking the database interface layer   246

11.3   Testing persistence code in isolation
    from the database   *247*

    Testing the execute method   248 ▪ Using expectations to verify state   256

11.4   Writing database integration unit tests   *260*

    Filling the requirements for database integration tests   260
    Presetting database data   261

11.5   Running the Cactus test using Ant   *265*

    Reviewing the project structure   265 ▪ Introducing the Cactus/Ant integration module   266 ▪ Creating the Ant build file step by step   267 ▪ Executing the Cactus tests   274

11.6   Tuning for build performance   *275*

    Factoring out read-only data   275 ▪ Grouping tests in functional test suites   277 ▪ Using an in-memory database   278

11.7   Overall database unit-testing strategy   *278*

    Choosing an approach   278
    Applying continuous integration   279

11.8   Summary   *280*

12   *Unit-testing EJBs   281*

12.1   Defining a sample EJB application   *282*

12.2   Using a façade strategy   *283*

12.3   Unit-testing JNDI code using mock objects   *284*

12.4   Unit-testing session beans   *285*

    Using the factory method strategy   289
    Using the factory class strategy   293
    Using the mock JNDI implementation strategy   297

12.5   Using mock objects to test message-driven beans   *307*

12.6   Using mock objects to test entity beans   *310*

12.7   Choosing the right mock-objects strategy   *312*

12.8   Using integration unit tests   *313*

12.9 Using JUnit and remote calls *314*

Requirements for using JUnit directly 315 ▪ *Packaging the Petstore application in an ear file 315* ▪ *Performing automatic deployment and execution of tests 319* ▪ *Writing a remote JUnit test for PetstoreEJB 325* ▪ *Fixing JNDI names 326 Running the tests 327*

12.10 Using Cactus *328*

Writing an EJB unit test with Cactus 328 ▪ *Project directory structure 329* ▪ *Packaging the Cactus tests 329 Executing the Cactus tests 333*

12.11 Summary *334*

A The source code *335*

A.1 Getting the source code *336*

A.2 Source code overview *336*

A.3 External libraries *338*

A.4 Jar versions *339*

A.5 Directory structure conventions *340*

B Eclipse quick start *341*

B.1 Installing Eclipse *342*

B.2 Setting up Eclipse projects from the sources *342*

B.3 Running JUnit tests from Eclipse *343*

B.4 Running Ant scripts from Eclipse *344*

B.5 Running Cactus tests from Eclipse *345*

references 346
index 351

preface

To date tests are still the best solution mankind has found to deliver working software. This book is the sum of four years of research and practice in the testing field. The practice comes from my IT consulting background, first at Octo Technology and then at Pivolis; the research comes from my involvement with open source development at night and on weekends.

Since my early programming days in 1982, I've been interested in writing tools to help developers write better code and develop more quickly. This interest has led me into domains such as software mentoring and quality improvement. These days, I'm setting up continuous-build platforms and working on development best practices, both of which require strong suites of tests. The closer these tests are to the coding activity, the faster you get feedback on your code—hence my interest in unit testing, which is so close to coding that it's now as much a part of development as the code that's being written.

This background led to my involvement in open source projects related to software quality:

- Cactus for unit-testing J2EE components (http://jakarta.apache.org/cactus/)
- Mock objects for unit-testing any code (http://www.mockobjects.com/)
- Gump for continuous builds (http://jakarta.apache.org/gump/)
- Maven for builds and continuous builds (http://maven.apache.org/)

- The Pattern Testing proof of concept for using Aspect-Oriented Programming (AOP) to check architecture and design rules (http://patterntesting.sf.net/).[1]

JUnit in Action is the logical conclusion to this involvement.

Nobody wants to write sloppy code. We all want to write code that works—code that we can be proud of. But we're often distracted from our good intentions. How often have you heard this: "We wanted to write tests, but we were under pressure and didn't have enough time to do it"; or, "We started writing unit tests, but after two weeks our momentum dropped, and over time we stopped writing them."

This book will give you the tools and techniques you need to happily write quality code. It demonstrates in a hands-on fashion how to use the tools in an effective way, avoiding common pitfalls. It will empower you to write code that works. It will help you introduce unit testing in your day-to-day development activity and develop a rhythm for writing robust code.

Most of all, this book will show you how to control the entropy of your software instead of being controlled by it. I'm reminded of some verses from the Latin writer Lucretius, who, in 94–55 BC wrote in his *On the Nature of Things* (I'll spare you the original Latin text):

> Lovely it is, when the winds are churning up the waves on the great sea, to gaze out from the land on the great efforts of someone else; not because it's an enjoyable pleasure that somebody is in difficulties, but because it's lovely to realize what troubles you are yourself spared.

This is exactly the feeling you'll experience when you know you're armed with a good suite of tests. You'll see others struggling, and you'll be thankful that you have tests to prevent anyone (including yourself) from wreaking havoc in your application.

Vincent Massol
Richeville (close to Paris), France

---

[1] As much as I wanted to, I haven't included a chapter on unit-testing code using an AOP framework. The existing AOP frameworks are still young, and writing unit tests with them leads to verbose code. My prediction is that specialized AOP/unit-testing frameworks will appear in the very near future, and I'll certainly cover them in a second edition. See the following entry in my blog about unit-testing an EJB with JUnit and AspectJ: http://blogs.codehaus.org/people/vmassol/archives/000138.html.

acknowledgments

This book was one year in the making. I am eternally grateful to my wife, Marie-Albane, and my kids, Pierre-Olivier and Jean. During that year, they accepted that I spent at least half of my free time writing the book instead of being with them. I had to promise that I won't write another book... for a while....

Thank you to Ted Husted, who stepped up to the plate and helped make the first part of the book more readable by improving on my English, reshuffling the chapters, and adding some parsley here and there where I had made shortcuts.

JUnit in Action would not exist without Kent Beck and Erich Gamma, the authors of JUnit. I thank them for their inspiration; and more specially I thank Erich, who agreed to read the manuscript while under pressure to deliver Eclipse 2.1 and who came up with a nice quote for the book.

Again, the book would not be what it is without Tim Mackinnon and Steve Freeman, the original creators of the mock objects unit-testing strategy, which is the subject of a big part of this book. I thank them for introducing me to mock objects while drinking beer (it was cranberry juice for me!) at the London Extreme Tuesday Club.

The quality of this book would not be the same without the reviewers. Many thanks to Mats Henricson, Bob McWhirter, Erik Hatcher, William Brogden, Brendan Humphreys, Robin Goldsmith, Scott Stirling, Shane Mingins, and Dorothy Graham. I'd like to express special thanks to Ilja Preuß, Kim Topley, Roger D. Cornejo, and J. B. Rainsberger, who gave extremely thorough review comments and provided excellent suggestions.

With this first book, I have discovered the world of publishing. I have been extremely impressed by Manning's professionalism and obsession with perfection. Whenever I thought the book was done and I could relax, it had to go through another phase of verifications of some sort! Many thanks to publisher Marjan Bace for his continuing trust even though I kept pushing the delivery date. Developmental editor Marilyn Smith was an example of responsiveness, giving me back corrected chapters and suggestions just a few hours after I submitted chapters. Copy editor Tiffany Taylor fixed an incredible number of errors (I could almost not recognize my chapters after Tiffany stormed through them). Tony Roberts had the hard task of typesetting the book and supporting my numerous requests; thanks, Tony. Technical proofreader Robert McGovern did an excellent job of catching all my technical mistakes.

Last but not least, a big thank-you to Francois Hisquin, CEO of Octo Technology and Pivolis, the two companies I have been working for while writing *JUnit in Action*, for letting me write some parts of the book during the day!

about this book

JUnit in Action is an example-driven, how-to book on unit-testing Java applications, including J2EE applications, using the JUnit framework and its extensions. This book is intended for readers who are software architects, developers, members of testing teams, development managers, extreme programmers, or anyone practicing any agile methodology.

JUnit in Action is about solving tough real-world problems such as unit-testing legacy applications, writing real tests for real objects, employing test metrics, automating tests, testing in isolation, and more.

Special features

Several special features appear throughout the book.

Best practices

The JUnit community has already adopted several best practices. When these are introduced in the book, a callout box summarizes the best practice.

Design patterns in action

The JUnit framework puts several well-known design patterns to work. When we first discuss a component that makes good use of a design pattern, a callout box defines the pattern and points out its use in the JUnit framework.

Software directory

Throughout the book, we cover how to use extensions and tools with JUnit. For your convenience, references to all of these software packages have been collected in a directory in the references section at the end of this book. A bibliography of other books we mention is also provided in the references section.

Roadmap

The book is divided into three parts. Part 1 is "JUnit distilled." Here, we introduce you to unit testing in general and JUnit in particular. Part 2, "Testing strategies," investigates different ways of testing the complex objects found in professional applications. Part 3, "Testing components," explores strategies for testing common subsystems like servlets, filters, JavaServer Pages, databases, and even EJBs.

Part 1: JUnit distilled

Chapter 1 walks through creating a test for a simple object. We introduce the benefits, philosophy, and technology of unit testing along the way. As the tests grow more sophisticated, we present JUnit as the solution for creating better tests.

Chapter 2 delves deeper into the JUnit classes, life cycle, and architecture. We take a closer look at the core classes and the overall JUnit life cycle. To put everything into context, we look at several example tests, like those you would write for your own classes.

Chapter 3 presents a sophisticated test case to show how JUnit works with larger components. The subject of the case study is a component found in many applications: a controller. We introduce the case-study code, identify what code to test, and then show how to test it. Once we know that the code works as expected, we create tests for exceptional conditions, to be sure the code behaves well even when things go wrong.

Chapter 4 looks at the various types of software tests, the role they play in an application's life cycle, how to design for testability, and how to practice test-first development.

Chapter 5 explores the various ways you can integrate JUnit into your development environment. We look at automating JUnit with Ant, Maven, and Eclipse.

Part 2: Testing strategies

Chapter 6 describes how to perform unit tests using stubs. It introduces a sample application that connects to a web server and demonstrates how to unit-test the method calling the remote URL using a stub technique.

Chapter 7 demonstrates a technique called mock objects that lets you unit test code in isolation from the surrounding domain objects. This chapter carries on with the sample application (opening an HTTP connection to a web server); it shows how to write unit tests for the application and highlights the differences between stubs and mock objects.

Chapter 8 demonstrates another technique which is useful for unit-testing J2EE components: in-container testing. This chapter covers how to use Cactus to run unit tests from within the container. In addition, we explain the pros and cons of using an in-container approach versus a mock-objects approach, and when to use each.

Part 3: Testing components

Chapter 9 shows how to unit-test servlets and filters using both the mock-objects approach and the in-container approach. It highlights how they complement each other and gives strategies on when to use them.

Chapter 10 carries us into the world of unit-testing JSPs and taglibs. It shows how to use the mock-objects and in-container strategies.

Chapter 11 touches on a difficult but crucial subject: unit-testing applications that call databases using JDBC. It also demonstrates how to unit-test database code in isolation from the database.

Chapter 12 investigates how to unit-test all kind of EJBs using mock objects, pure JUnit test cases, and Cactus.

Code

The source code for the examples in this book has been donated to the Apache Software Foundation. It is available on SourceForge (http://sourceforge.net/projects/junitbook/). A link to the source code is also provided from the book's web page at http://www.manning.com/massol. Check appendix A for details on how the source code is organized and for software version requirements.

The Java code listings that we present have the Java keywords shown in bold to make the code more readable. In addition, when we highlight changes in a new listing, the changes are shown in bold font to draw attention to them. In that case, the Java keywords are displayed in standard, non-bold code font. Often, numbers and annotations appear in the code. These numbers refer to the discussion of that portion of the code directly following the listing.

In the text, a monotype font is used to denote code (JSP, Java, and HTML) as well as Java methods, JSP tag names, and most other source code identifiers:

- A reference to a method in the text may not include the signature because there may be more than one form of the method call.

- A reference to an XML element or JSP tag in the text usually does not include the braces or the attributes.

References

Bibliographic references are indicated in footnotes or in the body of text. Full publication details and/or URLs are provided in the references section at the end of this book. Web site URLs are given in the text of the book and cross-referenced in the index.

Author online

Purchase of *JUnit in Action* includes free access to a private web forum run by Manning Publications where you can make comments about the book, ask technical questions, and receive help from the author and from other users. To access the forum and subscribe to it, point your web browser to http://www.manning.com/massol. This page provides information on how to get on the forum once you are registered, what kind of help is available, and the rules of conduct on the forum.

Manning's commitment to our readers is to provide a venue where a meaningful dialog between individual readers and between readers and the author can take place. It is not a commitment to any specific amount of participation on the part of the author, whose contribution to the AO remains voluntary (and unpaid). We suggest you try asking the author some challenging questions lest his interest stray!

The Author Online forum and the archives of previous discussions will be accessible from the publisher's web site as long as the book is in print.

about the authors

Vincent Massol is the creator of the Jakarta Cactus framework. He is also an active member of the Maven, Gump, and MockObjects development teams. After having spent four years as a technical architect on several major projects (mostly J2EE), Vincent is now the co-founder and CTO of Pivolis, a company specialized in applying agile methodologies to offshore software development. A consultant and lecturer during the day and open source developer at night, Vincent currently lives in Paris, France. He can be contacted through his blog at http://blogs.code-haus.org/people/vmassol/.

Ted Husted is an active member of the Struts development team, manager of the JGuru Struts Forum, and the lead author of *Struts in Action*.[2] As a consultant, lecturer, and trainer, Ted has worked with Java development teams throughout the United States. Ted's latest development project used test-driven development throughout and is available as open source (http://sourceforge.net/projects/wqdata/). Ted lives in Fairport, NY, with his wife, two children, four computers, and an aging cat.

---

[2] Ted Husted, Cedric Dumoulin, George Franciscus, and David Winterfeldt, *Struts in Action* (Greenwich, CT: Manning, 2002).

about the title

Manning's *in Action* books combine an overview with how-to examples to encourage learning *and* remembering. Cognitive science tells us that we remember best through discovery and exploration. At Manning, we think of exploration as "playing." Every time computer scientists build a new application, we believe they play with new concepts and new techniques—to see if they can make the next program better than the one before. An essential element of an *in Action* book is that it is example-driven. *In Action* books encourage the reader to play with new code and explore new ideas. At Manning, we are convinced that permanent learning comes through exploring, playing, and most importantly, *sharing* what we have discovered with others. People learn best *in action*.

There is another, more mundane, reason for the title of this book: Our readers are busy. They use books to do a job or solve a problem. They need books that allow them to jump in and jump out easily—books that will help them *in action*. The books in this series are designed for these "impatient" readers. You can start reading an *in Action* book at any point, to learn just what you need just when you need it.

about the cover illustration

The figure on the cover of *JUnit in Action* is a "Burco de Alpeo," taken from a Spanish compendium of regional dress customs first published in Madrid in 1799. The book's title page states:

> *Coleccion general de los Trages que usan actualmente todas las Nacionas del Mundo desubierto, dibujados y grabados con la mayor exactitud por R.M.V.A.R. Obra muy util y en special para los que tienen la del viajero universal*

which we translate, as literally as possible, thus:

> *General collection of costumes currently used in the nations of the known world, designed and printed with great exactitude by R.M.V.A.R. This work is very useful especially for those who hold themselves to be universal travelers*

Although nothing is known of the designers, engravers, and workers who colored this illustration by hand, the "exactitude" of their execution is evident in this drawing, which is just one of many in this colorful collection. Their diversity speaks vividly of the uniqueness and individuality of the world's towns and regions just 200 years ago. This was a time when the dress codes of two regions separated by a few dozen miles identified people uniquely as belonging to one or the other. The collection brings to life a sense of isolation and distance of that period‹and of every other historic period except our own hyperkinetic present. Dress codes have changed since then and the diversity by region, so rich at the time, has faded away. It is now often hard to tell the inhabitant of one continent from another. Perhaps, trying to view it optimistically, we have traded a cultural and visual diversity for a more varied personal life. Or a more varied and interesting intellectual and technical life.

We at Manning celebrate the inventiveness, the initiative, and, yes, the fun of the computer business with book covers based on the rich diversity of regional life of two centuries ago, brought back to life by the pictures from this collection.

At the time of publication, we were unable to decipher the meaning of the caption "Burco de Alpeo" but will keep you posted on our progress on the *JUnit in Action* web page. The first reader to come up with the correct translation will be thanked with a free copy of another Manning book of his or her choice. Please make postings to the Author Online forum at www.manning.com/massol.

Part 1

JUnit distilled

In part 1, you'll become test-infected! Through a simple example, chapter 1 will teach you what the JUnit framework is and what problems it solves. Chapter 2 will take you on a discovery tour of the core JUnit classes and how to best use them. In chapter 3, you'll practice your new JUnit knowledge on a real-world example. You'll also learn how to set up a JUnit project and how to execute the unit tests. Chapter 4 steps back and explains why unit test are important and how they fit in the global testing ecosystem. It also presents the Test-Driven Development methodology and provides guidance on measuring your test coverage. Chapter 5 demonstrates how to automate unit testing using three popular tools: Eclipse, Ant, and Maven.

At the end of part 1, you'll have a good general knowledge of JUnit, how to write unit tests, and how to run them easily. You'll be ready to start learning about the different strategies required to unit-test full-fledged applications: stubs, mock objects, and in-container testing.

JUnit jumpstart 1

This chapter covers

- Writing simple tests by hand
- Installing JUnit and running tests
- Writing better tests with JUnit

Never in the field of software development was so much owed by so many to so few lines of code.

　　—Martin Fowler

All code is tested.

During development, the first thing we do is run our own programmer's "acceptance test." We code, compile, and run. And when we run, we test. The "test" may just be clicking a button to see if it brings up the expected menu. But, still, every day, we code, we compile, we run…and *we test*.

When we test, we often find issues—especially on the first run. So we code, compile, run, and test again.

Most of us will quickly develop a pattern for our informal tests: We add a record, view a record, edit a record, and delete a record. Running a little test suite like this by hand is easy enough to do; so we do it. *Over and over again.*

Some programmers like doing this type of repetitive testing. It can be a pleasant break from deep thought and hard coding. And when our little click-through tests finally succeed, there's a real feeling of accomplishment: *Eureka! I found it!*

Other programmers dislike this type of repetitive work. Rather than run the test by hand, they prefer to create a small program that runs the test automatically. Play-testing code is one thing; running automated tests is another.

If you are a "play-test" developer, this book is meant for you. We will show you how creating automated tests can be easy, effective, and even fun!

If you are already "test-infected," this book is also meant for you! We cover the basics in part 1, and then move on to the tough, real-life problems in parts 2 and 3.

1.1 *Proving it works*

Some developers feel that automated tests are an essential part of the development process: A component cannot be *proven* to work until it passes a comprehensive series of tests. In fact, two developers felt that this type of "unit testing" was so important that it deserved its own framework. In 1997, Erich Gamma and Kent Beck created a simple but effective unit testing *framework* for Java, called JUnit. The work followed the design of an earlier framework Kent Beck created for Smalltalk, called SUnit.

DEFINITION   *framework*—A framework is a semi-complete application.[1] A framework provides a reusable, common structure that can be shared between applications. Developers incorporate the framework into their own application and extend it to meet their specific needs. Frameworks differ from toolkits by providing a coherent structure, rather than a simple set of utility classes.

If you recognize those names, it's for good reason. Erich Gamma is well known as one of the "Gang of Four" who gave us the now classic *Design Patterns* book.[2] Kent Beck is equally well known for his groundbreaking work in the software discipline known as Extreme Programming (http://www.extremeprogramming.org).

JUnit (junit.org) is open source software, released under IBM's Common Public License Version 1.0 and hosted on SourceForge. The Common Public License is business-friendly: People can distribute JUnit with commercial products without a lot of red tape or restrictions.

JUnit quickly became the de facto standard framework for developing unit tests in Java. In fact, the underlying testing model, known as xUnit, is on its way to becoming the standard framework for *any* language. There are xUnit frameworks available for ASP, C++, C#, Eiffel, Delphi, Perl, PHP, Python, REBOL, Smalltalk, and Visual Basic—just to name a few!

Of course, the JUnit team did not invent software testing or even the unit test. Originally, the term *unit test* described a test that examined the behavior of a single *unit of work*.

Over time, usage of the term *unit test* broadened. For example, IEEE has defined unit testing as "Testing of individual hardware or software units *or groups of related units*" (emphasis added).[3]

In this book, we use the term *unit test* in the narrower sense of a test that examines a single unit in isolation from other units. We focus on the type of small, incremental test that programmers apply to their own code. Sometimes these are called *programmer tests* to differentiate them from quality assurance tests or customer tests (http://c2.com/cgi/wiki?ProgrammerTest).

---

[1] Ralph Johnson and Brian Foote, "Designing Reusable Classes," *Journal of Object-Oriented Programming* 1.5 (June/July 1988): 22–35; http://www.laputan.org/drc/drc.html.

[2] Erich Gamma et al., *Design Patterns* (Reading, MA: Addison-Wesley, 1995).

[3] *IEEE Standard Computer Dictionary: A Compilation of IEEE Standard Computer Glossaries* (New York: IEEE, 1990).

Here's a generic description of a typical unit test from our perspective: "Confirm that the method accepts the expected range of input, and that the method returns the expected value for each test input."

This description asks us to test the behavior of a method through its interface. If we give it value *x*, will it return value *y*? If we give it value *z* instead, will it throw the proper exception?

> **DEFINITION**   *unit test*—A unit test examines the behavior of a distinct *unit of work*. Within a Java application, the "distinct unit of work" is often (but not always) a single method. By contrast, *integration tests* and *acceptance tests* examine how various components interact. A *unit of work* is a task that is not directly dependent on the completion of any other task.

Unit tests often focus on testing whether a method is following the terms of its *API contract*. Like a written contract by people who agree to exchange certain goods or services under specific conditions, an API contract is viewed as a formal agreement made by the interface of a method. A method requires its callers to provide specific objects or values and will, in exchange, return certain objects or values. If the contract cannot be fulfilled, then the method throws an exception to signify that the contract cannot be upheld. If a method does not perform as expected, then we say that the method has broken its contract.

> **DEFINITION**   *API contract*—A view of an Application Programming Interface (API) as a formal agreement between the caller and the callee. Often the unit tests help define the API contract by demonstrating the expected behavior. The notion of an API contract stems from the practice of *Design by Contract*, popularized by the Eiffel programming language (http://archive.eiffel.com/doc/manuals/technology/contract).

In this chapter, we'll walk through creating a unit test for a simple class from scratch. We'll start by writing some tests manually, so you can see how we *used* to do things. Then, we will roll out JUnit to show you how the right tools can make life much simpler.

1.2 *Starting from scratch*

Let's say you have just written the Calculator class shown in listing 1.1.

Listing 1.1   The Calculator class

```java
public class Calculator
{
  public double add(double number1, double number2)
  {
    return number1 + number2;
  }
}
```

Although the documentation is not shown, the intended purpose of the Calcula-tor's add(double, double) method is to take two doubles and return the sum as a double. The compiler can tell you that it compiles, but you should also make sure it works at runtime. A ycore tenet of unit testing is: "Any program feature without an automated test simply doesn't exist."[4] The add method represents a core fea-ture of the calculator. You have some code that allegedly implements the feature. What's missing is an automated test that proves your implementation works.

> ### But isn't the add method "too simple to possibly break"?
>
> The current implementation of the add method is too simple to break. If add were a minor utility method, then you might not test it directly. In that case, if add did fail, then tests of the methods that used add would fail. The add method would be tested indirectly, but tested nonetheless.
>
> In the context of the calculator program, add is not just a method, it's a *program feature*. In order to have confidence in the program, most developers would expect there to be an automated test for the add feature, no matter how simple the implementation appears.
>
> In some cases, you can prove program features through automatic functional tests or automatic acceptance tests. For more about software tests in general, see chapter 4.

Yet testing anything at this point seems problematic. You don't even have a user interface with which to enter a pair of doubles. You could write a small command-line program that waited for you to type in two double values and then displayed the result. Of course, then you would also be testing your own ability to type a number and add the result ourselves. This is much more than you want to do. You just want to know if this "unit of work" will actually add two doubles and return the correct sum. You don't necessarily want to test whether programmers can type numbers!

---

[4] Kent Beck, *Extreme Programming Explained: Embrace Change* (Reading, MA: Addison-Wesley, 1999).

Meanwhile, if you are going to go to the effort of testing your work, you should also try to preserve that effort. It's good to know that the add(double,double) method worked when you wrote it. But what you really want to know is whether the method works when you ship the rest of the application.

As shown in figure 1.1, if we put these two requirements together, we come up with the idea of writing a simple test program for the method. The test program could pass known values to the method and see if the result matches our expectations.

Figure 1.1 Justifying JUnit: Putting the two testing requirements together gives an idea for a simple test program.

You could also run the program again later to be sure the method continues to work as the application grows.

So what's the simplest possible test program you could write? How about the simple TestCalculator program shown in listing 1.2?

Listing 1.2 A simple TestCalculator program

```java
public class TestCalculator
{
  public static void main(String[] args)
  {
    Calculator calculator = new Calculator();
    double result = calculator.add(10,50);
    if (result != 60)
    {
      System.out.println("Bad result: " + result);
    }
  }
}
```

The first TestCalculator is simple indeed! It creates an instance of Calculator, passes it two numbers, and checks the result. If the result does not meet your expectations, you print a message on standard output.

If you compile and run this program now, the test will quietly pass, and all will seem well. But what happens if you change the code so that it fails? You will have to carefully watch the screen for the error message. You may not have to supply the input, but you are still testing your own ability to monitor the program's output. You want to test the code, not yourself!

The conventional way to handle error conditions in Java is to throw an exception. Since failing the test is an error condition, let's try throwing an exception instead.

Meanwhile, you may also want to run tests for other Calculator methods that you haven't written yet, like subtract or multiply. Moving to a more modular design would make it easier to trap and handle exceptions and make it easier to extend the test program later. Listing 1.3 shows a slightly better TestCalculator program.

Listing 1.3 A (slightly) better TestCalculator program

```
public class TestCalculator
{
  private int nbErrors = 0;

  public void testAdd()
  {
    Calculator calculator = new Calculator();              ❶
    double result = calculator.add(10, 50);
    if (result != 60)
    {
      throw new RuntimeException("Bad result: " + result);
    }
  }

  public static void main(String[] args)
  {
    TestCalculator test = new TestCalculator();
    try
    {
      test.testAdd();                                       ❷
    }
    catch (Throwable e)
    {
      test.nbErrors++;
      e.printStackTrace();
    }

    if (test.nbErrors > 0)
    {
      throw new RuntimeException("There were " + test.nbErrors
        + " error(s)");
    }
  }
}
```

Working from listing 1.3, at ❶ you move the test into its own method. It's now easier to focus on what the test does. You can also add more methods with more unit tests later, without making the main block harder to maintain. At ❷, you change the main block to print a stack trace when an error occurs and then, if there are any errors, to throw a summary exception at the end.

1.3 *Understanding unit testing frameworks*

There are several best practices that unit testing frameworks should follow. These seemingly minor improvements in the TestCalculator program highlight three rules that (in our experience) all unit testing frameworks should observe:

- Each unit test must run independently of all other unit tests.
- Errors must be detected and reported test by test.
- It must be easy to define which unit tests will run.

The "slightly better" test program comes close to following these rules but still falls short. For example, in order for each unit test to be truly independent, each should run in a different classloader instance.

Adding a class is also only slightly better. You can now add new unit tests by adding a new method and then adding a corresponding try/catch block to main.

A definite step up, but still short of what you would want in a *real* unit test suite. The most obvious problem is that large try/catch blocks are known to be maintenance nightmares. You could easily leave a unit test out and never know it wasn't running!

It would be nice if you could just add new test methods and be done with it. But how would the program know which methods to run?

Well, you could have a simple registration procedure. A registration method would at least inventory which tests are running.

Another approach would be to use Java's *reflection* and *introspection* capabilities. A program could look at itself and decide to run whatever methods are named in a certain way—like those that begin with the letters *test*, for example.

Making it easy to add tests (the third rule in our earlier list) sounds like another good rule for a unit testing framework.

The support code to realize this rule (via registration or introspection) would not be trivial, but it would be worthwhile. There would be a lot of work up front, but that effort would pay off each time you added a new test.

Happily, the JUnit team has saved you the trouble. The JUnit framework already supports registering or introspecting methods. It also supports using a different *classloader* instance for each test, and reports all errors on a case-by-case basis.

Now that you have a better idea of why you need unit testing frameworks, let's set up JUnit and see it in action.

1.4 Setting up JUnit

JUnit comes in the form of a jar file (`junit.jar`). In order to use JUnit to write your application tests, you'll simply need to add the junit jar to your project's compilation classpath and to your execution classpath when you run the tests.

Let's now download the JUnit (JUnit 3.8.1 or newer[5]) distribution, which contains several test samples that you will run to get familiar with executing JUnit tests. Follow these steps:

1 Download the latest version of JUnit from junit.org, referred to in step 2 as `http://junit.zip`.

2 Unzip the `junit.zip` distribution file to a directory on your computer system (for example, `C:\` on Windows or `/opt/` on UNIX).

3 Underneath this directory, unzip will create a subdirectory for the JUnit distribution you downloaded (for example, `C:\junit3.8.1` on Windows or `/opt/junit.3.8.1` on UNIX).

You are now ready to run the tests provided with the JUnit distribution. JUnit comes complete with Java programs that you can use to view the result of a test. There is a *graphical*, Swing-based test runner (figure 1.2) as well as a *textual* test runner (figure 1.3) that can be used from the command line.

To run the graphical test runner, open a shell in `C:\junit3.8.1` on Windows or in `/opt/junit3.8.1` on UNIX, and type the appropriate command:

Windows:
```
java -cp junit.jar;. junit.swingui.TestRunner junit.samples.AllTests
```

UNIX:
```
java -cp junit.jar:. junit.swingui.TestRunner junit.samples.AllTests
```

To run the text test runner, open a shell in `C:\junit3.8.1` on Windows or in `/opt/junit3.8.1` on UNIX, and type the appropriate command:

Windows:
```
java -cp junit.jar;. junit.textui.TestRunner junit.samples.AllTests
```

UNIX:
```
java -cp junit.jar:. junit.textui.TestRunner junit.samples.AllTests
```

---

[5] Earlier versions of JUnit will not work with all of our sample code.

Figure 1.2
Execution of the JUnit
distribution sample tests using
the graphical Swing test runner

Notice that for the text test runner, tests that pass are shown with a dot. Had there been errors, they would have been displayed with an *E* instead of a dot.

As you can see from the figures, the runners report equivalent results. The textual test runner is easier to run, especially in batch jobs, though the graphical test runner can provide more detail.

The graphical test runner also uses its own classloader instance (a reloading classloader). This makes it easier to use interactively, because you can reload classes (after changing them) and quickly run the test again without restarting the test runner.

```
C:\WINDOWS\System32\cmd.exe                                    _ □

C:\junit3.8.1>java -cp junit.jar;. junit.textui.TestRunner junit.samples.AllTests
................................................................
................................................................
............................
Time: 1.022

OK (119 tests)


C:\junit3.8.1>
```

Figure 1.3   Execution of the JUnit distribution sample tests using the text test runner

In chapter 5, "Automating JUnit," we look at running tests using the Ant build tool and from within integrated development environments, like Eclipse.

1.5 *Testing with JUnit*

JUnit has many features that make tests easier to write and to run. You'll see these features at work throughout this book:

- Alternate front-ends, or test runners, to display the result of your tests. Command-line, AWT, and Swing test runners are bundled in the JUnit distribution.
- Separate classloaders for each unit test to avoid side effects.
- Standard resource initialization and reclamation methods (setUp and tear-Down).
- A variety of assert methods to make it easy to check the results of your tests.
- Integration with popular tools like Ant and Maven, and popular IDEs like Eclipse, IntelliJ, and JBuilder.

Without further ado, let's turn to listing 1.4 and see what the simple Calculator test looks like when written with JUnit.

Listing 1.4   The TestCalculator program written with JUnit

```
import junit.framework.TestCase;

public class TestCalculator extends TestCase          ❶
{
  public void testAdd()                               ❷
  {
    Calculator calculator = new Calculator();         ❸
    double result = calculator.add(10, 50);           ❹
    assertEquals(60, result, 0);                      ❺
  }
}
```

Pretty simple, isn't it? Let's break it down by the numbers.

In listing 1.4 at ❶, you start by extending the test class from the standard JUnit junit.framework.TestCase. This base class includes the framework code that JUnit needs to automatically run the tests.

At ❷, you simply make sure that the method name follows the pattern test*XXX*(). Observing this naming convention makes it clear to the framework that the method is a unit test and that it can be run automatically. Following the test*XXX* naming convention is not strictly required, but it is strongly encouraged as a best practice.

At ❸, you start the test by creating an instance of the Calculator class (the "object under test"), and at ❹, as before, you execute the test by calling the method to test, passing it two known values.

At ❺, the JUnit framework begins to shine! To check the result of the test, you call an assertEquals method, which you inherited from the base TestCase. The Javadoc for the assertEquals method is:

```
/**
 * Asserts that two doubles are equal concerning a delta. If the
 * expected value is infinity then the delta value is ignored.
 */

static public void assertEquals(double expected, double actual,
    double delta)
```

In listing 1.4, you passed assertEquals these parameters:

- expected = 60
- actual = result
- delta = 0

Since you passed the calculator the values 10 and 50, you tell assertEquals to expect the sum to be 60. (You pass 0 as you are adding integer numbers, so there is no delta.) When you called the calculator object, you tucked the return value into a local double named result. So, you pass that variable to assertEquals to compare against the expected value of 60.

Which brings us to the mysterious delta parameter. Most often, the delta parameter can be zero, and you can safely ignore it. It comes into play with calculations that are not always precise, which includes many floating-point calculations. The delta provides a plus/minus factor. So if the actual is within the range (expected-delta) and (expected+delta), the test will still pass.

If you want to enter the test program from listing 1.4 into your text editor or IDE, you can try it using the graphical test runner. Let's assume you have entered the code from listings 1.1 and 1.4 in the C:\junitbook\jumpstart directory (/opt/junitbook/jumpstart on UNIX). Let's first compile the code by opening a shell prompt in that directory and typing the following (we'll assume you have the javac executable on your PATH):

JUnit Design Goals

The JUnit team has defined three discrete goals for the framework:

- The framework must help us write useful tests.
- The framework must help us create tests that retain their value over time.
- The framework must help us lower the cost of writing tests by reusing code.

In listing 1.4, we tried to show how easy it can be to write tests with JUnit. We'll return to the other goals in chapter 2.

Windows:

```
javac -cp ..\..\junit3.8.1\junit.jar *.java
```

UNIX:

```
javac -cp ../../junit3.8.1/junit.jar *.java
```

You are now ready to start the Swing test runner, by typing the following:

Windows:

```
java -cp .;..\..\junit3.8.1\junit.jar
    ➔ junit.swingui.TestRunner TestCalculator
```

UNIX:

```
java -cp .:../../junit3.8.1/junit.jar
    ➔ junit.swingui.TestRunner TestCalculator
```

The result of the test is shown in figure 1.4.

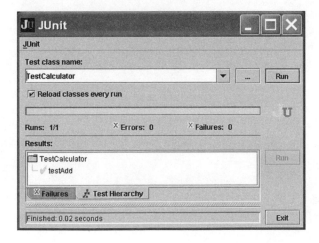

Figure 1.4
Execution of the first JUnit test
`TestCalculator` **using the Swing test runner**

The remarkable thing about the JUnit `TestCalculator` class in listing 1.4 is that the code is every bit as easy to write as the first `TestCalculator` program in listing 1.2, but you can now run the test automatically through the JUnit framework.

> **NOTE** If you are maintaining any tests written prior to JUnit version 3.8.1, you will need to add a constructor, like this:
>
> ```
> public TestCalculator(String name) { super(name); }
> ```
>
> It is no longer required with JUnit 3.8 and later.

1.6 Summary

Every developer performs some type of test to see if new code actually works. Developers who use automatic unit tests can repeat these tests on demand to ensure the code still works later.

Simple unit tests are not difficult to write by hand, but as tests become more complex, writing and maintaining tests can become more difficult. JUnit is a unit testing framework that makes it easier to create, run, and revise unit tests.

In this chapter, we scratched the surface of JUnit by installing the framework and stepping through a simple test. Of course, JUnit has much more to offer.

In chapter 2, we take a closer look at the JUnit framework classes and how they work together to make unit testing efficient and effective. (Not to mention just plain fun!)

Exploring JUnit

2

This chapter covers

- Using the core JUnit classes
- Understanding the JUnit life cycle

Mistakes are the portals of discovery.

—James Joyce

In chapter 1, we decided that we need an automatic testing program so that we can replicate our tests. As we add new classes, we often want to make changes to classes under test. Of course, experience has taught us that sometimes classes interact in unexpected ways. So, we'd really like to keep running all of our tests on all of our classes, whether they've been changed or not. But how can we run multiple test cases? And what do we use to run all these tests?

In this chapter, we will look at how JUnit provides the functionality to answer those questions. We will begin with an overview of the core JUnit classes TestCase, TestSuite, and BaseTestRunner. Then we'll take a closer look at test runners and TestSuite, before we revisit our old friend TestCase. Finally, we'll examine how the core classes work together.

2.1 *Exploring core JUnit*

The TestCalculator program from chapter 1, shown in listing 2.1, can run a single test case on demand. As you see, to create a single test case, you can extend the TestCase class.

Listing 2.1   The TestCalculator program written with JUnit

```
import junit.framework.TestCase;

public class TestCalculator extends TestCase
{
  public void testAdd()
  {
    Calculator calculator = new Calculator();
    double result = calculator.add(10, 50);
    assertEquals(60, result, 0);
  }
}
```

When you need to write more test cases, you create more TestCase objects. When you need to run several TestCase objects at once, you create another object called a TestSuite. To run a TestSuite, you use a TestRunner, as you did for a single TestCase object in the previous chapter. Figure 2.1 shows this trio in action.

These three classes are the backbone of the JUnit framework. Once you understand how TestCase, TestSuite, and BaseTestRunner work, you will be able to

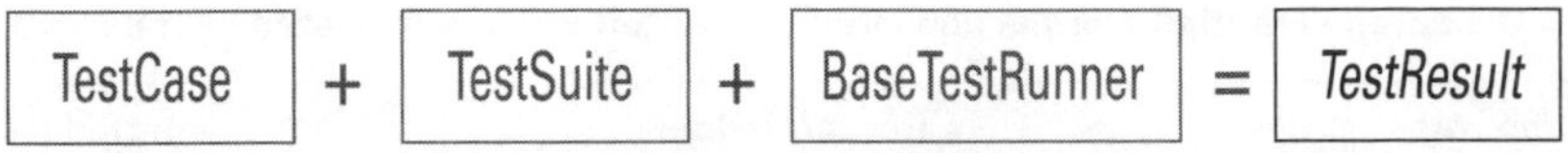

Figure 2.1 **The members of the JUnit trio work together to render a test result.**

DEFINITION *TestCase (or test case)*—A class that extends the JUnit `TestCase` class. It contains one or more tests represented by test*XXX* methods. A test case is used to group together tests that exercise common behaviors. In the remainder of this book, when we mention a *test,* we mean a test*XXX* method; and when we mention a *test case,* we mean a class that extends `TestCase`—that is, a set of tests.

TestSuite (or test suite)—A group of tests. A test suite is a convenient way to group together tests that are related. For example, if you don't define a test suite for a `TestCase`, JUnit automatically provides a test suite that includes all the tests found in the `TestCase` (more on that later).

TestRunner (or test runner)—A launcher of test suites. JUnit provides several test runners that you can use to execute your tests. There is no `TestRunner` interface, only a `BaseTestRunner` that all test runners extend. Thus when we write `TestRunner` we actually mean any test runner class that extends `BaseTestRunner`.

write whatever tests you need. On a daily basis, you only need to write test cases. The other classes work behind the scenes to bring your tests to life. These three classes work closely with four other classes to create the core JUnit framework. Table 2.1 summarizes the responsibilities of all seven core classes.

Table 2.1 **The seven core JUnit classes and interfaces (interfaces are indicated by italics)**

Class / *interface*	Responsibilities	Introduced in...
`Assert`	An assert method is silent when its proposition succeeds but throws an exception if the proposition fails.	Section 2.6.2
`TestResult`	A `TestResult` collects any errors or failures that occur during a test.	Section 2.4
Test	A *Test* can be run and passed a `TestResult`.	Section 2.3.2
TestListener	A *TestListener* is apprised of events that occur during a test, including when the test begins and ends, along with any errors or failures.	Section 2.5

continued on next page

Table 2.1 **The seven core JUnit classes and interfaces (interfaces are indicated by italics)** *(continued)*

Class / *interface*	Responsibilities	Introduced in...
TestCase	A TestCase defines an environment (or *fixture*) that can be used to run multiple tests.	Section 2.1
TestSuite	A TestSuite runs a collection of test cases, which may include other test suites. It is a composite of *Tests*.	Section 2.3
BaseTestRunner	A test runner is a user interface for launching tests. BaseTestRunner is the superclass for all test runners.	Section 2.2.2

Figure 2.2 shows the relationships among the seven core JUnit classes. You'll see how these core classes and interfaces work together in this chapter and throughout the book.

2.2 Launching tests with test runners

Writing tests can be fun, but what about the grunt work of running them? When you are first writing tests, you want them to run as quickly and easily as possible. You should be able to make testing part of the development cycle—*code : run : test : code* (or *test : code : run : test* if you are test-first inclined). There are IDEs and compilers for quickly building and running applications, but what can you use to run the tests?

2.2.1 Selecting a test runner

To make running tests as quick and easy as possible, JUnit provides a selection of test runners. The test runners are designed to execute your tests and provide you with statistics regarding the outcome. Because they are specifically designed for this purpose, the test runners can be very easy to use. Figure 2.3 shows the Swing test runner in action.

   The progress indicator running across the screen is the famous JUnit green bar. *Keep the bar green to keep the code clean* is the JUnit motto.

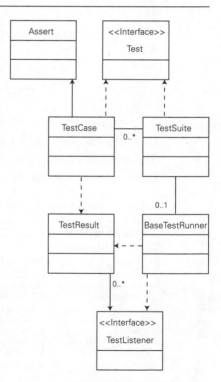

Figure 2.2 **The core JUnit classes used to run any JUnit test program**

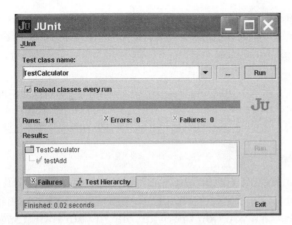

**Figure 2.3
The graphical test
runner in action**

When tests fail, the bar shows up red instead. JUnit testers tend to refer to passing tests as *green-bar* and failing tests as *red-bar.*

The JUnit distribution includes three `TestRunner` classes: one for the text console, one for Swing, and even one for AWT (the latter being a legacy that few people still use).

2.2.2 *Defining your own test runner*

Unlike other elements of the JUnit framework, there is no `TestRunner` interface. Instead, the various test runners bundled with JUnit all extend `BaseTestRunner`. If you needed to write your own test runner for any reason, you could also extend this class yourself. For example, the Cactus framework that we'll discuss in later chapters extends `BaseTestRunner` to create a `ServletTestRunner` that can run JUnit tests from a browser.

2.3 *Composing tests with TestSuite*

Simple things should be simple ... and complex things should be possible. Suppose you compile the simple calculator test program from listing 2.1 and hand it to a graphical test runner, like this:

```
>java junit.swingui.TestRunner TestCalculator
```

It should run just fine, assuming you have the correct classpath. (See figure 2.3 for the Swing test runner in action.) Altogether, this seems simple—at least as far as running a single test case is concerned.

But what happens when you want to run multiple test cases? Or just some of your test cases? How can you group test cases?

Between the `TestCase` and the `TestRunner`, it would seem that you need some type of container that can collect several tests together and run them as a set. But, by making it easier to run multiple cases, you don't want to make it harder to run a single test case.

JUnit's answer to this puzzle is the `TestSuite`. The `TestSuite` is designed to run one or more test cases. The test runner launches the `TestSuite`; which test cases to run is up to the `TestSuite`.

2.3.1 *Running the automatic suite*

You might wonder how you managed to run the example at the end of chapter 1, when you didn't define a `TestSuite`. To keep simple things simple, the test runner automatically creates a `TestSuite` if you don't provide one of your own. (*Sweet!*)

The default `TestSuite` scans your test class for any methods that start with the characters *test*. Internally, the default `TestSuite` creates an instance of your `TestCase` for each test*XXX* method. The name of the method being invoked is passed as the `TestCase` constructor, so that each instance has a unique identity.

For the `TestCalculator` in listing 2.1, the default `TestSuite` could be represented in code like this:

```java
public static Test suite()
{
    return new TestSuite(TestCalculator.class);
}
```

And this is again equivalent to the following:

```java
public static Test suite()
{
    TestSuite suite = new TestSuite();
    suite.addTest(new TestCalculator("testAdd"));
    return suite;
}
```

NOTE To use this form, the hypothetical `TestCalculator` class would need to define the appropriate constructor, like this:

```java
public TestCalculator(String name) { super(name); }
```

JUnit 3.8 made this constructor optional, so it is not part of the source code for the original `TestCalculator` class. Most developers now rely on the automatic `TestSuite` and rarely create manual suites, so they can omit this constructor.

If you added another test, like testSubtract, the default TestSuite would automatically include it too, saving you the trouble of maintaining yet another block of fluff:

```
public static Test suite()
{
    TestSuite suite = new TestSuite();
    suite.addTest(new TestCalculator("testAdd"));
    suite.addTest(new TestCalculator("testSubstract"));
    return suite;
}
```

This is trivial code and would be easy to copy, paste, and edit—but why bother with such drudgery when JUnit can do it for you? Most important, the automatic test suite ensures that you don't forget to add some test to the test suite.

2.3.2 *Rolling your own test suite*

The default TestSuite goes a long way toward keeping the simple things simple. But what happens when the default suite doesn't meet your needs? You may want to combine suites from several different packages as part of a master suite. If you're working on a new feature, then as you make changes, you may want to run a small set of relevant tests.

There are many circumstances in which you may want to run multiple suites or selected tests within a suite. Even the JUnit framework has a special case: In order to test the automatic suite feature, the framework needs to build its own suite for comparison!

If you check the Javadoc for TestSuite and TestCase, you'll notice that they both implement the Test interface, shown in listing 2.2.

> **Listing 2.2   The Test interface**

```
package junit.framework;

public interface Test {
    public abstract int countTestCases();
    public abstract void run(TestResult result);
}
```

If you are an over-achiever and also look up the Javadoc for TestSuite, you'll probably notice that the addTest signature doesn't specify a TestCase type—any old Test will do.

The ability to add both test suites and test cases to a suite makes it simple to create specialty suites as well as an aggregate TestAll class for your application.

JUnit design goals

The simple but effective combination of a `TestRunner` with a `TestSuite` makes it easy to run all your tests every day. At the same time, you can select a subset of tests that relate to the current development effort. This speaks to JUnit's second design goal:

The framework must create tests that retain their value over time.

When you continue to run your tests, you minimize your investment in testing and maximize your return on that investment.

Typically, the `TestAll` class is just a static `suite` method that registers whatever `Test` objects (`TestCase` objects or `TestSuite` objects) your application should be running on a regular basis. Listing 2.3 shows a typical `TestAll` class.

Listing 2.3   A typical TestAll class

```
import junit.framework.Test;
import junit.framework.TestSuite;
import junitbook.sampling.TestDefaultController;

public class TestAll
{
    public static Test suite()            ❶
    {
        TestSuite suite = new TestSuite("All tests from part 1");    ❷
        suite.addTestSuite(TestCalculator.class);         ❸
        suite.addTestSuite(TestDefaultController.class);
            // if TestDefaultController had a suite method
            // (or alternate suite methods) you could also use
            // suite.addTestSuite(TestDefaultController.suite());
        return suite;
    }
}
```

❶ Create a `suite` method to call all your other tests or suites.

❷ Give the `TestSuite` a legend to help identify it later.

❸ You call `addTestSuite` to add whatever `TestCase` objects or `TestSuite` objects you want to run together. It works for both types because the `addTestSuite` method accepts a `Test` object as a parameter, and `TestCase` and `TestSuite` both implement the `Test` interface.

In chapter 5, we look at several techniques for automating tasks like this one, so that you do not have to create and maintain a `TestAll` class. Of course, you still may want to create specialty suites for discrete subsets of your tests.

> ### Design patterns in action: Composite and Command
>
> *Composite pattern.* "Compose objects into tree structures to represent part-whole hierarchies. Composite lets clients treat individual objects and compositions of objects uniformly."[1] JUnit's use of the `Test` interface to run a single test or suites of suites of suites of tests is an example of the Composite pattern. When you add an object to a `TestSuite`, you are really adding a *Test*, not simply a *Test Case*. Because both `TestSuite` and `TestCase` implement `Test`, you can add either to a suite. If the `Test` is a `TestCase`, the single test is run. If the `Test` is a `TestSuite`, then a group of tests is run (which could include other `TestSuites`).
>
> *Command pattern.* "Encapsulate a request as an object, thereby letting you parameterize clients with different requests, queue or log requests, and support undoable operations."[2] The use of the `Test` interface to provide a common run method is an example of the Command pattern.

2.4 Collecting parameters with TestResult

Newton taught us that for every action there is an equal and opposite reaction. Likewise, for every `TestSuite`, there is a `TestResult`.

A `TestResult` collects the results of executing a `TestCase`. If all your tests always succeeded, what would be the point of running them? So, `TestResult` stores the details of all your tests, pass or fail.

The `TestCalculator` program (listing 2.1) includes a line that says

```
assertEquals(60, result, 0);
```

If the result did not equal 60, JUnit would create a `TestFailure` object to be stored in the `TestResult`.

The `TestRunner` uses the `TestResult` to report the outcome of your tests. If there are no `TestFailures` in the `TestResult` collection, then the code is clean, and the bar turns green. If there are failures, the `TestRunner` reports the failure

---

[1] Erich Gamma et al., *Design Patterns* (Reading, MA: Addison-Wesley, 1995).

[2] Ibid.

count and the stack trace for failing tests. Figure 2.4 shows what a failed test looks like in the Swing test runner.

JUnit distinguishes between failures and errors. *Failures* are to be expected. From time to time changes in the code will cause an assertion to fail. When it does, you fix the code so the failure goes away. An *error* is an unexpected condition that is not expected by the test, such as an exception in a conventional program.

Of course, an error may indicate a failure in the underlying environment. The test itself may not be broken. A good heuristic in the face of an error is the following:

- Check the environment. (Is the database up? What about the network?)
- Check the test.
- Check the code.

Figure 2.5 shows what an error condition looks like in the Swing test runner. At the end of a suite, the test runner provides a tally of how many tests passed and failed, along with details of any test that failed.

With JUnit 3.8.1, you can use the automatic suite mechanism to ensure that any new tests you write are included in the run. If you'd like to retain the results

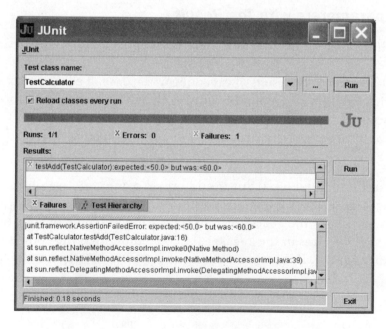

Figure 2.4
Oops—time to fix the code!

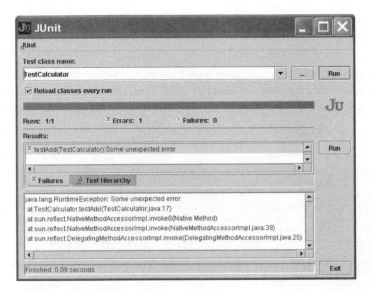

**Figure 2.5
Oh, no! You have to
fix the test!**

for later review, you can do so using Ant, Eclipse, and other tools. See chapter 5 for more about using automated tools.

The TestResult is used by almost all the JUnit classes internally. As a JUnit test writer, you won't interact with the TestResult directly; but in trying to understand how JUnit works, it's helpful to know that it exists.

> **Design patterns in action: Collecting Parameter**
>
> "When you need to collect results over several methods, you should add a parameter to the method and pass an object that will collect the results for you."[3] The TestResult class is an example of the Collecting Parameter pattern.

2.5 *Observing results with TestListener*

The TestResult collects information about the test, and the TestRunner reports it. But does an object have to be a TestRunner to report on a test? Can more than one object report on a test at once?

The JUnit framework provides the TestListener interface to help objects access the TestResult and create useful reports. The TestRunners implement TestListener, as do many of the special JUnit extensions. Any number of TestListeners can register with the framework and do whatever they need to do

---

[3] Kent Beck, *Smalltalk Best Practice Patterns* (Upper Saddle River, NJ: Prentice Hall, 1996).

with the information provided by the `TestResult`. Table 2.2 describes the `TestListener` interface.

> **NOTE**   Although the `TestListener` interface is an essential part of the JUnit framework, it is not an interface that you will implement when writing your own tests. We provide this section for completeness only.

Table 2.2   The `TestListener` interface

Method	Description
void **addError**(Test test, Throwable t)	Called when an error occurs
void **addFailure**(Test test, AssertionFailedError e)	Called when a failure occurs
void **endTest**(Test test)	Called when a test ends
void **startTest**(Test test)	Called when a test begins

As mentioned, although the `TestListener` interface is an interesting bit of plumbing, you would only need to implement it if you were extending the JUnit framework, rather than just using it.

> ### Design patterns in action: Observer
>
> "Define a one-to-many dependency between objects so that when one object changes state, all its dependants are notified and updated automatically."[4] The `TestRunner` registering as a `TestListener` with the `TestResult` is an example of the Observer pattern.

2.6 *Working with TestCase*

The JUnit big picture is that the `TestRunner` runs a `TestSuite`, which contains one or more `TestCases` (or other `TestSuites`). On a daily basis, you usually work only with the `TestCases`.

The framework ships with ready-to-use graphical and textual `TestRunners`. The framework can also generate a default runtime `TestSuite` for you. So, the only class you absolutely must provide yourself is the `TestCase`. A typical `TestCase` includes two major components: the fixture and the unit tests.

---

[4]   Ibid.

2.6.1 *Managing resources with a fixture*

Some tests require resources that can be a bother to set up. A prime example is something like a database connection. Several tests in a `TestCase` may need a connection to a test database and access to a number of test tables. Another series of tests may require complex data structures or a long series of random inputs.

Putting common setup code in your tests doesn't make sense. You are not testing your ability to create a resource—you just need a stable background environment in which to run tests. The set of background resources that you need to run a test is commonly called a *test fixture*.

> **DEFINITION** *fixture*—The set of common resources or data that you need to run one or more tests.

A fixture is automatically created and destroyed by a `TestCase` through its `setUp` and `tearDown` methods. The `TestCase` calls `setUp` before running *each* of its tests and then calls `tearDown` when *each* test is complete. A key reason why you put more than one test method into the same `TestCase` is to share the fixture code. The `TestCase` life cycle is depicted in figure 2.6.

In practice, many developers now use *mock objects* or *stubs* to simulate database connections and other complex resources. For more about mock objects and stubs, see chapters 6 and 7, respectively.

A database connection is a good example of why you might need a fixture. If a `TestCase` includes several database tests, they each need a fresh connection to the database. A fixture makes it easy for you to open a new connection for each test without replicating code. For more about testing databases, see chapter 11. You can also use a fixture to generate input files; doing this means you do not have to carry your test files with your tests, and you always have a known state before the test is executed.

JUnit also reuses code through the utility methods provided by the `Assert` interface, as we'll explain in the next section.

Figure 2.6 The `TestCase` life cycle re-creates your fixture, or scaffolding, for each test method.

> ### JUnit design goals
>
> When it is easy to reuse a fixture between tests, you can write tests more quickly. Each time you reuse the fixture, you decrease the initial investment made when the fixture was created. The TestCase fixtures speak to JUnit's third design goal:
>
> *The framework must lower the cost of writing tests by reusing code.*

2.6.2 Creating unit test methods

Fixtures are a great way to reuse setup code. But there are many other common tasks that many tests perform over and over again. The JUnit framework encapsulates the most common testing tasks with an array of assert methods. The assert methods can make writing unit tests much easier.

The Assert supertype

In listing 2.2, we introduced the Test interface that both TestSuite and TestCase implement. The Test interface specifies only two methods, countTestCases and run. But in writing the TestCalculator case, you also used an assert method inherited from the base TestCase class.

The assert methods are defined in a utility class named (you guessed it) Assert. This class contains many of the nuts and bolts you use to construct tests.

If you look at the Javadoc or the source, you'll see that, with 38 signatures, the Assert interface is longer than most. But if you look a little closer, you'll notice that Assert has only eight public methods, as shown in table 2.3.

Table 2.3   The eight core methods provided by the Assert superclass

Method	Description
assertTrue	Asserts that a condition is true. If it isn't, the method throws an AssertionFailedError with the given message (if any).
assertFalse	Asserts that a condition is true. If it isn't, the method throws an AssertionFailedError with the given message (if any).
assertEquals	Asserts that two objects are equal. If they are not, the method throws an AssertionFailedError with the given message (if any).
assertNotNull	Asserts that an object isn't null. If it is, the method throws an Assertion-FailedError with the message (if any).

continued on next page

Table 2.3 The eight core methods provided by the `Assert` superclass *(continued)*

Method	Description
`assertNull`	Asserts that an object is null. If it isn't, the method throws an `Assertion-FailedError` with the given message (if any).
`assertSame`	Asserts that two objects refer to the same object. If they do not, the method throws an `AssertionFailedError` with the given message (if any).
`assertNotSame`	Asserts that two objects do not refer to the same object. If they do, the method throws an `AssertionFailedError` with the given message (if any).
`fail`	Fails a test with the given message.

The Javadoc is bulked up by convenience forms of these eight methods. The convenience forms make it easy to pass whatever type you need in your test. The assertEquals method, for example, has 20 forms! Most of the assertEquals forms are conveniences that end up calling the core assertEquals(String message, Object expected, Object actual) form.

The TestCase members

Along with the methods provided by `Assert`, `TestCase` implements 10 methods of its own. Table 2.4 overviews the 10 `TestCase` methods *not* provided by the `Assert` interface.

Table 2.4 The 10 additional methods provided by `TestCase`

Method	Description
`countTestCases`	Counts the number of `TestCases` executed by `run(TestResult result)`. (Specified by the `Test` interface.)
`createResult`	Creates a default `TestResult` object.
`getName`	Gets the name of a `TestCase`.
`run`	Runs the `TestCase` and collects the results in `TestResult`. (Specified by the `Test` interface.)
`runBare`	Runs the test sequence without any special features, like automatic discovery of test methods.
`runTest`	Override to run the test and assert its state.
`setName`	Sets the name of a `TestCase`.
`setUp`	Initializes the fixture, for example, to open a network connection. This method is called before a test is executed. (Specified by the `Test` interface.)

continued on next page

Table 2.4 The 10 additional methods provided by `TestCase` *(continued)*

Method	Description
`tearDown`	De-initializes the fixture, for example, to close a network connection. This method is called after a test is executed. (Specified by the `Test` interface.)
`toString`	Returns a string representation of the `TestCase`.

In practice, many `TestCases` use the `setUp` and `tearDown` methods. The other methods in table 2.4 are mainly of interest to developers creating JUnit extensions. Used together, the 18 methods in tables 2.3 and 2.4 provide you with all the functionality you need to write tests with JUnit.

Keeping tests independent

As you begin to write your own tests, remember the first rule: *Each unit test must run independently of all other unit tests.* Unit tests must be able to be run in any order. One test must not depend on some side effect caused by a previous test (for example, a member variable being left in a certain state). If tests begin to depend on one another, you are inviting trouble. Here are some of the problems with co-dependent tests:

- *Not portable*—By default, JUnit finds test methods by reflection. The reflection API does not guarantee an order in which it returns the method names. If your tests depend on an ordering, then your suite may work in one Java Virtual Machine (JVM) but fail in another.

- *Hard to maintain*—When you modify one test, you may find that a number of other tests are affected. If you need to change the other tests, you spend time maintaining tests—time that could have been spent developing code.

- *Not legible*—To understand how co-dependent tests work, you must understand how each one works in turn. Tests become more difficult to read and harder to maintain. A good test must be easy to read and simple to maintain.

2.7 *Stepping through TestCalculator*

Let's demonstrate how all the core JUnit classes work together, using the `TestCalculator` test from listing 2.1 as an example. This is a very simple test class with a single test method:

```
import junit.framework.TestCase;

public class TestCalculator extends TestCase
```

```
{
  public void testAdd()
  {
    Calculator calculator = new Calculator();
    double result = calculator.add(10, 50);
    assertEquals(60, result, 0);
  }
}
```

When you start a JUnit test runner by typing `java junit.swingui.TestRunner TestCalculator`, the JUnit framework performs the following actions:

- Creates a `TestSuite`
- Creates a `TestResult`
- Executes the test methods (`testAdd` in this case)

We'll present these steps using standard Universal Modeling Language (UML) sequence diagrams.

More about UML and design patterns

As the sage said, a picture tells a thousand words; a symbol tells ten thousand more. Today many developers rely on UML to represent software components and design patterns to symbolize the deeper meanings of designs. To learn more about UML, we recommend *UML Distilled: A Brief Guide to the Standard Object Modeling Language,* by Martin Fowler and Kendall Scott (Reading, MA: Addison-Wesley, 1999). For more about design patterns, we recommend the classic *Design Patterns,* by Erich Gamma et al (Reading, MA: Addison-Wesley, 1995); and *Patterns of Enterprise Application Architecture,* by Martin Fowler (Boston: Addison-Wesley, 2003). You don't need to understand UML or design patterns to test your code, but both disciplines can help you design code to test.

2.7.1 Creating a TestSuite

NOTE In the UML diagrams that follow, we refer to a `TestRunner` class. Although there is no `TestRunner` interface, the JUnit test runners all extend the `BaseTestRunner` class and are named `TestRunner`: `junit.swingui.TestRunner` for the Swing test runner and `junit.textui.TestRunner` for the text test runner. By extrapolation, we are giving the name `TestRunner` to any class that extends `BaseTestRunner`. This means whenever we mention `TestRunner`, you can mentally replace it with any JUnit test runner.

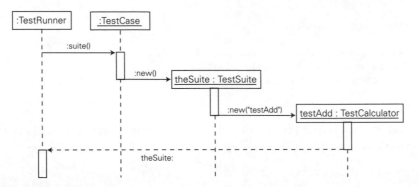

Figure 2.7 JUnit creates an explicit test suite (when the `suite` method is defined in the test case).

The `TestRunner` begins by looking for a `suite` method in the `TestCalculator` class. Had one existed, the `TestRunner` would have called it, as shown in figure 2.7. Then this `suite` method would have created the different `TestCase` classes, adding them to the test suite (see section 2.3).

Because there is no `suite` method in the `TestCalculator` class, the `TestRunner` creates a default `TestSuite` object, as shown in figure 2.8.

The main difference between figures 2.7 and 2.8 is that in figure 2.8, the discovery of the `TestCalculator` test methods is done using Java introspection, whereas in figure 2.7, the `suite` method explicitly defines the `TestCalculator` test methods. For example:

```java
public static Test suite()
{
    TestSuite suite = new TestSuite();
    suite.addTest(new TestCalculator("testAdd"));
    return suite;
}
```

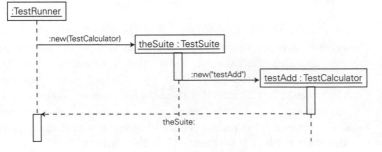

**Figure 2.8
JUnit creates an
automatic test suite
(when the `suite`
method is not defined
in the test case).**

2.7.2 Creating a TestResult

Figure 2.9 demonstrates the steps that JUnit follows to create a TestResult object that contains the test results (success or failures or errors).

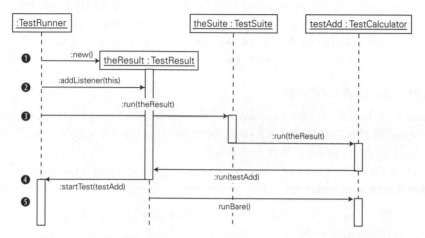

Figure 2.9   JUnit creates a `TestResult` object to collect the test results (good or bad).

These steps are as follows:

1 At ❶ in the figure, the TestRunner instantiates the TestResult object that will hold the test results as the tests are executed one after another.

2 The TestRunner registers against the TestResult so that it will receive events that happen during the execution of the tests (❷). This is a typical example of the Observer pattern in action. A TestResult advertises these methods:

- A test has been started (startTest; see ❹).
- A test has failed (addFailure; see figure 2.10).
- A test has thrown an unexpected exception (addError; see figure 2.10).
- A test has ended (endTest; see figure 2.10).

3 Knowing about these events allows the TestRunner to display a progress bar as the tests progress and to display failures and errors as they happen (instead of having to wait until the end of all the tests).

4 The TestRunner starts the tests by calling the TestSuite's run(TestResult) method (❸).

5 The `TestSuite` calls the `run(TestResult)` method for each of the `TestCase` instances it holds.

6 The `TestCase` uses the `TestResult` instance that was passed to it to call its `run(Test)` method, passing itself as a parameter so that the `TestResult` can then call it back with `runBare` (**❺**). The reason is that JUnit needs to give the control to the `TestResult` instance so that it can alert all its listeners that the test has started (**❹**).

2.7.3 *Executing the test methods*

You have seen in the previous section that for each `TestCase` in the `TestSuite`, the `runBare` method is called. In this case, because you have a single `testAdd` test in `TestCalculator`, it will be called only once.

Figure 2.10 highlights the steps for executing a single test method. The steps in figure 2.10 are as follows:

1 At **❶** in the figure, the `runBare` method executes the `setUp`, `testAdd`, and `tearDown` methods.

2 If any test failure or test error happens during the execution of any of these three methods, the `TestResult` notifies its listeners by calling `addFailure` (**❷**) and `addError` (**❸**), respectively.

3 If any errors occur, the `TestRunner` lists them. Otherwise, the bar turns green—and you know the code is clean.

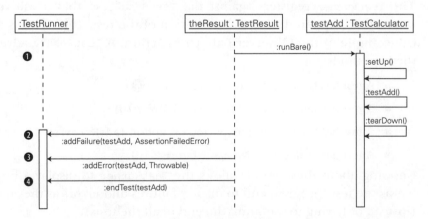

Figure 2.10   JUnit executes a test method and notifies test listeners about failure, errors, and the end of the test.

4   When the `tearDown` method has finished executing, the test is finished. The `TestResult` signals this fact to its listeners by calling the `endTest` method (❹).

2.7.4 *Reviewing the full JUnit life cycle*

The full JUnit life cycle we have described in the previous sections is shown in figure 2.11.

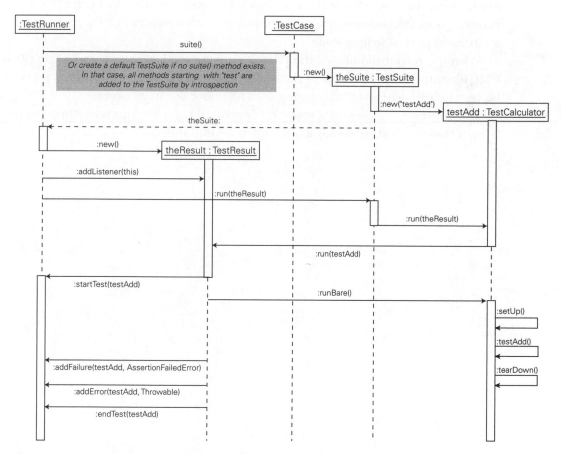

Figure 2.11   The full JUnit life cycle applied on the `TestCalculator` class

2.8 Summary

As you saw in chapter 1, it's not hard to jump in and begin writing JUnit tests for your applications. In this chapter, we zoomed in and took a closer look at how JUnit works under the hood.

A key feature of JUnit is that it provides a convenient spot to hang the scaffolding (or fixture) that you need for a test. Also built into JUnit are several convenient assert methods that make tests quick and easy to build. With the JUnit test runners, unit tests become so convenient that some developers have made testing an integral part of writing code.

With the responsibilities of the JUnit classes defined, we presented a complete UML diagram of the JUnit life cycle. Being able to visualize the JUnit life cycle can be very helpful when you're creating tests for more complex objects.

In chapter 3, we present a more sophisticated use case and walk through the type of tests you will create for a package of related objects.

Sampling JUnit

This chapter covers

- Testing larger components
- Project infrastructure

Tests are the Programmer's Stone, transmuting fear into boredom.
—Kent Beck, *Test First Development*

Now that you've had an introduction to JUnit, you're ready to see how it works on a practical application. Let's walk through a case study of testing a single, significant component, like one your team leader might assign to you. We should choose a component that is both useful *and* easy to understand, common to many applications, large enough to give us something to play with, but small enough that we can cover it here. How about a *controller*?

In this chapter, we'll first introduce the case-study code, identify what code to test, and then show how to test it. Once we know that the code works as expected, we'll create tests for exceptional conditions, to be sure the code behaves well even when things go wrong.

3.1 *Introducing the controller component*

Core J2EE Patterns describes a controller as a component that "interacts with a client, controlling and managing the handling of each request," and tells us that it is used in both presentation-tier and business-tier patterns.[1]

In general, a controller does the following:

- Accepts requests
- Performs any common computations on the request
- Selects an appropriate request handler
- Routes the request so that the handler can execute the relevant business logic
- May provide a top-level handler for errors and exceptions

A controller is a handy class and can be found in a variety of applications. For example, in a presentation-tier pattern, a web controller accepts HTTP requests and extracts HTTP parameters, cookies, and HTTP headers, perhaps making the HTTP elements easily accessible to the rest of the application. A web controller determines the appropriate business logic component to call based on elements in the request, perhaps with the help of persistent data in the HTTP session, a database, or some other resource. The Apache Struts framework is an example of a web controller.

---

[1] Deepak Alur, John Crupi, and Dan Malks, *Core J2EE Patterns: Best Practices and Design Strategies* (Upper Saddle River, NJ: Prentice Hall, 2001).

Another common use for a controller is to handle applications in a business-tier pattern. Many business applications support several presentation layers. Web applications may be handled through HTTP clients. Desktop applications may be handled through Swing clients. Behind these presentation tiers there is often an application controller, or *state machine*. Many Enterprise JavaBean (EJB) applications are implemented this way. The EJB tier has its own controller, which connects to different presentation tiers through a business façade or *delegate*.

Given the many uses for a controller, it's no surprise that controllers crop up in a number of enterprise architecture patterns, including Page Controller, Front Controller, and Application Controller.[2] The controller you will design here could be the first step in implementing any of these classic patterns.

Let's work through the code for the simple controller, to see how it works, and then try a few tests. If you would like to follow along and run the tests as you go, all the source code for this chapter is available at SourceForge (http://junit-book.sf.net). See appendix A for more about setting up the source code.

3.1.1 Designing the interfaces

Looking over the description of a controller, four objects pop out: the `Request`, the `Response`, the `RequestHandler`, and the `Controller`. The `Controller` accepts a `Request`, dispatches a `RequestHandler`, and returns a `Response` object. With a description in hand, you can code some simple starter interfaces, like those shown in listing 3.1.

Listing 3.1   Request, Response, RequestHandler, and Controller interfaces

```
public interface Request
{
    String getName();        ❶
}

public interface Response    ❷
{
}

public interface RequestHandler
{
    Response process(Request request) throws Exception;    ❸
}

public interface Controller
{
    Response processRequest(Request request);    ❹
```

---

[2] Martin Fowler, *Patterns of Enterprise Application Architecture* (Boston: Addison-Wesley, 2003).

```
    void addHandler(Request request, RequestHandler requestHandler);    5
}
```

1 Define a `Request` interface with a single `getName` method that returns the request's unique name, just so you can differentiate one request from another. As you develop the component you will need other methods, but you can add those as you go along.

2 Here you specify an empty interface. To begin coding, you only need to return a `Response` object. What the `Response` encloses is something you can deal with later. For now, you just need a `Response` type you can plug into a signature.

3 Define a `RequestHandler` that can process a `Request` and return your `Response`. `RequestHandler` is a helper component designed to do most of the dirty work. It may call upon classes that throw any type of exception. So, `Exception` is what you have the `process` method throw.

4 Define a top-level method for processing an incoming request. After accepting the request, the controller dispatches it to the appropriate `RequestHandler`. Notice that `processRequest` does not declare any exceptions. This method is at the top of the control stack and should catch and cope with any and all errors internally. If it did throw an exception, the error would usually go up to the Java Virtual Machine (JVM) or servlet container. The JVM or container would then present the user with one of those nasty white screens. Better you handle it yourself.

5 This is a very important design element. The `addHandler` method allows you to extend the `Controller` without modifying the Java source.

> ### Design patterns in action: Inversion of Control
> Registering a handler with the controller is an example of Inversion of Control. This pattern is also known as the *Hollywood Principle*, or "Don't call us, we'll call you." Objects register as handlers for an event. When the event occurs, a hook method on the registered object is invoked. Inversion of Control lets frameworks manage the event life cycle while allowing developers to plug in custom handlers for framework events.[3]

---

[3] John Earles, "Frameworks! Make Room for Another Silver Bullet": http://www.cbd-hq.com/PDFs/cbdhq_000301je_frameworks.pdf.

3.1.2 *Implementing the base classes*

Following up on the interfaces in listing 3.1, listing 3.2 shows a first draft of the simple controller class.

Listing 3.2   The generic controller

```java
package junitbook.sampling;

import java.util.HashMap;
import java.util.Map;

public class DefaultController implements Controller
{
    private Map requestHandlers = new HashMap();            ❶

    protected RequestHandler getHandler(Request request)    ❷
    {
        if (!this.requestHandlers.containsKey(request.getName()))
        {
            String message = "Cannot find handler for request name "
                + "[" + request.getName() + "]";
            throw new RuntimeException(message);            ❸
        }
        return (RequestHandler) this.requestHandlers.get(   ❹
            request.getName());
    }

    public Response processRequest(Request request)         ❺
    {
        Response response;
        try
        {
            response = getHandler(request).process(request);
        }
        catch (Exception exception)
        {
            response = new ErrorResponse(request, exception);
        }
        return response;
    }

    public void addHandler(Request request,
        RequestHandler requestHandler)
    {
        if (this.requestHandlers.containsKey(request.getName()))
        {
            throw new RuntimeException("A request handler has "   ❻
                + "already been registered for request name "
                + "[" + request.getName() + "]");
        }
        else
```

```
        {
            this.requestHandlers.put(request.getName(),
                requestHandler);
        }
    }
}
```

1 Declare a HashMap (java.util.HashMap) to act as the registry for your request handlers.

2 Add a protected method, getHandler, to fetch the RequestHandler for a given request.

3 If a RequestHandler has not been registered, you throw a RuntimeException (java.lang.RuntimeException), because this happenstance represents a programming mistake rather than an issue raised by a user or external system. Java does not require you to declare the RuntimeException in the method's signature, but you can still catch it as an exception. An improvement would be to add a specific exception to the controller framework (NoSuitableRequestHandlerException, for example).

4 Your utility method returns the appropriate handler to its caller.

5 This is the core of the Controller class: the processRequest method. This method dispatches the appropriate handler for the request and passes back the handler's Response. If an exception bubbles up, it is caught in the ErrorResponse class, shown in listing 3.3.

6 Check to see whether the name for the handler has been registered, and throw an exception if it has. Looking at the implementation, note that the signature passes the request object, but you only use its name. This sort of thing often occurs when an interface is defined *before* the code is written. One way to avoid over-designing an interface is to practice Test-Driven Development (see chapter 4).

Listing 3.3   Special response class signaling an error

```
package junitbook.sampling;

public class ErrorResponse implements Response
{
    private Request originalRequest;
    private Exception originalException;

    public ErrorResponse(Request request, Exception exception)
    {
        this.originalRequest = request;
        this.originalException = exception;
```

```
    }
    public Request getOriginalRequest()
    {
        return this.originalRequest;
    }
    public Exception getOriginalException()
    {
        return this.originalException;
    }
}
```

At this point, you have a crude but effective skeleton for the controller. Table 3.1 shows how the requirements at the top of this section relate to the source code.

Table 3.1 Resolving the base requirements for the component

Requirement	Resolution
Accept requests	`public Response processRequest(Request request)`
Select handler	`this.requestHandlers.get(request.getName())`
Route request	`response = getRequestHandler(request).process(request);`
Error-handling	Subclass `ErrorResponse`

The next step for many developers would be to cobble up a stub application to go with the skeleton controller. But not us! As "test-infected" developers, we can write a test suite for the controller without fussing with a stub application. That's the beauty of unit testing! You can write a package and verify that it works, all outside of a conventional Java application.

3.2 *Let's test it!*

A fit of inspiration has led us to code the four interfaces shown in listing 3.1 and the two starter classes shown in listings 3.2 and 3.3. If we don't write an automatic test now, the Bureau of Extreme Programming will be asking for our membership cards back!

Listings 3.2 and 3.3 began with the simplest implementations possible. So, let's do the same with the new set of unit tests. What's the simplest possible test case we can explore?

3.2.1 *Testing the DefaultController*

How about a test case that instantiates the DefaultController class? The first step in doing anything useful with the controller is to construct it, so let's start there.

Listing 3.4 shows the bootstrap test code. It constructs the DefaultController object and sets up a framework for writing tests.

Listing 3.4 TestDefaultController—a bootstrap iteration

```
package junitbook.sampling;

import junit.framework.TestCase;

public class TestDefaultController extends TestCase    ❶
{
    private DefaultController controller;

    protected void setUp() throws Exception     ❷
    {
        controller = new DefaultController();
    }

    public void testMethod()     ❸
    {
        throw new RuntimeException("implement me");     ❹
    }
}
```

❶ Start the name of the test case class with the prefix *Test*. Doing so marks the class as a test case so that you can easily recognize test classes and possibly filter them in build scripts.

❷ Use the default setUp method to instantiate DefaultController. This is a built-in extension point that the JUnit framework calls between test methods.

❸ Here you insert a dummy test method, just so you have something to run. As soon as you are sure the test infrastructure is working, you can begin adding real test methods. Of course, although this test runs, it also fails. The next step will be to fix the test!

❹ Use a "best practice" by throwing an exception for test code that has not yet been implemented. This prevents the test from passing and reminds you that you must implement this code.

3.2.2 *Adding a handler*

Now that you have a bootstrap test, the next step is to decide what to test first. We started the test case with the DefaultController object, because that's the point of this exercise: to create a controller. You wrote some code and made sure it compiled. But how can you test to see if it works?

The purpose of the controller is to process a request and return a response. But before you process a request, the design calls for adding a `RequestHandler` to do the actual processing. So, first things first: You should test whether you can add a `RequestHandler`.

The tests you ran in chapter 1 returned a known result. To see if the test succeeded, you compared the result you expected with whatever result the object you were testing returned. The signature for `addHandler` is

```
void addHandler(Request request, RequestHandler requestHandler)
```

To add a `RequestHandler`, you need a `Request` with a known name. To check to see if adding it worked, you can use the `getHandler` method from `DefaultController`, which uses this signature:

```
RequestHandler getHandler(Request request)
```

This is possible because the `getHandler` method is protected, and the test classes are located in the same package as the classes they are testing.

For the first test, it looks like you can do the following:

1 Add a `RequestHandler`, referencing a `Request`.

2 Get a `RequestHandler` and pass the same `Request`.

3 Check to see if you get the same `RequestHandler` back.

Where do tests come from?

Now you know what objects you need. The next question is, where do these objects come from? Should you go ahead and write some of the objects you will use in the application, like a logon request?

The point of unit testing is to test one object at a time. In an object-oriented environment like Java, objects are designed to interact with other objects. To create a unit test, it follows that you need two flavors of objects: the *domain object* you are testing and *test objects* to interact with the object under test.

> **DEFINITION** *domain object*—In the context of unit testing, the term *domain object* is used to contrast and compare the objects you use *in* your application with the objects that you use to *test* your application (*test objects*). Any object under test is considered to be a domain object.

If you used another domain object, like a logon request, and a test failed, it would be hard to identify the culprit. You might not be able to tell if the problem was with the controller or the request. So, in the first series of tests, the only class you will use in production is `DefaultController`. Everything else should be a special test class.

> ### JUnit best practices: unit-test one object at a time
>
> A vital aspect of unit tests is that they are finely grained. A unit test independently examines each object you create, so that you can isolate problems as soon as they occur. If more than one object is put under test, you cannot predict how the objects will interact when changes occur to one or the other. When an object interacts with other complex objects, you can surround the object under test with predictable test objects.
>
> Another form of software test, integration testing, examines how working objects interact with each other. See chapter 4 for more about other types of tests.

Where do test classes live?

Where do you put the test classes? Java provides several alternatives. For starters, you could do one of the following:

- Make them public classes in your package
- Make them inner classes within your test case class

If the classes are simple and likely to stay that way, then it is easiest to code them as inner classes. The classes in this example are pretty simple.

Listing 3.5 shows the inner classes you can add to the `TestDefaultController` class.

Listing 3.5   Test classes as inner classes

```
public class TestDefaultController extends TestCase
{
[...]
    private class TestRequest implements Request        ❶
    {
        public String getName()
        {
            return "Test";
        }
    }

    private class TestHandler implements RequestHandler    ❷
    {
        public Response process(Request request) throws Exception
```

```
        {
            return new TestResponse();
        }
    }

    private class TestResponse implements Response      ❸
    {
        // empty
    }
[...]
```

❶ Set up a request object that returns a known name (Test).

❷ Implement a TestHandler. The interface calls for a process method, so you have
to code that, too. You're not testing the process method right now, so you have it
return a TestResponse object to satisfy the signature.

❸ Go ahead and define an empty TestResponse just so you have something to
instantiate.

With the scaffolding from listing 3.5 in place, let's look at listing 3.6, which shows
the test for adding a RequestHandler.

Listing 3.6   TestDefaultController.testAddHandler

```
public class TestDefaultController extends TestCase
{
[...]
    public void testAddHandler()      ❶
    {
        Request request = new TestRequest();
        RequestHandler handler = new TestHandler();      ❷

        controller.addHandler(request, handler);      ❸

        RequestHandler handler2 = controller.getHandler(request);      ❹

        assertSame(handler2, handler);      ❺
    }
}
```

❶ Pick an obvious name for the test method.

❷ Instantiate your test objects.

❸ This code gets to the point of the test: controller (the object under test) adds the
test handler. Note that the DefaultController object is instantiated by the setUp
method (see listing 3.4).

④ Read back the handler under a new variable name.

⑤ Check to see if you get back the same object you put in.

> ### JUnit best practices: choose meaningful test method names
>
> You must be able to understand what a method is testing by reading the name. A good rule is to start with the test*Xxx* naming scheme, where *Xxx* is the name of the method to test. As you add other tests against the same method, move to the test*XxxYyy* scheme, where *Yyy* describes how the tests differ.

Although it's very simple, this unit test confirms the key premise that the mechanism for storing and retrieving `RequestHandler` is alive and well. If `addHandler` or `getRequest` fails in the future, the test will quickly detect the problem.

As you create more tests like this, you will notice that you follow a pattern of steps:

1 Set up the test by placing the environment in a known state (create objects, acquire resources). The pre-test state is referred to as the *test fixture*.

2 Invoke the method under test.

3 Confirm the result, usually by calling one or more assert methods.

3.2.3 *Processing a request*

Let's look at testing the core purpose of the controller, processing a request. Because you know the routine, we'll just present the test in listing 3.7 and review it.

Listing 3.7   testProcessRequest

```
public class TestDefaultController extends TestCase
{
[...]
    public void testProcessRequest()          ❶
    {
        Request request = new TestRequest();
        RequestHandler handler = new TestHandler();     ❷
        controller.addHandler(request, handler);

        Response response = controller.processRequest(request);   ❸
        assertNotNull("Must not return a null response", response);   ❹

        assertEquals(TestResponse.class, response.getClass());   ❺
    }
}
```

❶ First give the test a simple, uniform name.

❷ Set up the test objects and add the test handler.

❸ Here the code diverges from listing 3.6 and calls the processRequest method.

❹ You verify that the returned Response object is not null. This is important because in **❺** you call the getClass method on the Response object. It will fail with a dreaded NullPointerException if the Response object is null. You use the assert-NotNull(String, Object) signature so that if the test fails, the error displayed is meaningful and easy to understand. If you had used the assertNotNull(Object) signature, the JUnit runner would have displayed a stack trace showing an AssertionFailedError exception with no message, which would be more difficult to diagnose.

❺ Once again, compare the result of the test against the expected TestResponse class.

> ### JUnit best practices: explain the failure reason in assert calls
> Whenever you use the assertTrue, assertNotNull, assertNull, and assertFalse methods, make sure you use the signature that takes a String as the first parameter. This parameter lets you provide a meaningful textual description that is displayed in the JUnit test runner if the assert fails. Not using this parameter makes it difficult to understand the reason for a failure when it happens.

Factorizing setup logic

Because both tests do the same type of setup, you can try moving that code into the JUnit setUp method. As you add more test methods, you may need to adjust what you do in the standard setUp method. For now, eliminating duplicate code as soon as possible helps you write more tests more quickly. Listing 3.8 shows the new and improved TestDefaultController class (changes are shown in bold).

Listing 3.8 TestDefaultController after some refactoring

```
package junitbook.sampling;

import junit.framework.TestCase;

public class TestDefaultController extends TestCase
{
    private DefaultController controller;
    private Request request;
    private RequestHandler handler;
```

```
    protected void setUp() throws Exception
    {
        controller = new DefaultController();
        request = new TestRequest();
        handler = new TestHandler();
        controller.addHandler(request, handler);
    }

    private class TestRequest implements Request
    {
        // Same as in listing 3.5
    }

    private class TestHandler implements RequestHandler
    {
        // Same as in listing 3.5
    }

    private class TestResponse implements Response
    {
        // Same as in listing 3.5
    }

    public void testAddHandler()          ❷
    {
        RequestHandler handler2 = controller.getHandler(request);
        assertSame(handler2, handler);
    }

    public void testProcessRequest()          ❸
    {
        Response response = controller.processRequest(request);
        assertNotNull("Must not return a null response", response);
        assertEquals(TestResponse.class, response.getClass());
    }
}
```

❶ The instantiation of the test Request and RequestHandler objects is moved to setUp. This saves you repeating the same code in testAddHandler ❷ and testProcessRequest ❸.

>   **DEFINITION**   *refactor*—To improve the design of existing code. For more about refactoring, see Martin Fowler's already-classic book.[4]

Note that you do *not* try to share the setup code by testing more than one operation in a test method, as shown in listing 3.9 (an anti-example).

---

[4] Martin Fowler, *Refactoring: Improving the Design of Existing Code* (Reading, MA: Addison-Wesley, 1999).

Listing 3.9 Do *not* combine test methods this way.

```java
public class TestDefaultController extends TestCase
{
[...]
    public void testAddAndProcess()
    {
        Request request = new TestRequest();
        RequestHandler handler = new TestHandler();
        controller.addHandler(request, handler);

        RequestHandler handler2 = controller.getHandler(request);
        assertEquals(handler2,handler);

        // DO NOT COMBINE TEST METHODS THIS WAY
        Response response = controller.processRequest(request);
        assertNotNull("Must not return a null response", response);
        assertEquals(TestResponse.class, response.getClass());
    }
}
```

JUnit best practices: one unit test equals one testMethod

Do not try to cram several tests into one method. The result will be more complex test methods, which will become increasingly difficult to read and understand. Worse, the more logic you write in your test methods, the more risk there is that it will not work and will need debugging. This is a slippery slope that can end with writing tests to test your tests!

Unit tests give you confidence in a program by alerting you when something that had worked now fails. If you put more than one unit test in a method, it makes it more difficult to zoom in on exactly what went wrong. When tests share the same method, a failing test may leave the fixture in an unpredictable state. Other tests embedded in the method may not run, or may not run properly. Your picture of the test results will often be incomplete or even misleading.

Because all the test methods in a TestCase share the same fixture, and JUnit can now generate an automatic test suite (see chapter 2), it's really just as easy to place each unit test in its own method. If you need to use the same block of code in more than one test, extract it into a utility method that each test method can call. Better yet, if all methods can share the code, put it into the fixture.

For best results, your test methods should be as concise and focused as your domain methods.

Each test method must be as clear and focused as possible. This is why JUnit provides a setUp method: so you can share fixtures between tests without combining test methods.

3.2.4 *Improving testProcessRequest*

When we wrote the testProcessRequest method in listing 3.7, we wanted to confirm that the response returned is the expected response. The implementation confirms that the object returned is the object that we expected. But what we would really like to know is whether the response returned equals the expected response. The response could be a different class. What's important is whether the class identifies itself as the correct response.

The assertSame method confirms that both references are to the same object. The assertEquals method utilizes the equals method, inherited from the base Object class. To see if two different objects have the same identity, you need to provide your own definition of identity. For an object like a response, you can assign each response its own command token (or name).

The empty implementation of TestResponse didn't have a name property you can test. To get the test you want, you have to implement a little more of the Response class first. Listing 3.10 shows the enhanced TestResponse class.

Listing 3.10   A refactored TestResponse

```
public class TestDefaultController extends TestCase
{
[...]
    private class TestResponse implements Response
    {
        private static final String NAME = "Test";

        public String getName()
        {
            return NAME;
        }

        public boolean equals(Object object)
        {
            boolean result = false;
            if (object instanceof TestResponse)
            {
                result = ((TestResponse) object).getName().equals(
                    getName());
            }
            return result;
        }
```

```
        public int hashCode()
        {
            return NAME.hashCode();
        }
    }
[...]
```

Now that `TestResponse` has an identity (represented by `getName()`) and its own `equals` method, you can amend the test method:

```
public void testProcessRequest()
{
    Response response = controller.processRequest(request);
    assertNotNull("Must not return a null response", response);
    assertEquals(new TestResponse(), response);
}
```

We have introduced the concept of identity in the `TestResponse` class for the purpose of the test. However, the tests are really telling you that this should have existed in the proper `Response` class. Thus you need to modify the `Response` interface as follows:

```
public interface Response
{
    String getName();
}
```

3.3 *Testing exception-handling*

So far, your tests have followed the main path of execution. If the behavior of one of your objects under test changes in an unexpected way, this type of test points to the root of the problem. In essence, you have been writing *diagnostic tests* that monitor the application's health.

But sometimes, bad things happen to healthy programs. Say an application needs to connect to a database. Your diagnostics may test whether you are following the database's API. If you open a connection but don't close it, a diagnostic can note that you have failed to meet the expectation that all connections are closed after use.

But what if a connection is not available? Maybe the connection pool is tapped out. Or, perhaps the database server is down. If the database server is configured properly and you have all the resources you need, this may never happen. But all resources are finite, and someday, instead of a connection, you may be handed an exception. "Anything that can go wrong, will" (http://www.geo-cities.com/murphylawsite/).

If you are testing an application by hand, one way to test for this sort of thing is to turn off the database while the application is running. Forcing actual error conditions is an excellent way to test your disaster-recovery capability. Creating error conditions is also very time-consuming. Most of us cannot afford to do this several times a day—or even once a day. And many other error conditions are not easy to create by hand.

Testing the main path of execution is a good thing, and it needs to be done. But testing exception-handling can be even more important. If the main path does not work, your application will not work either (a condition you are likely to notice).

> **JUnit best practices: test anything that could possibly fail**
>
> Unit tests help ensure that your methods are keeping their API contracts with other methods. If the contract is based solely on other components' keeping their contracts, then there *may* not be any useful behavior for you to test. But if the method changes the parameter's or field's value in any way, then you are providing unique behavior that you should test. The method is no longer a simple go-between—it's a filtering or munging method with its own behavior that future changes could conceivably break. If a method is changed so it is not so simple anymore, then you should add a test *when that change takes place,* but not before. As the JUnit FAQ puts it, "The general philosophy is this: if it can't break *on its own,* it's too simple to break."
>
> But what about things like JavaBean getters and setters? Well, that depends. If you are coding them by hand in a text editor, then yes, you might want to test them. It's surprisingly easy to miscode a setter in a way that the compiler won't catch. But if you are using an IDE that watches for such things, then your team might decide not to test simple JavaBean properties.

We are all too human, and often we tend to be sloppy when it comes to exception cases. Even textbooks scrimp on error-handling so as to simplify the examples. As a result, many otherwise great programs are not error-proofed before they go into production. If properly tested, an application should not expose a screen of death but should trap, log, and explain all errors gracefully.

3.3.1 Simulating exceptional conditions

The exceptional test case is where unit tests really shine. Unit tests can simulate exceptional conditions as easily as normal conditions. Other types of tests, like functional and acceptance tests, work at the production level. Whether these tests encounter systemic errors is often a matter of happenstance. A unit test can produce exceptional conditions on demand.

During our original fit of inspired coding, we had the foresight to code an error handler into the base classes. As you saw back in listing 3.2, the `processRequest` method traps all exceptions and passes back a special error response instead:

```
try
{
    response = getHandler(request).process(request);
}
catch (Exception exception)
{
    response = new ErrorResponse(request, exception);
}
```

How do you simulate an exception to test whether your error handler works? To test handling a normal request, you created a `TestRequestHandler` that returned a `TestRequest` (see listing 3.5). To test the handling of error conditions, you can create a `TestExceptionHandler` that throws an exception instead, as shown in listing 3.11.

Listing 3.11   RequestHandler for exception cases

```
public class TestDefaultController extends TestCase
{
[...]
    private class TestExceptionHandler implements RequestHandler
    {
        public Response process(Request request) throws Exception
        {
            throw new Exception("error processing request");
        }
    }
}
```

This just leaves creating a test method that registers the handler and tries processing a request—for example, like the one shown in listing 3.12.

Listing 3.12   testProcessRequestAnswersErrorResponse, first iteration

```
public class TestDefaultController extends TestCase
{
[...]
    public void testProcessRequestAnswersErrorResponse()
    {
```

```
        TestRequest request = new TestRequest();                    1
        TestExceptionHandler handler = new TestExceptionHandler();
        controller.addHandler(request, handler);        2
        Response response = controller.processRequest(request);
        assertNotNull("Must not return a null response", response);  3
        assertEquals(ErrorResponse.class, response.getClass());
    }
}
```

1 Create the request and handler objects.

2 You reuse the `controller` object created by the default fixture (see listing 3.8).

3 Test the outcome against your expectations.

But if you run this test through JUnit, you get a red bar! (See figure 3.1.) A quick look at the message tells you two things. First, you need to use a different name for the test request, because there is already a request named `Test` in the fixture. Second, you may need to add more exception-handling to the class so that a `RuntimeException` is not thrown in production.

As to the first item, you can try using the `request` object in the fixture instead of your own, but that fails with the same error. (Moral: Once you have a test, use it to explore alternative coding strategies.) You consider changing the fixture. If you remove from the fixture the code that registers a default `TestRequest` and `TestHandler`, you introduce duplication into the other test methods. Not good. Better to fix the `TestRequest` so it can be instantiated under different names. Listing 3.13 is the refactored result (changes from listing 3.11 and 3.12 are in bold).

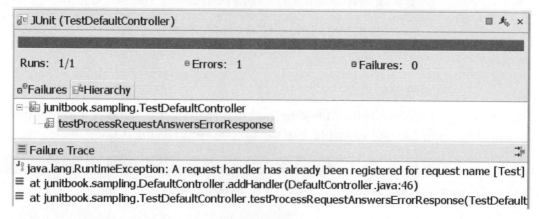

Figure 3.1   Oops, red bar—time to add exception-handling!

Listing 3.13 testProcessRequestExceptionInHandler, fixed and refactored

```
public class TestDefaultController extends TestCase
{
[...]
    private class TestRequest implements Request
    {
        private static final String DEFAULT_NAME = "Test";      ❶
        private String name;

        public TestRequest(String name)      ❷
        {
            this.name = name;
        }

        public TestRequest()      ❸
        {
            this(DEFAULT_NAME);
        }

        public String getName()
        {
            return this.name;
        }
    }
[...]
    public void testProcessRequestAnswersErrorResponse()
    {
        TestRequest request = new TestRequest("testError");      ❹
        TestExceptionHandler handler = new TestExceptionHandler();
        controller.addHandler(request, handler);
        Response response = controller.processRequest(request);
        assertNotNull("Must not return a null response", response);
        assertEquals(ErrorResponse.class, response.getClass());
    }
}
```

❶ Introduce a member field to hold the request's name and set it to the previous version's default.

❷ Introduce a new constructor that lets you pass a name to the request, to override the default.

❸ Here you introduce an empty constructor, so existing calls will continue to work.

❹ Call the new constructor instead, so the exceptional request object does not conflict with the fixture.

Of course, if you added another test method that also used the exception handler, you might move its instantiation to the setUp method, to eliminate duplication.

> **JUnit best practices: let the test improve the code**
>
> Writing unit tests often helps you write better code. The reason is simple: A test case is a user of your code. And, it is only when using code that you find its shortcomings. Thus, do not hesitate to listen to your tests and refactor your code so that it is easier to use. The practice of *Test-Driven Development (TDD)* relies on this principle. By writing the tests first, you develop your classes from the point of view of a user of your code. See chapter 4 for more about TDD.

But because the duplication hasn't happened yet, let's resist the urge to anticipate change, and let it stand. *("Don't anticipate, navigator!" the captain barked.)*

3.3.2 *Testing for exceptions*

During testing, you found that addHandler throws an undocumented RuntimeException if you try to register a request with a duplicate name. (By *undocumented*, we mean that it doesn't appear in the signature.) Looking at the code, you see that getHandler throws a RuntimeException if the request hasn't been registered.

Whether you *should* throw undocumented RuntimeException exceptions is a larger design issue. (You can make that a to-do for later study.) For now, let's write some tests that prove the methods will behave as designed.

Listing 3.14 shows two test methods that prove addHandler and getHandler will throw runtime exceptions when expected.

Listing 3.14   Testing methods that throw an exception

```
public class TestDefaultController extends TestCase
{
[...]
    public void testGetHandlerNotDefined()          ❶
    {
        TestRequest request = new TestRequest("testNotDefined");   ❷
        try
        {
            controller.getHandler(request);          ❸
            fail("An exception should be raised if the requested "
                + "handler has not been registered");              ❹
        }
        catch (RuntimeException expected)           ❺
        {
            assertTrue(true);          ❻
        }
    }

    public void testAddRequestDuplicateName()          ❼
```

```
    {
        TestRequest request = new TestRequest();
        TestHandler handler = new TestHandler();
        try
        {
            controller.addHandler(request, handler);      ⑧
            fail("An exception should be raised if the default "
                + "TestRequest has already been registered");
        }
        catch (RuntimeException expected)
        {
            assertTrue(true);
        }
    }
}
```

❶ Give the test an obvious name. Because this test represents an exceptional case, append `NotDefined` to the standard `testGetHandler` prefix. Doing so keeps all the `getHandler` tests together and documents the purpose of each derivation.

❷ You create the `request` object for the test, also giving it an obvious name.

❸ Pass the (unregistered) request to the default `getHandler` method.

❹ Introduce the `fail` method, inherited from the `TestCase` superclass. If a test ever reaches a `fail` statement, the test (unsurprisingly) will fail, just as if an assertion had failed (essentially, `assertTrue(false)`). If the `getHandler` statement throws an exception, as you expect it will, the `fail` statement will not be reached.

❺ Execution proceeds to the `catch` statement, and the test is deemed a success.

❻ You clearly state that this is the expected success condition. Although this line is not necessary (because it always evaluates to true), we have found that it makes the test easier to read. For the same reason, at ❺ you name the exception variable `expected`.

❼ In the second test, you again use a descriptive name. (Also note that you do not combine tests, but write a separate test for each case.)

❽ You follow the same pattern as the first method:

    1 Insert a statement that should throw an exception.

    2 Follow it with a `fail` statement (in case the exception isn't thrown).

    3 Catch the exception you expect, naming the exception `expected` so the reader can easily guess that the exception is expected!

    4 Proceed normally.

JUnit best practices: make exception tests easy to read

Name the exception variable in the `catch` block `expected`. Doing so clearly tells readers that an exception is expected to make the test pass. It also helps to add an `assertTrue(true)` statement in the `catch` block to stress even further that this is the correct path.

The controller class is by no means done, but you have a respectable first iteration and a test suite proving that it works. Now you can commit the controller package, along with its tests, to the project's code repository and move on to the next task on your list.

JUnit best practices: let the test improve the code

An easy way to identify exceptional paths is to examine the different branches in the code you're testing. By *branches*, we mean the outcome of `if` clauses, `switch` statements, and `try/catch` blocks. When you start following these branches, sometimes you may find that testing each alternative is painful. If code is difficult to test, it is usually just as difficult to use. When testing indicates a poor design (called a *code smell*, http://c2.com/cgi/wiki?CodeSmell), you should stop and refactor the domain code.

In the case of too many branches, the solution is usually to split a larger method into several smaller methods.[5] Or, you may need to modify the class hierarchy to better represent the problem domain.[6] Other situations would call for different refactorings.

A test is your code's first "customer," and, as the maxim goes, "the customer is always right."

3.4 Setting up a project for testing

Because this chapter covers testing a fairly realistic component, let's finish up by looking at how you set up the controller package as part of a larger project. In chapter 1, you kept all the Java domain code and test code in the same folder. They were introductory tests on an example class, so this approach seemed simplest for everyone. In this chapter, you've begun to build real classes with real

---

[5] Fowler, *Refactoring*, "Extract Method."

[6] Ibid., "Extract Hierarchy."

tests, as you would for one of your own projects. Accordingly, you've set up the source code repository just like you would for a real project.

So far, you have only one test case. Mixing this in with the domain classes would not have been a big deal. But, experience tells us that soon you will have at least as many test classes as you have domain classes. Placing all of them in the same directory will begin to create file-management issues. It will become difficult to find the class you want to edit next.

Meanwhile, you want the test classes to be able to unit-test protected methods, so you want to keep everything in the same Java package. The solution? One package, two folders. Figure 3.2 shows a snapshot of how the directory structure looks in a popular integrated development environment (IDE).

This is the code for the "sampling" chapter, so we used `sampling` for the top-level project directory name (see appendix A). The IDE shows it as `junitbook-sampling`, because this is how we named the project. Under the `sampling` directory we created separate `java` and `test` folders. Under each of these, the actual package structure begins.

In this case, all of the code falls under the `junitbook.sampling` package. The working interfaces and classes go under `src/java/junitbook/sampling`; the classes we write for testing only go under the `src/test/junitbook/sampling` directory.

Beyond eliminating clutter, a "separate but equal" directory structure yields several other benefits. Right now, the only test class has the convenient `Test` prefix. Later you may need other helper classes to create more sophisticated tests.

Figure 3.2
A "separate but equal" filing system keeps tests in the same package but in different directories.

These might include stubs, mock objects, and other helpers. It may not be convenient to prefix all of these classes with `Test`, and it becomes harder to tell the domain classes from the test classes.

Using a separate test folder also makes it easy to deliver a runtime jar with only the domain classes. And, it simplifies running all the tests automatically.

> ### JUnit best practices: same package, separate directories
>
> Put test classes in the same package as the class they test but in a parallel directory structure. You need tests in the same package to allow access to protected methods. You want tests in a separate directory to simplify file management and to clearly delineate test and domain classes.

3.5 Summary

In this chapter, we created a test case for a simple but complete application controller. Rather than test a single component, the test case examined how several components worked together. We started with a bootstrap test case that could be used with any class. Then we added new tests to `TestCase` one by one until all of the original components were under test.

We expect this package to grow, so we created a second source code directory for the test classes. Because the test and domain source directories are part of the same package, we can still test protected and package default members.

Knowing that even the best-laid plans go astray, we were careful to test the exception- and error-handling as thoroughly as the main path of execution. Along the way, we let the tests help us improve our initial design. At the end, we had a good start on the `Controller` class, and the tests to prove it!

In the next chapter, we will put unit testing in perspective with other types of tests that you need to perform to fully test your applications. We will also talk about how unit testing fits in the development life cycle.

Examining software tests

4

This chapter covers

- The need for unit tests
- Understanding the different types of tests
- Test coverage: how much is enough?
- Practicing Test-Driven Development
- Testing in the development cycle

A crash is when your competitor's program dies. When your program dies, it is an 'idiosyn-crasy'. Frequently, crashes are followed with a message like 'ID 02'. 'ID' is an abbreviation for idiosyncrasy and the number that follows indicates how many more months of testing the product should have had.

—Guy Kawasaki

Earlier chapters in this book took a very pragmatic approach to designing and deploying unit tests. This chapter steps back and looks at the various types of software tests, the role they play in the application's life cycle, how to design for testability, and how to practice test-first development.

Why would you need to know all this? Because performing unit testing is not just something you do out of the blue. In order to be a good developer, you have to understand why you are doing it and why you are writing unit tests instead of (or to complement) functional, integration, or other kinds of tests. Once you understand why you are writing unit tests, then you need to know how far you should go and when you have enough tests. Testing is not an end goal.

Finally, we'll show you how Test-Driven Development (TDD) can substantially improve the quality and design of your application by placing unit tests at the center of the development process.

4.1 The need for unit tests

Writing unit tests is good. Understanding why you write them is even better! The main goal is to verify that your application works and to try to catch bugs early. Functional testing does that; however, unit tests are extremely powerful and versatile beasts that offer much more than simply verifying that the application works:

- They allow greater test coverage than functional tests. u
- They enable teamwork.
- They prevent regression and limit the need for debugging.
- They give us the courage to refactor.
- They improve the implementation design.
- They serve as the developer's documentation.
- They're fun!

4.1.1 *Allowing greater test coverage*

Functional tests are the first type of tests any application should have. If you had to choose between writing unit tests or functional tests, you should choose the latter. In our experience, functional tests are able to cover about 70% of the application code. If you wish to go further and provide more test coverage (see section 4.3), you need to write unit tests.

Unit tests can easily simulate error conditions, which is extremely difficult to do with functional tests (it's impossible in some instances). However, making a decision about your need for unit tests based solely on test coverage criteria is a mistake. Unit tests provide much more than just testing, as explained in the following sections.

4.1.2 *Enabling teamwork*

Imagine you are part of a team, working on some part of the overall application. Unit tests allow you to deliver quality code (tested code) without having to wait for all the other parts to be complete (you wouldn't dream of delivering code without it being tested, right?). On the other hand, functional tests are more coarse-grained and need the full application (or a good part of it) to be ready before you can test it.

4.1.3 *Preventing regression and limiting debugging*

A good unit-test suite gives you confidence that your code works. It also gives you the courage to modify your existing code, either for refactoring purposes or to add/modify new features. As a developer, there's no better feeling than knowing that someone is watching your back and will warn you if you break something.

A corollary is that a good suite of unit tests reduces the need to debug an application to find out what's failing. Whereas a functional test will tell you that a bug exists somewhere in the implementation of a use case, a unit test will tell you that a specific method is failing for a specific reason. You no longer need to spend hours trying to find the error.

JUnit best practices: refactor

Throughout the history of computer science, many great teachers have advocated iterative development. Nikolas Wirth, for example, who gave us the now-ancient languages Algol and Pascal, championed techniques like *stepwise refinement.*

For a time, these techniques seemed difficult to apply to larger, layered applications. Small changes can reverberate throughout a system. Project managers looked to up-front planning as a way to minimize change, but productivity remained low.

The rise of the xUnit framework has fueled the popularity of *agile methodologies* that once again advocate iterative development. Agile methodologists favor writing code in vertical slices to produce a fully working use case, as opposed to writing code in horizontal slices to provide services layer by layer.

When you design and write code for a single use case or functional chain, your design may be adequate for this feature, but it may not be adequate for the next feature. To retain a design across features, agile methodologies encourage *refactoring* to adapt the code base as needed.

But how do you ensure that refactoring, or improving the design of existing code, does not break the existing code? Answer: unit tests that tell you when code breaks. In short, unit tests give you the courage to refactor.

The agile methodologies try to lower project risks by providing the ability to cope with change. They allow and embrace change by standardizing on quick iterations and applying principles like YAGNI (You Ain't Gonna Need It) and The Simplest Thing That Could Possibly Work. But the foundation upon which all these principles rest is a solid bed of unit tests.

4.1.4 Enabling refactoring

Without unit tests, it is difficult to justify refactoring, because there is always a relatively high chance that you may break something. Why would you risk spending hours of debugging time (and putting the delivery at risk) only to improve the implementation design, change a variable name, and so on? Unit tests provide a safety net that gives you the courage to refactor.

4.1.5 *Improving implementation design*

Unit tests are a first-rate client of the code they test. They force the API under test to be flexible and to be unit-testable in isolation. You usually have to refactor your code under test to make it unit-testable (or use the TDD approach, which by definition spawns code that can be unit-tested; see section 4.4).

It is important to listen to your unit tests and be tuned to the melody they are singing. If a unit test is too long and unwieldy, it usually means the code under test has a design smell and should be refactored. If the code cannot be easily tested in isolation (see chapter 7), it usually means the code isn't flexible enough and should be refactored. Modifying runtime code so that it can be tested is absolutely normal.

4.1.6 *Serving as developer documentation*

Imagine you're trying to learn a new API. On one side is a 300-page document describing the API, and on the other side are some simple examples showing how to use it. Which would you choose to learn the API?

The power of examples is well known and doesn't need to be demonstrated. Unit tests are exactly this: samples that show how to use the API and how it behaves. As such, they make excellent developer documentation. Because unit tests must be kept in synch with the working code, unlike other forms of documentation, they must always be up to date.

Listing 4.1 illustrates how unit tests can help provide documentation. The testTransferWithoutEnoughFunds() method shows that an AccountInsufficientFundsException is thrown when an account transfer is performed without enough funds.

Listing 4.1   Unit tests as automatic documentation

```java
import junit.framework.TestCase;

public class TestAccount extends TestCase
{
[...]
    public void testTranferWithoutEnoughFunds()
    {
        long balance = 1000;
        long amountToTransfer = 2000;
        Account credit = new Account(balance);
        Account debit = new Account();
        try
        {
            credit.transfer(debit, amountToTransfer);
```

```
            fail("The debited account doesn't have enough funds"
                + " and an exception should have been thrown");
        }
        catch (AccountInsufficientFundsException expected)
        {
            assertTrue(true); // We get the exception as expected
        }
    }
}
```

4.1.7 Having fun

Unit tests are addictive. Once you get hooked on the JUnit green bar, it's hard to do without. It gives you peace of mind: "The bar is green, and I'm happy because I know my code is OK." Alternating between red bar and green bar becomes a challenging, productive pastime. Like any good contest, there's a prize at the end: automated tests that, at the push of a button, tell you if everything still works.

You may be skeptical at first, but you once you are test-infected, it becomes difficult to write any piece of code without writing a test. (Kent Beck, king of test infection, said, "Any program feature without an automated test simply doesn't exist."[1]) The test runner's green bar, shown in figure 4.1, becomes a familiar friend. You miss it when it's gone. For a programmer, there's no greater pleasure than *knowing your code is of good quality and doing what it is supposed to do.*

To help keep the fun going, you can add metrics, such as showing the progress in a number of unit tests across iterations. Test-coverage reports (see section 4.3) showing the part of the code being exercised are another good strategy to keep up the momentum.

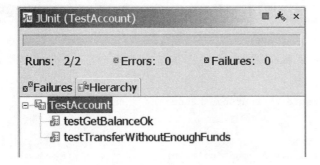

Figure 4.1
The famous green bar that appears when all tests pass

---

[1] Kent Beck, *Extreme Programming Explained: Embrace Change* (Reading, MA: Addison-Wesley, 1999), p. 57.

4.2 Different kinds of tests

Figure 4.2 outlines our five categories of software tests. There are other ways of categorizing software tests, but we find these most useful for the purposes of this text. Please note that this section is discussing *software tests in general,* not just the automated unit tests covered elsewhere in the book.

In figure 4.2, the outermost software tests are broadest in scope. The innermost software tests are narrowest in scope. As you move from the inner boxes to the outer boxes, the software tests get more and more functional and require that more and more of the application already be built.

Here, we'll first look at the general software test types. Then, we'll focus on the flavors of unit tests.

4.2.1 The four flavors of software tests

We've mentioned that unit tests focus on each distinct unit of work. But what about testing what happens when different units of work are combined into a workflow? Will the end result of the workflow do what you expect? How well will the application work when many people are using it at once? Will the application meet everyone's needs?

Each of these questions is answered by a different "flavor" of software test. For the purposes of this discussion, we can categorize software tests into four varieties:

- Integration tests
- Functional tests
- Stress/load tests
- Acceptance tests

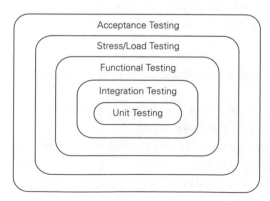

**Figure 4.2
The five flavors of tests within
the application life cycle**

Let's look at each of the test types encompassing software testing, starting with the innermost after unit testing and working our way out.

Integration software testing

Individual unit tests are an essential quality control, but what happens when different units of work are combined into a workflow? Once you have the tests for a class up and running, the next step is to hook up with other methods and with other services. Examining the interaction between components, possibly when they run in their target environment, is the stuff of integration testing.

Because there are many things with which you might want to integrate, the word *integration* can mean different things under different circumstances. Some of these circumstances are laid out in table 4.1.

Table 4.1   Testing how objects, services, and subsystems interact

Circumstance	Description
How objects interact	The test instantiates one or more objects and calls methods on one object from another.
How services interact	Tests are run while the application is hosted within a servlet or EJB container, connected to a live database, or attached to any other external resource or device.
How subsystems interact	A layered application may have a front-end subsystem to handle the presentation and a back-end subsystem to execute the business logic. Tests can verify that a request passes through the front end and returns an appropriate response from the back end.

Just as more traffic collisions occur at intersections, the points where units interact are major contributors of software accidents. Ideally, integration tests should be defined before the units are coded. Being able to code to the test dramatically increases a programmer's ability to write well-behaved objects.

Functional software testing

Testing interactions between objects is essential. But will the end result be what you expect?

Functional tests examine the code at the boundary of its public API. In general, this amounts to testing the application use cases.

Functional tests are often combined with integration tests. You may have a secure web page that should only be accessed by authorized clients. If the client is not logged in, then trying to access the page should result in a redirect to the login page. A functional unit test can examine this case by sending an HTTP request to the page to see whether a redirect (302) response code comes back.

Depending on the application, you can use several types of functional testing, as shown in table 4.2.

Table 4.2 Testing frameworks, GUIs, and subsystems

Circumstance	Description
Whether the application being built uses a framework	Functional testing within a framework focuses on testing the framework API that is used by users of the framework (end users or service providers).
Whether the application has a GUI	Functional testing of a GUI is about verifying that all features can be accessed and provide expected results. The tests are exercised directly on the GUI (which may in turn call several other components or a back end).
Whether the application is made of subsystems	A layered system tries to separate systems by roles. There may be a presentation subsystem, a business logic subsystem, and a data subsystem. Layering provides flexibility and the ability to access the back end with several different front ends. Each layer defines an API for other layers to use. Functional tests verify that the API contract is enforced.

Stress/load testing

It's important to have an application that functions correctly, but how well will the application perform when many people are using it at once? Most stress tests examine whether the application can process a large number of requests within a short period of time. Usually, this is done with special software like JMeter (http://jakarta.apache.org/jmeter), which can automatically send pre-programmed requests and track how quickly the application responds. Whether the response is correct is not usually tested. (That's why we have the other tests.) Figure 4.3 shows a JMeter throughput graph.

The stress tests are usually performed in a separate environment. A stress-test environment is generally more controlled than a typical development environment. It must be as close as possible to the production environment. If the production and stress-test environments are not very similar, then the tests are meaningless.

Other types of performance tests can be performed within the development environment. A profiler can look for bottlenecks in an application, which the developer can try to optimize. A number of Java profilers are available, and a search on Google will bring up several candidates.

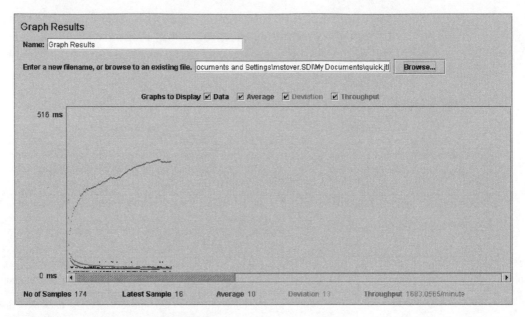

Figure 4.3   A JMeter throughput graph

From a testing perspective, using a profiler helps you to be proactive and can identify potential issues before the actual stress/load tests are performed. First you must be able to prove that a specific bottleneck exists, and then you must be able to prove that the bottleneck has been eliminated. A profiler is an essential tool in either case.

Unit tests can also help you profile an application as a natural part of development. JUnit extensions like JUnitPerf (http://www.clarkware.com/software/ JUnitPerf.html) are available to help you create a suite of performance tests to match your unit tests. You might want to assert that a critical method never takes too long to execute. You can specify a threshold duration as part of the performance unit test. As the application is refactored, you will be alerted if any change causes the critical method to cross your threshold.

Listing 4.2 shows the source for a timed test, taken from the JUnitPerf distribution examples. This test ensures that the `ExampleTestCase` never takes more than one second to run.

Listing 4.2 Timed test example

```
package com.clarkware.junitperf;

import junit.framework.Test;
import junit.framework.TestSuite;

public class ExampleTimedTest {

    public static final long toleranceInMillis = 100;

    public static Test suite() {

        long maxElapsedTimeInMillis = 1000 + toleranceInMillis;

        Test testCase =
            new ExampleTestCase("testOneSecondResponse");
        Test timedTest =
            new TimedTest(testCase, maxElapsedTimeInMillis);

        TestSuite suite = new TestSuite();
        suite.addTest(timedTest);

        return suite;
    }

    public static void main(String args[]) {
        junit.textui.TestRunner.run(suite());
    }
}
```

Acceptance software testing

It's important that an application perform well; but, in the end, the only question that matters is *Does the application meet the customer's needs?* Acceptance tests are the final sphere of tests. These tests are usually conducted directly by the customer or someone acting as the customer's proxy. Acceptance tests ensure that the application has met whatever goals the customer or stakeholder defined.

Acceptance tests are a superset of all other tests. Usually they start as functional and performance tests, but they may include subjective criteria like "ease of use" and "look and feel." Sometimes, the acceptance suite may include a subset of the tests run by the developers, the difference being that this time the tests are run by the customer or a QA team.

For more about using acceptance tests with an agile software methodology, visit the Wiki site regarding Ward Cunningham's *fit* framework (http://fit.c2.com/).

4.2.2 *The three flavors of unit tests*

The focus of this book is automatic unit tests used by programmers. *Unit testing*, as we use the term, concentrates on testing the code from the inside (*white box testing*; see section 4.3.1). This activity is inextricably linked with coding and happens at the same time. Unit tests can ensure that your application is under test from the very beginning.

Of course, your application should undergo other forms of software testing, starting with unit tests and ending with acceptance tests. The previous section outlined the other types of software tests that should be applied to your application.

Most applications are divided into subsystems. As a developer, you want to ensure that each of your subsystems works correctly. As you write code, your first tests will probably be logic unit tests. As you write more tests and more code, you will begin to add integration and functional unit tests. At any one time, you will probably be working on a logic unit test, an integration unit test, or a functional unit test. Table 4.3 summarizes the different types of unit tests.

Table 4.3   Three flavors of unit tests: logic, integration, and functional

Test type	Description
Logic unit tests	Unit tests that focus on exercising the code logic. These tests are usually meant to exercise only a single method and no other. You can control the boundaries of a given method using mock objects or stubs (see chapters 6 and 7).
Integration unit tests	Unit tests that focus on testing the interaction between components in their real environment (or part of the real environment). For example, code that accesses a database has tests that effectively call the database, thus proving that the code-database interaction works (see chapter 11).
Functional unit tests	Unit tests that extend the boundaries of integration unit testing to confirm a stimulus-response. For example, imagine a web page that is protected and that you can access only after being logged in. If you are not logged in, accessing the page results in a redirect to the login page. A functional unit test verifies that behavior by sending an HTTP request to the page and verifying that the result is a 302 response code. It does not, however, verify that the full workflow leads to the login page. Workflow is the domain of pure, software functional testing (see section 4.2.1).

Figure 4.4 illustrates how these three flavors of unit tests interact. The sliders define the boundaries between the types of unit tests. The tests can be defined by the locations of the sliders. All three types of tests are needed to ensure your code works. If you use them, you can sleep well at night and come in the next day, well rested and eager to create more great code!

Strictly speaking, the functional unit tests are not pure unit tests, but neither are they pure functional tests. They are more dependent on an external environment than pure unit tests are, but they do not test a complete workflow, as

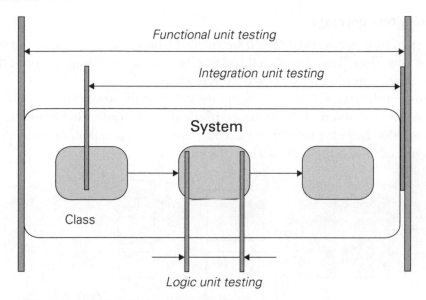

Figure 4.4   Unit testing within the application life cycle

expected by pure functional tests. We put functional unit tests in our scope because they are often useful as part of the battery of tests run in development.

An example is the `StrutsTestCase` (http://strutstestcase.sourceforge.net/) framework, which provides functional unit testing of the runtime Struts configuration. These tests tell a developer that the controller is invoking the appropriate software action and forwarding to the expected presentation page, but they do not confirm that the page is actually present and renders correctly.

4.3 *Determining how good tests are*

When you test a rivet, you can apply simple, objective standards. You can look at its dimensions, its weight, and whether it can withstand a certain amount of pressure. You can say that your tests cover just these aspects, and let the builder decide if the test coverage is sufficient.

But how do you express what aspects an application's unit tests cover? "Everything that could possibly fail" is a fine standard, but it's rather subjective. What kind of metrics can we apply?

4.3.1 *Measuring test coverage*

One metric of test coverage would be to count how many methods are being called by your tests. This doesn't tell you whether the test is doing the right thing, but it does tell you whether you have a test in place.

Without unit tests, you can only write tests against the application's public API methods. Because you don't need to see inside the application to create the tests, these are called *black box tests*. Figure 4.5 diagrams what an application's test coverage might look like using only black box tests.

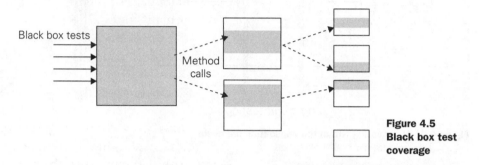

**Figure 4.5
Black box test
coverage**

Unit tests can be written with an intimate knowledge of how a method is implemented. If a conditional branch exists within the method, you can write two unit tests: one for each branch. Because you need to see into the method to create such a test, this is called *white box testing*. Figure 4.6 shows what an application's test coverage might look like using white box unit tests.

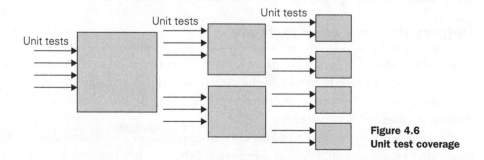

**Figure 4.6
Unit test coverage**

With white box unit tests, it's easier to achieve a higher test coverage metric, mainly because you have access to more methods and because you can control both the inputs to each method and the behavior of secondary objects called (using stubs or mock objects, as you'll see in later chapters). White box unit tests can be written against both package-protected and public methods.

4.3.2 Generating test coverage reports

Tools are available for JUnit that can analyze your application and provide an exact report of your application's test coverage. Figure 4.7 shows one such report generated by the Clover tool (http://www.thecortex.net/clover/).[2] It is the result of applying Clover on the `Controller` sample from chapter 3.

Knowing what classes are tested (`DefaultController`) and what classes are not tested (`ErrorResponse`) is useful information. However, it's even better to know why the `DefaultController` has only 94.7% test coverage. Fortunately, Clover is able to drill down at the level of the method implementation, as shown in figure 4.8.

The report shown in figure 4.8 itemizes how many times a given line of source code has been executed by our tests (this is the number in the second column from the left—for example, the `getHandler` method at line 10 has been called three times). But more important, the report shows the lines of code that have *not* been tested. In our example, the case when an `Exception` is thrown by `process-Request` is not being tested (line 32).

Knowing what code is untested is good. However, a good test-coverage tool (such as Clover) should also provide historical reports showing the progression (or regression) of tests across development iterations and integration with your favorite build system (such as Ant). It should have the ability to stop the build if coverage criteria are not met—for example, if the coverage for such a package is below 70%.

On our own projects, we like to check the coverage percentage after a development iteration (say, every two weeks). We adjust the build failure criteria so that the next iteration must have at least the same coverage percentage as the previous iteration. This strategy helps to ensure that our test coverage steadily improves.

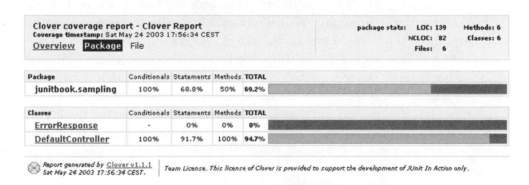

Figure 4.7 A class coverage report generated by the popular Clover product

---

[2] Clover is a commercial application that is free for noncommercial activities (especially the open source community).

Source file	Conditionals	Statements	Methods	TOTAL	
DefaultController.java	100%	91.7%	100%	94.7%	

```
 1    package junitbook.sampling;
 2
 3    import java.util.HashMap;
 4
 5    public class DefaultController implements Controller
 6    {
 7        private java.util.Map requestHandlers = new HashMap(); // (1)
 8
 9        // (2)
10  3   public RequestHandler getHandler(Request request)
11      {
12  3       if (!this.requestHandlers.containsKey(request.getName()))
13          {
14  1           String message = "Cannot find handler for request name " +
15                  "[" + request.getName() + "]";
16  1           throw new RuntimeException(message); // (3)
17          }
18  2       return (RequestHandler)
19                  this.requestHandlers.get(request.getName()); // (4)
20      }
21
22        // (5)
23  1   public Response processRequest(Request request)
24      {
25  1       Response response;
26  1       try
27          {
28  1           response =
29                  getHandler(request).process(request); // (6)
30          } catch (Exception exception)
31          {
32  0           response = new ErrorResponse(request,exception); // (7)
33          }
34  1       return response; // (8)
35      }
```

Figure 4.8   A Clover report showing how many times lines of code have been tested and what portion of the code has not been tested (line 32)

Although they're both helpful and interesting, the reports we have shown do not tell you how "good" your tests are. They only tell you which methods are being tested and which are not. Your tests could be faulty and not test anything at all, and the reports would still be the same! Ascertaining the quality of tests is difficult, and tools such as Jester (http://jester.sourceforge.net) can help. Jester works by performing random mutations to the code being tested; it then verifies if your tests still pass. If they do, it means they were not good enough. Jester does this over several iterations and then produces a report showing the quality of the tests.

What is important to remember is that *100% test coverage does not guarantee that your application is 100% tested.* Your test coverage is only as good as your tests! If your tests are poorly conceived, your application will be inadequately tested, no matter how many tests you have.

4.3.3 *Testing interactions*

So, if we can achieve higher test coverage with white box unit tests, and we can generate some fancy reports to prove it, do we need to bother with black box tests at all?

If you think about the differences between figure 4.5 and figure 4.6, there's more going on than how many methods are being tested. The black box tests in figure 4.5 are testing the interactions between objects. The white box unit tests in figure 4.6, by definition, do not test object interactions. If a white box test does interact with another object, that object is usually a stub or a mock object (see chapters 6 and 7), designed to produce specific test behavior.

If you want to fully test your application, including how the runtime objects interact with each other, you need to include black box integration tests as part of your regimen. Each type of test has its own place in the scheme of things.

4.4 *Test-Driven Development*

In chapter 3, you designed an application controller and quickly wrote some tests to prove your design. As you wrote the tests, the tests helped improve the initial design. As you write more unit tests, positive reinforcement encourages you to write them earlier. Pretty soon, as you design the implementation, it becomes natural to wonder about how you will test a class. Following this methodology, more developers are making the quantum leap from test-friendly designs to Test-Driven Development.[3]

> **DEFINITION**   *Test-Driven Development* (TDD)—Test-Driven Development is a programming practice that instructs developers to write new code only if an automated test has failed, *and* to eliminate duplication. The goal of TDD is "clean code that works."

4.4.1 *Tweaking the cycle*

When you develop code, you design an application programming interface (API) and then implement the behavior promised by the interface. When you unit-test code, you verify the promised behavior through a method's API. The test is a client of the method's API, just as your domain code is a client of the method's API.

---

[3] Kent Beck, *Test Driven Development: By Example* (Boston: Addison-Wesley, 2003).

The conventional development cycle goes something like this: [code, *test*, (repeat), commit]. Developers practicing TDD make a seemingly slight but surprisingly effective adjustment: [*test*, code, (repeat), commit]. (More on this later.) The test drives the design and becomes the method's first client.

Listing 4.3 illustrates how unit tests can help design the implementation. The `testGetBalanceOk` method shows that the `getBalance` method of `Account` returns the account balance as a long and that this balance can be set in the `Account` constructor. At this point, the implementation of `Account` is purely hypothetical, but writing the unit tests allows you to focus on the design of the code. As soon as you implement the class, you can run the test to prove that the implementation works. If the test fails, then you can continue working on the implementation until it passes the test. When the test passes, you know that your contract is fulfilled and that the code works as advertised.

Listing 4.3   Unit tests as a design guide

```java
import junit.framework.TestCase;

public class TestAccount extends TestCase
{
    public void testGetBalanceOk ()
    {
        long balance = 1000;
        Account account = new Account(balance);
        long result = account.getBalance();
        assertEquals(balance, result);
    }
}
```

When you use the test as the method's first client, it becomes easier to focus purely on the API. Writing the tests first provides the following:

- Means to design the code
- Documentation as to how the code works
- Unit tests for the code (*waddyaknow*)

Someone new to the project can understand the system by studying the functional test suite (with the help of some high-level UML diagrams, for example). To analyze a specific portion of the application in detail, someone can drill down into individual unit tests.

4.4.2 *The TDD two-step*

Earlier, we said that TDD tweaks the development cycle to go something like [test, code, (repeat), ship]. The problem with this chant is that it leaves out a key step. It should go more like this: [test, code, *refactor*, (repeat), ship].

The core tenets of TDD are to:

1 Write a failing automatic test before writing new code

2 Eliminate duplication[4]

The *eliminate duplication* step ensures that you write code that is not only testable but also *maintainable*. When you eliminate duplication, you tend to increase cohesion and decrease dependency. These are hallmarks of code that is easier to maintain over time.

Other coding practices have encouraged us to write maintainable code by anticipating change. In contrast, TDD encourages us to write maintainable code *by eliminating duplication*. Developers following this practice have found that test-backed, well-factored code is, by its very nature, easy *and safe* to change. TDD gives us the confidence to solve today's problems today and tomorrow's problems tomorrow. *Carpe diem!*

> **JUnit best practice: test first (never write a line of new code without a failing test)**
>
> If you take the TDD development pattern to heart, an interesting thing happens: Before you can write any code, *you must write a test that fails.* Why does it fail? *Because you haven't written the code to make it succeed.*
>
> Faced with a situation like this, most of us begin by writing a simple implementation to let the test pass. Now that the test succeeds, you could stop and move on to the next problem. Being a professional, you would take a few minutes to *refactor* the implementation to remove redundancy, clarify intent, and optimize the investment in the new code. But as long as the test succeeds, technically, you're done.
>
> The end game? If you always test first, you will never write a line of new code without a failing test.

---

[4] Ibid.

4.5 *Testing in the development cycle*

Testing occurs at different places and times during the development cycle. Let's first introduce a development life cycle and then use it as a base for deciding what types of tests are executed when. Figure 4.9 shows a typical development cycle we have used effectively in small to large teams.

The life cycle is divided into four or five platforms:

- *Development platform*—This is where the coding happens. It consists of developers' workstations. One important rule is usually to commit (or *check in,* depending on the terminology used) several times per day to your common Source Control Management (SCM) tool (CVS, ClearCase, Visual SourceSafe, Starteam, and so on). Once you commit, others can begin using what you have committed. However, it is important to only commit something that "works." In order to know if it works, a typical strategy is to have an automated build (see chapter 5) and run it before each commit.

- *Integration platform*—The goal of this platform is to build the application from its different pieces (which may have been developed by different teams) and ensure that they all fit together. This step is extremely valuable, because problems are often discovered here. It is so valuable that we want to automate it. It is then called *continuous integration* (see http://www.martinfowler.com/articles/continuousIntegration.html) and can be achieved by automatically building the application as part of the build process (more on that in chapter 5 and later).

- *Acceptance platform / stress test platform*—Depending on how rich your project is, this can be one or two platforms. The stress test platform exercises the

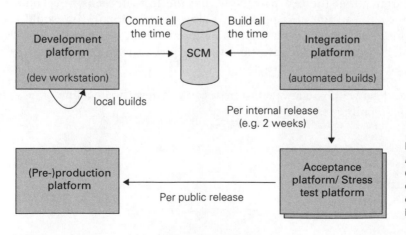

**Figure 4.9
A typical application development life cycle using the continuous integration principle**

application under load and verifies that it scales correctly (with respect to size and response time). The acceptance platform is where the project's customers accept (sign off on) the system. It is highly recommended that the system be deployed on the acceptance platform as often as possible in order to get user feedback.

- *(Pre-)production platform*—The pre-production platform is the last staging area before production. It is optional, and small or noncritical projects can do without it.

Let's see how testing fits in the development cycle. Figure 4.10 highlights the different types of tests you can perform on each platform:

- On the *development platform,* you execute logic unit tests (tests that can be executed in isolation from the environment). These tests execute very quickly, and you usually execute them from your IDE to verify that any change you have brought to the code has not broken anything. They are also executed by your automated build before you commit the code to your SCM. You could also execute integration unit tests; however, they often take much longer, because they need some part of the environment to be set up (database, application server, and so on). In practice, you would execute only a subset of all integration unit tests, including any new integration unit tests you have written.

- The *integration platform* usually runs the build process automatically to package and deploy the application and then executes unit and functional tests.

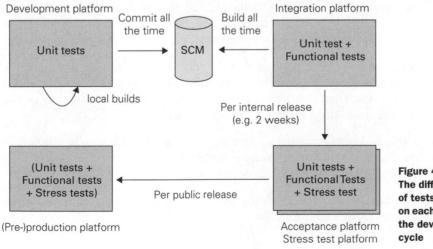

Figure 4.10
The different types of tests performed on each platform of the development cycle

Usually, only a subset of all functional tests is run on the integration platform, because compared to the target production platform it is a simple platform that lack elements (for example, it may be missing a connection to an external system being accessed). All types of unit tests are executed on the integration platform (logic unit tests, integration unit tests, and functional unit tests). Time is less important, and the whole build can take several hours with no impact on development.

- On the *acceptance platform / stress test platform*, you re-execute the same tests executed by the integration platform; in addition, you run stress tests (performance and load tests). The acceptance platform is extremely close to the production platform, and more functional tests can also be executed.

- It is always a good habit to try to run on the *(pre-)production platform* the tests you ran on the acceptance platform. Doing so acts as a sanity check to verify that everything is set up correctly.

JUnit best practice: continuous regression testing

Most tests are written for the here and now. You write a new feature, you write a new test. You see if the feature plays well with others, and if the users like it. If everyone is happy, you can lock the feature and move on to the next item on your list. Most software is written in a progressive fashion: You add one feature and then another.

Most often, each new feature is built over a path paved by existing features. If an existing method can service a new feature, you reuse the method and save the cost of writing a new one. Of course, it's never quite that easy. Sometimes you need to change an existing method to make it work with a new feature. When this happens, you need to confirm that all the old features still work with the amended method.

A strong benefit of JUnit is that the test cases are easy to automate. When a change is made to a method, you can run the test for that method. If that one passes, then you can run the rest. If any fail, you can change the code (or the tests) until everyone is happy again.

Using old tests to guard against new changes is a form of regression testing. Any kind of test can be used as a regression test, but running unit tests after every change is your first, best line of defense.

The best way to ensure that regression testing is done is to automate your test suites. See chapter 5 for more about automating JUnit.

4.6 Summary

The pace of change is increasing. Project time frames are getting shorter, and we need to react quickly to change. In addition, the development process is shifting—development as the art of writing code is not enough. Development must be the art of writing solutions.

To accommodate rapid change, we must break with asynchronous approaches where software testing is done after development by a separate team. Late testing does not scale when change and swiftness are paramount.

The agile approaches favor working in small vertical slices rather than big horizontal ones. This means small teams performing several activities at once (designing, testing, coding) and delivering solutions, slice by slice. Automated tests are hallmarks of applications that work. Tests enable refactoring, and refactoring enables the elegant addition of new solutions, slice by slice.

When it comes to unit-testing an application, you can use several types of tests: logic unit tests, integration unit tests, and functional unit tests. All are useful during development, and they complement each other. They also complement the other software tests that should be performed by quality assurance personnel and by the customer.

One of the great benefits of unit tests is that they are easy to automate. In the next chapter, we look at several tools to help you automate unit testing.

Automating JUnit

This chapter covers

- Integrating JUnit into your development environment
- Running JUnit from Ant, Maven, and Eclipse

It's supposed to be automatic, but you still have to press the button.

—John Brunner

In this chapter, we will look at three products with direct support for JUnit: Ant, Maven, and Eclipse. Ant and Maven are build tools that can be used with any Java programming environment. Eclipse is an integrated development environment (IDE). We will demonstrate how you can be productive with JUnit and these environments and how to automate running JUnit tests.

At the end of this chapter, you will know how to set up your environment on your machine to build Java projects, including execution of JUnit tests and generation of JUnit reports.

5.1 A day in the life

For unit tests to be effective, they should be part of the development routine. Most development cycles begin by checking out a module from the project's source-code repository. Before making any changes, prudent developers first run the full unit-test suite. Many teams have a rule that all the unit tests on the working repository must pass. Before starting any development of your own, you should see for yourself that no one has broken the all-green rule. You should always be sure that your work progresses from a known baseline.`

The next step is to write the code for a new use case (or modify an existing one). If you are a Test-Driven Development (TDD) practitioner, you'll start by writing new tests for the use case. (For more about TDD, see chapter 4.) Generally, the test will show that your use case isn't supported and either will not compile or will display a red bar when executed. Once you write the code to implement the use case, the bar turns green, and you can check in your code. Non-TDD practitioners will implement the use case and then write the tests to prove it. Once the bar turns green, the code and the tests can be checked in.

In any event, before you move on to code the next feature, you should have a test to prove the new feature works. After you code the next feature, you can run the tests for the prior feature too. In this way, you can ensure that new development does not break old development. If the old feature needs to change to accommodate the new feature, then you update its test and make the change.

If you test rigorously, both to help you design new code (TDD) and to ensure that old code works with new (regression testing), you must continually run the unit tests as a normal part of the development cycle. The test runners must become your best friends. And, like any best friend, the test runners should be on speed dial. You need to be able to run the tests automatically and effortlessly throughout the day.

> **DEFINITION**   *regression tests*—When new code is added to existing code, regression tests verify that the existing code continues to work correctly.[1]

In chapter 1, section 1.3, we discussed running JUnit from the command line. Running a single JUnit test case against a single class is not difficult. But it is not a practical approach for running continuous tests against a project with hundreds or even thousands of classes.

A project that is fully tested has at least as many test classes as production classes. Developers can't be expected to run an entire set of regression tests every day by hand. So, you must have a way to run key tests easily and automatically, without relying on already-overworked human beings.

Because you are writing so many tests, you need to write and run tests in the most effective way possible. Using JUnit should be seamless, like calling a build tool or plugging in a code highlighter.

Three tools that many developers already use are Ant, Maven, and Eclipse (or any other IDE). Ant is the de facto standard tool for building Java applications; it is an excellent tool for managing and automating JUnit tests. Maven extends Ant's features to provide broader project-management support. Like Ant, it is on its way to becoming a de facto standard.

Ant and Maven will happily build your applications, but they don't help write them. Although many Java applications are still written with text editors, more and more developers use full-featured IDEs. Several very competent IDEs are now available, both as open source and as retail products. We'll look at how one of these products, Eclipse, integrates JUnit into an omnibus development platform.

5.2 *Running tests from Ant*

Compiling and testing a single class, like the `DefaultController` class from chapter 3, is not difficult. Compiling a larger project with multiple classes can be a huge headache if your only tool is the stock javac compiler. Increasing numbers of classes refer to each other, and so more classes need to be on the classpath where the compiler can find them. On any one build, only a few classes will change, so

---

[1]   Derek Sisson, "Types of Tests": http://www.philosophe.com/testing/tests.html.

there is also the issue of which classes to build. Re-running your JUnit tests by hand after each build can be equally inconvenient, for all the same reasons.

Happily, the answer to both problems is the fabulous tool called Ant. Ant is not only an essential tool for building applications, but also a great way to run your JUnit regression tests.

5.2.1 Ant, indispensable Ant

Apache's Ant product (http://ant.apache.org/) is a build tool that lets you easily compile and test applications (among other things). It is the de facto standard for building Java applications. One reason for Ant's popularity is that it is more than a tool: Ant is a framework for running tools. In addition to using Ant to configure and launch a Java compiler, you can use it to generate code, invoke JDBC queries, and, as you will see, run JUnit test suites.

Like many modern projects, Ant is configured through an XML document. This document is referred to as the *buildfile* and is named build.xml by default. The Ant buildfile describes each task that you want to apply on your project. A task might be compiling Java source code, generating Javadocs, transferring files, querying databases, or running tests. A buildfile can have several *targets*, or entry points, so that you can run a single task or chain several together. Let's look at using Ant to automatically run tests as part of the build process. If *(gasp!)* you don't have Ant installed, see the following sidebars. For full details, consult the Ant manual (http://ant.apache.org/manual/).

> #### Installing Ant on Windows
>
> To install Ant on Windows, follow these steps:
>
> 1. Unzip the Zip distribution file to a directory on your computer system (for example, C:\Ant).
>
> 2. Under this directory, Unzip creates a subdirectory for the Ant distribution you downloaded—for example, C:\Ant\jakarta-ant-1.5.3. Add an ANT_HOME variable to your environment with this directory as the value. For example:
>
>    ```
>    Variable Name: ANT_HOME
>    Variable Value: C:\Ant\jakarta-ant-1.5.3
>    ```
>
> 3. Edit your system's PATH environment variable to include the ANT_HOME\bin folder:
>
>    ```
>    Variable Name: PATH
>    Variable Value: %ANT_HOME%\bin;…
>    ```

> **Installing Ant on Windows** (continued)
>
> 4   We recommend that you also specify the location of your Java Developer's Kit (JDK) as the JAVA_HOME environment variable:
>
> ```
> Variable Name: JAVA_HOME
> Variable Value: C:\j2sdk1.4.2
> ```
>
> This value, like the others, may vary depending on where you installed the JDK on your system.
>
> 5   To enable Ant's JUnit task, you must put junit.jar in the ANT_HOME\lib folder.

> **Installing Ant on UNIX (bash)**
>
> To install Ant on UNIX (or Linux), follow these steps:
>
> 1   Untar the Ant tarball to a directory on your computer system (for example, /opt/ant).
>
> 2   Under this directory, tar creates a subdirectory for the Ant distribution you downloaded—for example, /opt/ant/jakarta-ant-1.5.3. Add this subdirectory to your environment as ANT_HOME. For example:
>
> ```
> export ANT_HOME=/opt/ant/jakarta-ant-1.5.3
> ```
>
> 3   Add the ANT_HOME/bin folder to your system's command path:
>
> ```
> export PATH=${PATH}:${ANT_HOME}/bin
> ```
>
> 4   We recommend that you also specify the location of your JDK as the JAVA_HOME environment variable:
>
> ```
> export JAVA_HOME=/usr/java/j2sdk1.4.2
> ```
>
> 5   To enable Ant's JUnit task, you must put junit.jar in the ANT_HOME/lib folder.

5.2.2   *Ant targets, projects, properties, and tasks*

When you build a software project, you are often interested in more than just binary code. For a final distribution, you may want to generate Javadocs along with the binary classes. For an interim compile during development, you may skip that step. Sometimes, you want to run a clean build from scratch. Other times, you want to build the classes that have changed.

To help you manage the build process, Ant lets you create a buildfile for each of your projects. The buildfile may have several targets, encapsulating the different tasks needed to create your application and related resources. To make the build-files easier to configure and reuse, Ant lets you define dynamic property elements. These Ant essentials are as follows:

- *Buildfile*—Each buildfile is usually associated with a particular development project. Ant uses the `project` XML tag as the outermost element in `build.xml`. The `project` element defines a project. It also lets you specify a default target, so you can run Ant without any parameters.

- *Target*—When you run Ant, you can specify one or more targets for it to build. Targets can also declare that they depend on other targets. If you ask Ant to run one target, the buildfile might run several others first. This lets you create a distribution target that depends on other targets like `clean`, `compile`, `javadoc`, and `war`.

- *Property elements*—Many of the targets within a project will share the same settings. Ant lets you create property elements to encapsulate specific settings and reuse them throughout your buildfile. If a buildfile is carefully written, the property elements can make it easy to adapt the buildfile to a new environment. To refer to a property within a buildfile, you place the property within a special notation: `${property}`. To refer to the property named `target.dir`, you would write `${target.dir}`.

As mentioned, Ant is not so much a tool as a framework for running tools. You can use property elements to set the parameters a tool needs and a *task* to run the tool. A great number of tasks come bundled with Ant, and you can also write your own. For more about developing with Ant, we highly recommend *Java Development with Ant.*[2]

Listing 5.1 shows the top of the buildfile for the `sampling` project from chapter 3. This segment of the buildfile sets the default target and the properties your tasks will use.

Listing 5.1 The Ant buildfile project and property elements

```
<project name="sampling" default="test">          ❶

  <property file="build.properties"/>             ❷

  <property name="src.dir" location="src"/>
  <property name="src.java.dir" location="${src.dir}/java"/>   ❸
```

---

[2] Erik Hatcher and Steve Loughran, *Java Development with Ant* (Greenwich, CT: Manning, 2003); http://www.manning.com/hatcher/.

```
<property name="src.test.dir" location="${src.dir}/test"/>

<property name="target.dir" location="target"/>
<property name="target.classes.java.dir"
    location="${target.dir}/classes/java"/>
<property name="target.classes.test.dir"
    location="${target.dir}/classes/test"/>
[...]
```

❶ Give the project the name `sampling` and set the default `target` to `test`. (The `test` target appears in listing 5.3.)

❷ You include a `build.properties` file. This file contains Ant properties that may need to be changed on a user's system because they depend on the executing environment. For example, these properties can include the locations of redistributable jars. Because programmers may store jars in different locations, it is good practice to use a `build.properties` file to define them. Many open source projects provide a `build.properties.sample` file you can copy as `build.properties` and then edit to match your environment. For this project, you won't need to define any properties in it.

❸ ❹ As you will see, your targets need to know the location of your production and test source code. You use the Ant `property` task to define these values so that they can be reused and easily changed. At ❸, you define properties related to the source tree; at ❹, you define those related to the output tree (where the build-generated files will go). Notice that you use different properties to define where the compiled production and tests classes will be put. Putting them in different directories is a good practice because it allows you to easily package the production classes in a jar without mixing test classes.

An interesting thing about Ant properties is that they are *immutable*—once they are set, they cannot be modified. For example, if any properties are redefined after the `build.properties` file is loaded, the new value is ignored. The first definition always wins.

5.2.3 *The javac task*

For simple jobs, running the Java Compiler (javac) from the command line is easy enough. But for multipackage products, the care and feeding of javac and your classpath becomes a Herculean task. Ant's `javac` task tames the compiler and its classpath, making building projects effortless and automatic.

The Ant `javac` task is usually employed from within a target with a name like `compile`. Before and after running the `javac` task, you can perform any needed file management as part of the target. The `javac` task lets you set any of the standard options, including the destination directory. You can also supply a list of paths for your source files. The latter is handy for projects with tests, because you may tend to keep production classes in one folder and test classes in another.

Listing 5.2 shows the `compile` targets that call the Java Compiler for the sampling project, both for the production code and for the test code.

Listing 5.2 The buildfile compile targets

```
<target name="compile.java">                                    ❶
  <mkdir dir="${target.classes.java.dir}"/>                     ❷
  <javac destdir="${target.classes.java.dir}">                  ❸
    <src path="${src.java.dir}"/>                               ❹
  </javac>
</target>

<target name="compile.test" depends="compile.java">            ❺
  <mkdir dir="${target.classes.test.dir}"/>
  <javac destdir="${target.classes.test.dir}">
    <src path="${src.test.dir}"/>
    <classpath>                                                 ❻
      <pathelement location="${target.classes.java.dir}"/>
    </classpath>
  </javac>
</target>

<target name="compile" depends="compile.java,compile.test"/>   ❼
```

❶ Declare the target to compile the java production sources, naming it `compile.java`.

❷ Ensure that the directory where you will generate your production class files exists. Ant resolves the property you set at the top of the buildfile (see listing 5.1) and inserts it in place of the variable notation `${target.classes.java.dir}`. If the directory already exists, Ant quietly continues.

❸ Call the Java Compiler (javac) and pass it the destination directory to use.

❹ Tell the `javac` task what sources to compile.

❺ Compile the test sources exactly the same way you just did for the production sources. Your `compile.test` target has a dependency on the `compile.java` target, so you must add a `depends` element to that `compile.test` target definition (`depends="compile.java"`). You may have noticed that you don't explicitly add the JUnit jar to the classpath. Remember that when you installed Ant, you put the JUnit jar in ANT_HOME/lib (this is necessary in order to use the junit Ant task). As a consequence, junit.jar is already on your classpath, and you don't need to specify it in the javac task to properly compile your tests.

6 You need to add a nested classpath element in order to add the production classes you just compiled to the classpath. This is because test classes call production classes.

7 Create a compile target that automatically calls the compile.java and compile.test targets.

5.2.4 *The JUnit task*

In chapter 3, you ran the DefaultController tests by hand. That meant between any changes, you had to

- Compile the source code
- Run the TestDefaultController test case against the compiled classes

You can get Ant to perform both these steps as part of the same build target. Listing 5.3 shows the test target for the sampling buildfile.

Listing 5.3   The buildfile test target

```
<target name="test" depends="compile">                    ❶
  <junit printsummary="yes" haltonerror="yes" haltonfailure="yes"   ❷
    fork="yes">
    <formatter type="plain" usefile="false"/>             ❸
    <test name="junitbook.sampling.TestDefaultController"/>  ❹
    <classpath>                                           ❺
      <pathelement location="${target.classes.java.dir}"/>
      <pathelement location="${target.classes.test.dir}"/>
    </classpath>
  </junit>
</target>
</project>
```

❶ Give the target a name and declare that it relies on the compile target. If you ask Ant to run the test target, it will run the compile target before running test.

❷ Here you get into the JUnit-specific attributes. The printsummary attribute says to render a one-line summary at the end of the test. By setting fork to yes, you force Ant to use a separate Java Virtual Machine (JVM) for each test. This is always a good practice as it avoids interferences between test cases. The haltonfailure and haltonerror attributes say that the build should stop if any test returns a failure or an error (an error is an unexpected error, whereas a failure happens if one of the test asserts does not pass).

❸ Configure the junit task formatter to use plain text and output the test result to the console.

❹ Provide the class name of the test you want to run.

❺ Extend the classpath to use for this task to include the classes you just compiled.

5.2.5 *Putting Ant to the task*

Now that you've assembled the buildfile, you can run it from the command line by changing to your project directory and entering **ant**. Figure 5.1 shows what Ant renders in response.

You can now build and test the sampling project all at the same time. If any of the tests fail, the haltonfailure/haltonerror settings will stop the build, bringing the failure to your attention.

```
 C:\WINDOWS\System32\cmd.exe

C:\junitbook\sampling>ant
Buildfile: build.xml

compile.java:
    [mkdir] Created dir: C:\junitbook\sampling\target\classes\java
    [javac] Compiling 6 source files to C:\junitbook\sampling\target\classes\java

compile.test:
    [mkdir] Created dir: C:\junitbook\sampling\target\classes\test
    [javac] Compiling 9 source files to C:\junitbook\sampling\target\classes\test

compile:

test:
    [mkdir] Created dir: C:\junitbook\sampling\target\report
    [junit] Running junitbook.sampling.TestDefaultController
    [junit] Tests run: 5, Failures: 0, Errors: 0, Time elapsed: 0.201 sec
    [junit] Testsuite: junitbook.sampling.TestDefaultController
    [junit] Tests run: 5, Failures: 0, Errors: 0, Time elapsed: 0.201 sec

    [junit] Testcase: testAddHandler took 0.01 sec
    [junit] Testcase: testProcessRequest took 0 sec
    [junit] Testcase: testProcessRequestAnswersErrorResponse took 0 sec
    [junit] Testcase: testGetHandlerNotDefined took 0 sec
    [junit] Testcase: testAddRequestDuplicateName took 0 sec

BUILD SUCCESSFUL
Total time: 17 seconds
C:\junitbook\sampling>
```

Figure 5.1 Running the buildfile from the command line

> ### Running optional tasks
>
> The junit task is one of several components bundled in Ant's optional.jar. The optional.jar file should already be in your ANT_HOME/lib directory. Ant does not bundle a copy of JUnit, so you must be sure that junit.jar is on your system classpath or in the ANT_HOME/lib directory. (The optional.jar file is for tasks that depend on another package, like JUnit.) For more about installing Ant, see the sidebars on pages 89–90. If you have any trouble running the Ant buildfiles presented in this chapter, make sure the Ant optional.jar is in the ANT_HOME/lib folder and junit.jar is either on your system classpath or also in the ANT_HOME/lib folder.

The empty classpath

Given a tool like Ant, many developers don't bother with a system classpath anymore: You can let Ant take care of all that. Ant's classpath element makes it easy to build the classpath you need when you need it.

The only blind spot is the jars you need in order to run one of the optional Ant tasks, like junit. To provide the flexibility you need for other circumstances, Ant uses Sun's delegation model to create whatever classpath you need at runtime. In the case of the optional tasks, there's a bootstrap issue. To employ a task, whatever libraries a task needs must be on the *same* classpath as the code for the task. This means you need to load junit.jar in the same place you load optional.jar. Meanwhile, you also need to load the task (and any external libraries) before you can use the task in your buildfile. In short, you can't specify the path to junit.jar as part of the junit task.

The simplest solution is to move junit.jar to ANT_HOME/lib. There are alternative configurations, but they are usually more trouble than they are worth.[3]

So, to keep a clean classpath and use optional tasks like JUnit, you should move the jar for the external library to ANT_HOME/lib. Ant will then automatically load optional.jar and the external libraries together, enabling use of the optional tasks in your buildfiles. Just remember to update junit.jar in ANT_HOME/lib whenever you install a new version of either Ant or JUnit.

5.2.6 Pretty printing with JUnitReport

A report like the one in figure 5.1 is fine when you are running tests interactively. But what if you want to run a test suite and review the results later? For

---

[3] Ant 1.6 will let you put optional task jars in places other than ANT_HOME/lib.

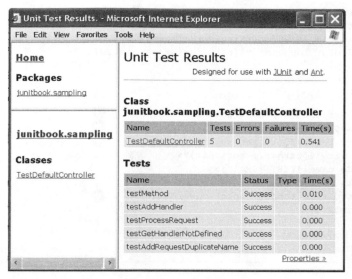

Figure 5.2 Output of the `junitreport` Ant task

example, the tests might be run automatically every day by a cron job (whether you liked it or not!).

Another optional Ant task, `junitreport`, is designed to output the result of the tests as XML. To finish the job, `junitreport` renders the XML into HTML using an XSL stylesheet. The result is an attractive and functional **report** that you (or your boss) can peruse with any browser. A `junitreport` page for the `sampling` project is shown in figure 5.2.

Listing 5.4 shows the changes (in bold) necessary in the buildfile to generate this report. To execute the script, type **ant report** on the command line in the sampling project.

Listing 5.4 Adding a JUnitReport task to the buildfile

```
<project name="sampling" default="test">
[...]
  <property name="target.report.dir"
      location="${target.dir}/report"/>                    ❶
[...]
  <target name="test" depends="compile">
    <mkdir dir="${target.report.dir}"/>                     ❷
    <junit printsummary="yes" haltonerror="yes" haltonfailure="yes"
        fork="yes">
      <formatter type="plain" usefile="false"/>
      <formatter type="xml"/>                               ❸
      <test name="junitbook.sampling.TestDefaultController"
```

```
              todir="${target.report.dir}"/>          ❹
        <classpath>
          <pathelement location="${target.classes.java.dir}"/>
          <pathelement location="${target.classes.test.dir}"/>
        </classpath>
      </junit>
    </target>

    <target name="report" depends="test">          ❺
      <mkdir dir="${target.report.dir}/html"/>          ❻
      <junitreport todir="${target.report.dir}">          ❼
        <fileset dir="${target.report.dir}">          ❽
          <include name="TEST-*.xml"/>
        </fileset>
        <report todir="${target.report.dir}/html"/>          ❾
      </junitreport>
    </target>

  </project>
```

❶ Define a property holding the target location where your reports will be generated.

❷ Create that directory.

❸ You need to modify the `junit` task so that it outputs the test results as XML. The `junitreport` task works by transforming the XML test result into an HTML report.

❹ Tell the `junit` task to create a report file in the `${target.report.dir}` directory.

❺ Introduce a new `report` target that generates the HTML report.

❻ You begin by creating the directory where the HTML will be generated.

❼ Call the `junitreport` task to create the report.

❽ The `junitreport` task works by scanning the list of XML test results you specify as an Ant `fileset`.

❾ Tell the `junitreport` task where to generate the HTML report.

5.2.7 *Automatically finding the tests to run*

The buildfile you have written is using the `test` element of the `junit` task to tell JUnit what test to execute. Although this is fine when there are only a few test cases, it becomes tiresome when your test suite grows. The biggest issue then becomes ensuring that you haven't forgotten to include a test in the buildfile. Fortunately, the `junit` task has a convenient `batchtest` element that lets you specify test cases using wildcards. Listing 5.5 shows how to use it (changes from listing 5.4 are shown in bold).

Listing 5.5   A better buildfile using batchtest

```
<project name="sampling" default="test">
[...]
  <target name="test" depends="compile">
    <mkdir dir="${target.report.dir}"/>
    <property name="tests" value="Test*"/>                    ❶
    <junit printsummary="yes" haltonerror="yes" haltonfailure="yes"
        fork="yes">
      <formatter type="plain" usefile="false"/>
      <formatter type="xml"/>
      <batchtest todir="${target.report.dir}">
        <fileset dir="${src.test.dir}">
          <include name="**/${tests}.java"/>                  ❷
          <exclude name="**/Test*All.java"/>
        </fileset>
      </batchtest>
      <classpath>
        <pathelement location="${target.classes.java.dir}"/>
        <pathelement location="${target.classes.test.dir}"/>
      </classpath>
    </junit>
  </target>
[...]
  <target name="clean">
    <delete dir="${target.dir}"/>                            ❸
  </target>
</project>
```

---

❶ You may wonder why you define a property here when you could have put the wildcards directly into the `fileset` element at ❷. Using this trick, you can define the `tests` property on the command line and run a single test (or a specific set of tests) instead. This is an easy way to run a test against the class you are working on right now. Of course, once it's working, you still run the full test suite to be sure everyone is on the same page. Here is an example that only executes the `TestDefaultController` test case:

```
ant –Dtests=TestDefaultController test
```

❷ You improve the buildfile by making the `test` target more flexible. Whereas before you had to explicitly name the different tests you wanted to execute, here you leverage the `junit` task's nested `batchtest` element. With `batchtest`, you can specify the test to run as a *fileset*, thus allowing the use of wildcards.

❸ Add the always-useful `clean` target to remove all build-generated files. Doing so lets you start with a fresh build with no side effects from obsolete classes. Typically, a `dist` target that generates the project distributable depends on the clean target.

> **Are automated unit tests a panacea?**
>
> Absolutely not! Automated tests can find a significant number of bugs, but manual testing is still required to find as many bugs as possible. In general, automated regression tests catch 15–30% of all bugs found; manual testing finds the other 70–85% (http://www.testingcraft.com/regression-test-bugs.html).
>
> **Are you sure about that?**
>
> Some test-first design / unit testing enthusiasts are now reporting remarkably low numbers of bug counts, on the order of one or two per month or fewer. But these results need to be substantiated by formal studies and replicated by other teams. Your mileage will definitely vary.

5.3 Running tests from Maven

Once you have used Ant on several projects, you'll notice that most projects almost always need the same Ant scripts (or at least a good percentage). These scripts are easy enough to reuse through cut and paste, but each new project requires a bit of fussing to get the Ant buildfiles working just right. In addition, each project usually ends up having several subprojects, each of which requires you to create and maintain an Ant buildfile.

Maven (http://maven.apache.org/) picks up where Ant leaves off, making it a natural fit for many teams. Like Ant, Maven is a tool for running other tools, but Maven is designed to take tool reuse to the next level. If Ant is a source-building framework, Maven is a source-building *environment*.

5.3.1 Maven the goal-seeker

Behind each target in every Ant buildfile lies a goal. The goal might be to generate the unit tests, to assemble the Javadocs, or to compile the distribution. The driving force behind Maven is that under the hood, each software project almost always does things the same way, following several years of best practices. Most differences are arbitrary, such as whether you call the target output directory `target` or `output`.

Instead of asking developers to write their own targets with tasks, Maven provides ready-to-use plugins to achieve the goals. At the time of this writing, Maven boasts more than 70 plugins. Once Maven is installed (see the sidebar on the next page), you can type `maven -g` to get the full list of the available plugins and goals. Reference documentation for the plugins is available at http://maven.apache.org/reference/plugins. The following list describes a few common Maven plugins:

- jar—Generates a project jar and deploys it to a local or remote jar repository
- junit—Executes JUnit tests
- site—Generates a project documentation web site that contains lots of useful reports and project information, in addition to containing any docs you wish to include
- changelog—Generates a change log report (CVS changelog, Starteam changelog, and so forth)
- checkstyle—Runs Checkstyle on the source code and generates a report
- clover—Runs Clover on the source code and generates a Clover report
- eclipse—Automatically generates Eclipse project files from the Maven project description
- ear—Packages the application as an ear file
- cactus—Automatically packages your code, deploys it in a container of your choice, starts the container, and runs Cactus tests (see chapter 8)
- jboss—Supports creation of JBoss Server configurations and deployments of war, ear, and EJB-jar in JBoss using a simple copy or JMX

Having well-defined plugins not only provides unprecedented ease of use, it also standardizes project builds, making it easy for developers to go from project to project.

Installing Maven

Installing Maven is a three-step process:

1 Download the latest distribution from http://maven.apache.org/builds/release/ and unzip/untar it in the directory of your choice (for example, c:\maven on Windows or /opt/maven on UNIX).

2 Define a MAVEN_HOME environment variable pointing to where you have installed Maven.

3 Add MAVEN_HOME\bin (MAVEN_HOME/bin on UNIX) to your PATH environment variable so that you can type **maven** from any directory.

You are now ready to use Maven. The first time you execute a plugin, make sure your Internet connection is on, because Maven will automatically download from the Web all the third-party jars the plugin requires.

5.3.2 *Configuring Maven for a project*

Using Ant alone, you describe your build at the level of the tasks. With Maven, you describe your project structure and the plugins use this directory structure, so you don't have to be an Ant wizard to set up your project. Maven handles the wizardry.

Let's look at a Maven description for a simple project based on the `sampling` project you wrote in chapter 3 and that you ran with Ant earlier in the chapter. The goal is to run your unit tests with Maven.

Configuring Maven for a project requires writing only one file: `project.xml` (also called the POM, short for project object model). It contains the full project description. Listing 5.6 shows the first part of this file, which contains background information about the project.

> **Listing 5.6 First part of project.xml showing background project information**

```
<?xml version="1.0" encoding="ISO-8859-1"?>

<project>
  <pomVersion>3</pomVersion>              ❶
  <id>junitbook-sampling</id>             ❷
  <name>JUnit in Action - Sampling JUnit</name>  ❸
  <currentVersion>1.0</currentVersion>    ❹
  <organization>
    <name>Manning Publications Co.</name>
    <url>http://www.manning.com/</url>
    <logo>http://www.manning.com/front/dance.gif</logo>
  </organization>
  <inceptionYear>2002</inceptionYear>
  <package>junitbook.sampling</package>
  <logo>/images/jia.jpg</logo>

  <description>                           ❺
    Chapter 3 presents a sophisticated test case to show how JUnit
    works with larger components. The subject of our case study is
    a component found in many applications: a controller. We
    introduce the case-study code, identify what code to test, and
    then show how to test it. Once we know that the code works as
    expected, we create tests for exceptional conditions, to be
    sure our code behaves well even when things go wrong.
  </description>
  <shortDescription>
    Chapter 3 of JUnit in Action: Sampling JUnit
  </shortDescription>

  <url>http://sourceforge.net/projects/junitbook/</url>

  <developers>                            ❻
    <developer>
      <name>Vincent Massol</name>
```

```
        <id>vmassol</id>                                        6
        <email>vmassol@users.sourceforge.net</email>
        <organization>Pivolis</organization>
        <roles>
          <role>Java Developer</role>
        </roles>
      </developer>
      <developer>
        <name>Ted Husted</name>
        <id>thusted</id>
        <email>thusted@users.sourceforge.net</email>
        <organization>Husted dot Com</organization>
        <roles>
          <role>Java Developer</role>
        </roles>
      </developer>
    </developers>
  [...]
</project>
```

❶ Tell Maven the version of the POM you are using to describe the project. As of this writing, the version to use is 3. Maven uses it to perform automatic migration of old POM versions to the new one if need be.

❷ Define the project ID. Several plugins use this ID to name files that are generated. For example, if you run the `jar` plugin on the project, it generates a jar named `junitbook-sampling-1.0.jar` (`<id>.<currentVersion>.jar`).

❸ Give a human-readable name for your project. It is used, for example, by the `site` plugin, which generates the documentation web site.

❹ This is the current version of your project. For example, the version suffixed to the jar name comes from the definition here.

❺ Describe background information about your project that is used by the `site` plugin for the web site.

❻ Describe the developers working on this project and their roles. This information is used in a report generated by the `site` plugin.

Executing Maven web-site generation

Let's use the Maven `site` plugin to generate the web site and see how the information you have provided is used. Open a command-line prompt in the `sampling/` project directory (see chapter 3, section 3.4 for details of setting up the project directory structure) and enter **maven site**, as shown in figure 5.3.

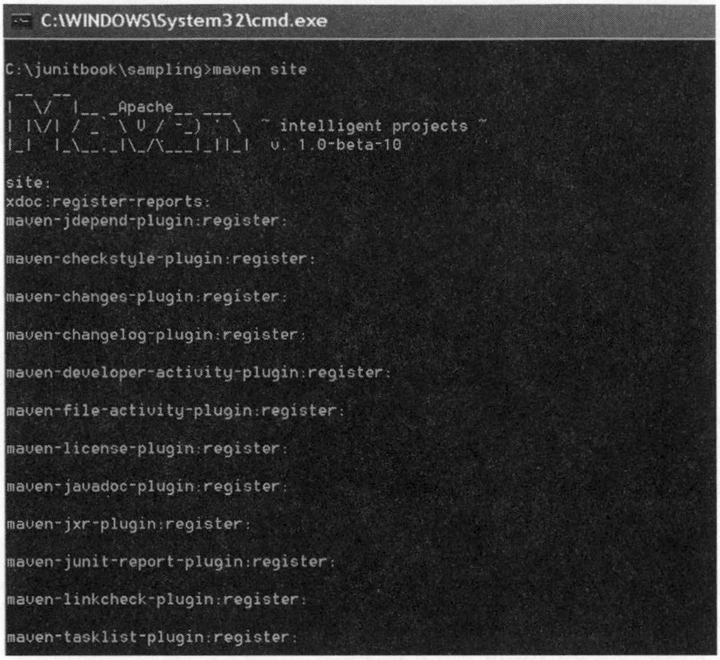

Figure 5.3   Beginning of the site-generation plugin execution showing the names of the different reports that will be generated

Figure 5.3 shows only the very beginning of the site plugin's execution. The website generation is quite rich. Maven generates several reports by default, as shown by figure 5.3. For example, you can see that it will generate metrics (maven-jepend-plugin), a Checkstyle report (maven-checkstyle-plugin), a change log report (maven-changelog-report), a JUnit report (maven-junit-report-plugin), a check for broken URL links in the documentation (maven-linkcheck-plugin), and so forth.

Figure 5.4 shows the welcome page of the generated web site. The generated web site makes good use of the information you entered in project.xml. For example, the images at the top are the ones you defined in listing 5.6 with the two logo elements. Each is linked to the URLs defined by the two corresponding url elements. The description comes from the description element, and the header is the project name (name element).

On the left are several menus, some of which contain submenus. For example, clicking Project Reports yields the screen in figure 5.5, showing all the generated default reports.

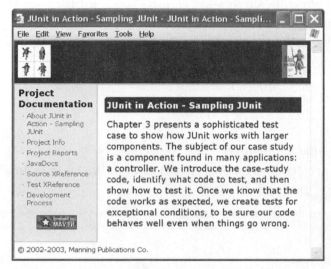

Figure 5.4   Welcome page of the generated site showing how the information entered in `project.xml` **is used**

Overview	
Document	**Description**
Metrics	Report on source code metrics.
Checkstyle	Report on coding style conventions.
Change Log	Report on the source control changelog.
Developer Activity	Report on the amount of developer activity.
File Activity	Report on file activity.
Project License	Displays the primary license for the project.
JavaDocs	JavaDoc API documentation.
JavaDoc Report	Report on the generation of JavaDoc.
Source Xref	A set of browsable cross-referenced sources.
Test Xref	A set of browsable cross-referenced test sources.
Unit Tests	Report on the results of the unit tests.
Link Check Report	Report on the validity of all links in the documentation.
Task List	Report on tasks specified in the source code.

Figure 5.5   List of Maven-generated default reports for the `sampling` **project**

It is possible to control exactly what reports you want for your web site by explicitly listing the desired reports in project.xml. For example, if you want only the unit test report and the checkstyle report, you can write the following at the end of project.xml:

```
<reports>
  <report>maven-junit-report-plugin</report>
  <report>maven-checkstyle-plugin</report>
</reports>
```

Describing build-related information

Let's complete the project object model (POM) by entering build-related information into project.xml (listing 5.7).

Listing 5.7   Second part of project.xml containing build-related information

```
<!--dependencies>
  <groupId>log4j</groupId>
  <artifactId>log4j</artifactId>                              ❶
  <version>1.2.8</version>
</dependencies-->

<build>
  <sourceDirectory>src/java</sourceDirectory>             ❷
  <unitTestSourceDirectory>src/test</unitTestSourceDirectory>  ❸
  <unitTest>
    <includes>
      <include>**/Test*.java</include>
    </includes>                                             ❹
    <excludes>
      <exclude>**/Test*All.java</exclude>
      <exclude>**/TestDefaultController?.java</exclude>
    </excludes>
  </unitTest>
</build>

</project>
```

❶ Describe the project's external dependencies. A dependency typically specifies a jar, but a dependency can be of any type. All jar dependencies are added to the classpath and used by the different plugins, such as the junit plugin. In this case, you have no external dependencies, which is why the log4j dependency is commented out in listing 5.7. In section 5.3.4, we describe in detail how Maven handles dependencies with the notion of local and remote *repositories*.

❷ Describe the location of the runtime sources.

❸ This is the location of the test sources.

④ Define the test classes you expect to include/exclude in the tests. Notice that you exclude the `TestDefaultController?.java` classes created in chapter 3 (the ? stands for any character), because they are unfinished tutorial classes and are not meant to be executed.

❸ ④ These code segments are used by the `junit` plugin.

Given just the description in listing 5.7, you can now run any of Maven's plugins to compile, package, and test your project, and more.

5.3.3 *Executing JUnit tests with Maven*

Executing JUnit tests in Maven is as simple as invoking the `junit` plugin with `maven test` from a command shell (see figure 5.6). This is close to the result of running the Ant script, back in figure 5.1—*but without writing a single line of script!* Generating a JUnit report is just as easy: Enter **maven site**, and the web site is generated, along with your JUnit report (among others). Figure 5.7 shows the JUnit report summary page for the `sampling` project.

5.3.4 *Handling dependent jars with Maven*

Maven solves another difficult issue: jar proliferation. You have probably noticed that more and more high-quality libraries are available in the Java community. Instead of reinventing the wheel, increasing numbers of projects import third-party libraries. The dark side is that building a project from its sources can be a nightmare, because you have to gather all the external jars, all in their correct versions.

Maven handles project *dependencies* (also called *artifacts*) through the use of two repositories: a remote repository and a local one. Figure 5.8 explains the workflow.

The first step for a project is to declare its dependencies in its `project.xml`. Although the `sampling` project does not depend on any external jars, let's imagine it needs to use Log4j. You would add the following to `project.xml`:

```
<dependency>
  <groupId>log4j</groupId>
  <artifactId>log4j</artifactId>
  <version>1.2.8</version>
</dependency>
```

When you execute a Maven goal on a project, here's what happens (following the numbers from figure 5.8):

❶ Check dependencies. Maven parses the dependencies located in `project.xml`.

❷ Check the dependency's existence in the local repository. For each dependency, Maven checks if it can be found in the local repository. This local repository is

```
C:\WINDOWS\System32\cmd.exe

C:\junitbook\sampling>maven test
  __  __
 |  \/  |__ _Apache__ ___
 | |\/| / _` \ v / _) ` \   ~ intelligent projects ~
 |_|  |_\__,_|\_/\___|_||_|  v. 1.0-beta-10

java:prepare-filesystem:
    [mkdir] Created dir: C:\junitbook\sampling\target\classes

java:compile:
    [echo] Compiling to C:\junitbook\sampling/target/classes
    [javac] Compiling 6 source files to C:\junitbook\sampling\target\classes

java:jar-resources:

test:prepare-filesystem:
    [mkdir] Created dir: C:\junitbook\sampling\target\test-classes
    [mkdir] Created dir: C:\junitbook\sampling\target\test-reports

test:test-resources:

test:compile:
    [javac] Compiling 9 source files to C:\junitbook\sampling\target\test-classes

test:test:
    [junit] dir attribute ignored if running in the same VM
    [junit] Running junitbook.sampling.TestDefaultController
    [junit] Tests run: 5, Failures: 0, Errors: 0, Time elapsed: 0.04 sec
BUILD SUCCESSFUL
Total time: 7 seconds

C:\junitbook\sampling>_
```

Figure 5.6   Results of executing maven test **on the** sampling **project**

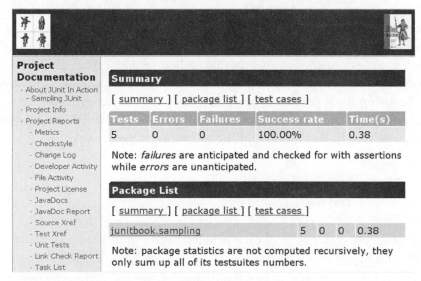

Project
Documentation

- About JUnit In Action
  - Sampling JUnit
- Project Info
- Project Reports
  - Metrics
  - Checkstyle
  - Change Log
  - Developer Activity
  - File Activity
  - Project License
  - JavaDocs
  - JavaDoc Report
  - Source Xref
  - Test Xref
  - Unit Tests
  - Link Check Report
  - Task List

Summary

[summary] [package list] [test cases]

Tests	Errors	Failures	Success rate	Time(s)
5	0	0	100.00%	0.38

Note: *failures* are anticipated and checked for with assertions while *errors* are unanticipated.

Package List

[summary] [package list] [test cases]

junitbook.sampling	5	0	0	0.38

Note: package statistics are not computed recursively, they only sum up all of its testsuites numbers.

Figure 5.7   JUnit report generated by Maven

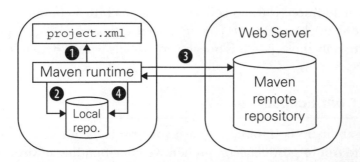

**Figure 5.8
How Maven resolves
external dependencies**

automatically created when you execute Maven the first time (it is located in your home user directory under `.maven/repository/`).

3 Download the dependency. If the dependency is not found in the local repository, Maven downloads it from a Maven remote repository. The default Maven remote repository is http://www.ibiblio.org/maven/. You can easily override this default by setting the `maven.repo.remote` property in a `project.properties` or `build.proper-ties` file in the same location as your `project.xml` file. This is especially useful if you wish to set up a project-wide or company-wide Maven remote repository.

4 Store the dependency. Once the dependency has been downloaded, Maven stores it in your local repository to prevent having to fetch it again next time.

The structure of the local and remote repositories is the same. Figure 5.9 shows a very simple repository.

In figure 5.9 you can see that jars are put in a `jars/` directory. The names are suffixed with the version to let you put several versions in the same directory and for easy identification. (For example, the `log4j` jar is available in versions 1.1.3,

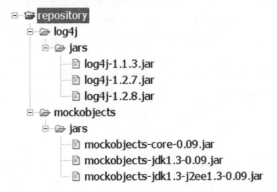

Figure 5.9   Very simple portion of a Maven repository (local or remote)

1.2.7, and 1.2.8.) In addition, you can collect several jars into a common group. Figure 5.9 also shows the MockObjects jars organized into a `mockobjects` group. Although the figure only shows jars, it is possible to put any type of dependency in a Maven repository.

5.4   *Running tests from Eclipse*

Ant gives you the ability to both build and test your projects in one fell swoop. Maven goes beyond Ant to provide a comprehensive code-building environment. But how do you go about creating the code to build?

Many excellent Java applications have been written using pure editors, like Emacs, JEdit, and TextPad, to name a few. Many applications are still being written with tools like these. But more and more developers are adopting one of the many IDEs now available for Java. The IDEs have come a long way over the last few years, and many developers now consider an IDE an indispensable tool.

Most of the Java IDEs work hand in hand with build tools like Ant and Maven. On a daily basis, many developers create and test code using an IDE and then use Ant or Maven to distribute or deploy the latest version. Sometimes, the developers on a team all use the same IDE; other times they don't. But as a rule, they all use the same build system (Ant or Maven).

The Java IDEs have also been quick to adopt JUnit as part of their toolset. Most IDEs let you launch JUnit from within the environment. Developers can now debug, edit, compile, and test a class, all from within a seamless environment.

Reviewing each Java IDE is out of the scope of this book. But to give you a feel for what these IDEs can do (or what your IDE *should* be doing), we will walk through setting up a project and running tests using Eclipse.

Eclipse (http://www.eclipse.org/) is a very popular open source project, available for download at no charge. That Eclipse has excellent support for JUnit should be no surprise. Erich Gamma, one of the original authors of JUnit, is a key member of the Eclipse team.

If you are not using Eclipse for development, don't worry—we won't use any features specific to Eclipse. In other words, you will be able to follow along using your favorite IDE.

5.4.1   *Creating an Eclipse project*

Eclipse comes with a full-featured installation program that makes setup a breeze. Detailed instructions for installing and configuring Eclipse for this book can be found in appendix B. This appendix demonstrates how to import this book's sources into Eclipse. We will demonstrate here how to create a new project from scratch in Eclipse (using the `sampling` project directory structure). We assume that you have all the book sources on your hard drive as explained in appendix A.

Follow these steps:

1 Create a new project by selecting File→New→Project.

2 In the dialog box that opens, select Java Project and click Next.

3 The screen that follows is shown in figure 5.10. Here you can choose a name for the project (for example, `junitbook-sampling`). You already have source files for this project, so be sure to *un*select the Use Default checkbox. You simply want to map your existing files to an Eclipse project.

4 Point the Directory field to where you put the `sampling` project on your local disk; for example, `C:\junitbook\sampling`. Click Next.

5 Eclipse asks whether it should automatically detect existing classpaths. Click Yes.

6 Eclipse should find your two source directories: `junitbook-sampling/src/java` and `junitbook-sampling/src/test`. You should have the same entries as are shown in figure 5.11.

7 You need the JUnit jar to compile your project, so the next step is to add it to your list of libraries. Click the Libraries tab and then click Add External Jars. Select the JUnit jar you already placed in the `C:\junitbook\repository\junit\jars` directory. Figure 5.12 shows the Libraries tab using the example paths.

8 Click Finish. Eclipse creates and compiles the project.

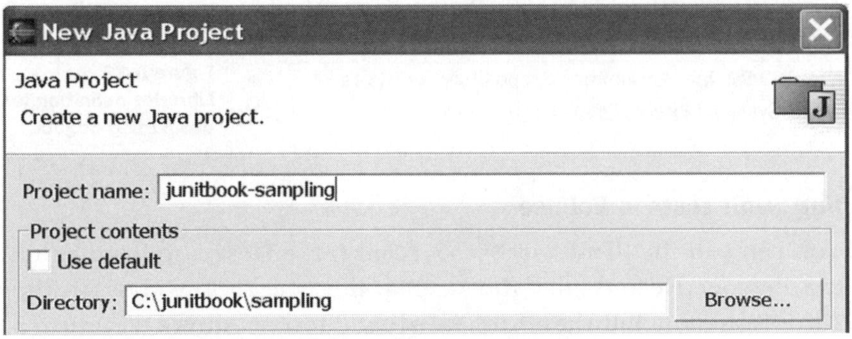

Figure 5.10 Enter the name and location of the new project in Eclipse.

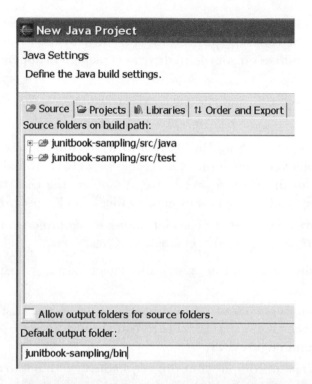

Figure 5.11
Source paths and build output
folder for the `sampling` **project**

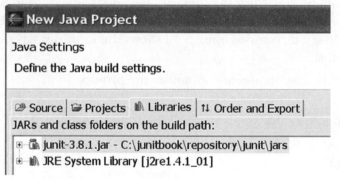

Figure 5.12
Libraries definition for the
`sampling` **project**

5.4.2 *Running JUnit tests in Eclipse*

Now you can run the JUnit `TestDefaultController` test case from Eclipse. Open the Java Perspective and click the `TestDefaultController` class. In the toolbar, select the Run icon and then Run As→JUnit Test, as shown in figure 5.13. The result of the execution is shown in figure 5.14.

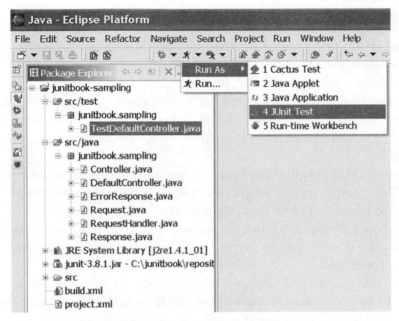

Figure 5.13   **Running the** `TestDefaultController` **JUnit test case**

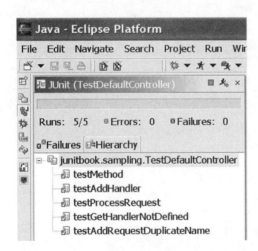

Figure 5.14
Result of executing the
`TestDefaultController`
test case

If a test fails, you can jump back to the editing window, make some changes, compile the class, and run the test again—all without leaving the Eclipse environment.

5.5 *Summary*

An essential element of a unit test is that, someday, it may fail. To realize the full value of your tests, you should run them continually, even when you don't expect anything to fail. Unit tests expect the unexpected.

Using the `sampling` project from chapter 3, we walked through compiling the project and running JUnit test cases using three popular products: Ant, Maven, and Eclipse. Ant and Maven are automation tools, and Eclipse is a productivity tool (an IDE).

These products all require very little effort to set up a stable unit-testing environment. The example is quite simple, but the same automation techniques apply equally well to larger and more complex projects.

However, the unit-testing techniques we've shown so far do not scale as well. As the classes we need to test become more complex and intertwined, we need better strategies to create tests.

In the second part of this book, we'll look at some of the strategies and tools we can use to test applications piece by piece. Or, as Julius Caesar said, *Divide et impera:* We must divide and conquer.

Part 2

Testing strategies

Part 1 was about learning the basics of unit-testing with JUnit. However, just knowing how JUnit works and how to use it on simple examples is not enough when it comes to testing a real application. For that, JUnit alone is not enough; you need to develop testing strategies that allow you to unit-test a full-fledged application. The main issue is testing in isolation. When you're writing unit tests, you want to test your application bit by bit. How do you separate bits of functionality so that they can be tested separately? Part 2 answers this crucial question.

Chapter 6 presents the stub strategy, which allows you to test relatively coarse-grained portions of code in isolation. In chapter 7, you'll learn about a relatively new technique called mock objects, which permits fine-grained testing in isolation. With mock objects, you'll discover not only a new way of unit-testing your code but also a new way of writing it. Chapter 8 takes you into the realm of unit-testing your code when it runs in its container (in-container testing). Nowadays, almost all code runs in some kind of container with which it interacts. You'll discover a strategy to unit-test J2EE code when it runs in its container, and you'll learn about the pros and cons of this strategy when compared with the mock-objects approach.

After reading part 2, you'll be familiar with these three strategies to unit-test code in isolation. You'll be ready to tackle the last step of our journey: unit-testing all types of J2EE components (servlets, filters, JSPs, taglibs, code accessing the database, and EJBs).

Coarse-grained testing
with stubs

6

This chapter covers

- Introducing stubs
- Using an embedded server in place of a real web server
- Unit-testing an HTTP connection sample with stubs

And yet it moves.

—Galileo

As you develop your applications, you will find that the code you want to test depends on other classes, which themselves depend on other classes, which depend on the environment. For example, you might be developing an application that uses JDBC to access a database, a J2EE application (one that relies on a J2EE container for security, persistence, and other services), an application that accesses a filesystem, or an application that connects to some resource using HTTP, SOAP, or another protocol.

For applications that depend on an environment, writing unit tests is a challenge. Your tests need to be stable, and when you run them over and over, they need to yield the same results. You need a way to control the environment in which they run. One solution is to set up the real required environment as part of the tests and run the tests from within that environment. In some cases, this approach is practical and brings real added value (see chapter 8, which discusses in-container testing). However, it works well only if you can set up the real environment on your development platform, which isn't always the case.

For example, if your application uses HTTP to connect to a web server provided by another company, you usually won't have that server application available in your development environment. So, you need a way to simulate that server so you can still write tests for your code.

Or, suppose you are working with other developers on a project. What if you want to test your part of the application, but the other part isn't ready? One solution is to simulate the missing part by replacing it with a fake that behaves the same way.

There are two strategies for providing these fake objects: stubbing and using mock objects. Stubs, the original solution, are still very popular, mostly because they allow you to test code without changing it to make it testable. This is not the case with mock objects. This chapter is dedicated to stubbing, and chapter 7 covers mock objects.

6.1 Introducing stubs

Stubs are a mechanism for faking the behavior of real code that may exist or that may not have been written yet. Stubs allow you to test a portion of a system without the other part being available. They usually do not change the code you're testing but instead adapt to provide seamless integration.

DEFINITION   *stub*—A stub is a portion of code that is inserted at runtime in place of
the real code, in order to isolate calling code from the real implementation. The intent is to replace a complex behavior with a simpler one
that allows independent testing of some portion of the real code.

Here are some examples of when you might use stubs:

- When you cannot modify an existing system because it is too complex and
  fragile
- For coarse-grained testing, such as integration testing between different
  subsystems

Stubs usually provide very good confidence in the system being tested. With stubs,
you are not modifying the objects under test, and what you are testing is the same
as what will execute in production. Tests involving stubs are usually executed in
their running environment, providing additional confidence.

On the downside, stubs are usually hard to write, especially when the system to
fake is complex. The stub needs to implement the same logic as the code it is
replacing, and that is difficult to get right for complex logic. This issue often leads
to having to debug the stubs! Here are some cons of stubbing:

- Stubs are often complex to write and need debugging themselves.
- Stubs can be difficult to maintain because they're complex.
- A stub does not lend itself well to fine-grained unit testing.
- Each situation requires a different strategy.

In general, stubs are better adapted for replacing coarse-grained portions of code.
You would usually use stubs to replace a full-blown external system like a filesystem, a connection to a server, a database, and so forth. Using stubs to replace a
method call to a single class can be done, but it is more difficult. (We will demonstrate how to do this with mock objects in chapter 7.)

6.2 *Practicing on an HTTP connection sample*

To demonstrate what stubs can do, let's build some stubs for a simple application
that opens an HTTP connection to a URL and reads its content. Figure 6.1 shows
the sample application (limited to a `WebClient.getContent` method) performing
an HTTP connection to a remote web resource. We have supposed that the remote

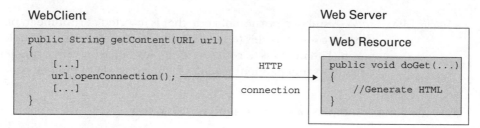

Figure 6.1 **The sample application makes an HTTP connection to a remote web resource. This is the real code in the stub definition.**

web resource is a servlet, which by some means (say, by calling a JSP) generates an HTML response. Figure 6.1 is what we called the *real code* in the stub definition.

Our goal in this chapter is to unit-test the getContent method by stubbing the remote web resource, as demonstrated in figure 6.2. As you can see, you replace the servlet web resource with the stub, a simple HTML page returning whatever you need for the TestWebClient test case.

This approach allows you to test the getContent method independently of the implementation of the web resource (which in turn could call several other objects down the execution chain, possibly up to a database).

The important point to notice with stubbing is that getContent has not been modified to accept the stub. It is transparent to the application under test. In order to allow this, the external code to be replaced needs to have a well-defined

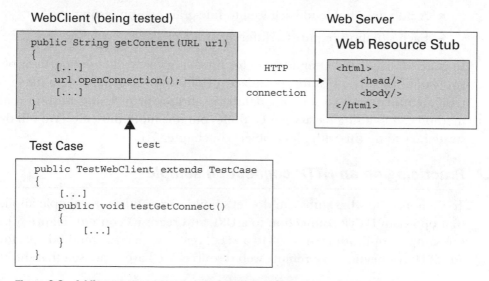

Figure 6.2 **Adding a test case and replacing the real web resource with a stub**

interface and allow plugging of different implementations (the stub one, for example). In the example in figure 6.1, the interface is URLConnection, which cleanly isolates the implementation of the page from its caller.

Let's see a stub in action using the simple HTTP connection sample. The example in listing 6.1 from the sample application demonstrates a code snippet opening an HTTP connection to a given URL and reading the content found at that URL. Imagine the method is one part of a bigger application that you want to unit-test, and let's unit-test that method.

> **Listing 6.1 Sample method opening an HTTP connection**

```
package junitbook.coarse.try1;

import java.net.URL;
import java.net.HttpURLConnection;
import java.io.InputStream;
import java.io.IOException;

public class WebClient
{
    public String getContent(URL url)
    {
        StringBuffer content = new StringBuffer();

        try
        {
            HttpURLConnection connection =                      ❶ Open HTTP
                (HttpURLConnection) url.openConnection();          connection
            connection.setDoInput(true);                          to URL

            InputStream is = connection.getInputStream();      ❷ Start reading
                                                                  remote data
            byte[] buffer = new byte[2048];
            int count;
            while (-1 != (count = is.read(buffer)))
            {                                                     Read all
                content.append(new String(buffer, 0, count));  ❸ data in
            }                                                     stream
        }
        catch (IOException e)
        {
            return null;        ❹ Return null
        }                          on error

        return content.toString();
    }
}
```

❶ Open an HTTP connection using the HttpURLConnection class.

❷ ❸ Read the content until there is nothing more to read.

❹ If an error occurs, you return `null`. One might argue that a better implementation might instead return a runtime exception (or a checked exception). However, for testing purposes, returning `null` is good enough.

6.2.1 *Choosing a stubbing solution*

There are two possible scenarios in the sample application: the remote web server (see figure 6.1) could be located outside of the development platform (such as on a partner site), or it could be part of the platform where your application is deployed. However, in both cases, you need to introduce a server into your development platform in order to be able to unit-test the `WebClient` class. One relatively easy solution would be to install an Apache test server and drop some test web pages in its document root. This is a typical, widely used stubbing solution. However, it has several drawbacks:

- *Reliance on the environment*—You need to be sure the full environment is up and running before the test. If the web server is down, and the test is executed, it will fail! You will then try to debug why it is failing. Next, you will discover that the code is working fine—it was only an environmental issue generating a false warning. This kind of thing is time consuming and annoying. When you're unit testing, it is important to be able to control as much as possible of the environment in which the test executes, so that test results are reproducible.

- *Separated test logic*—The test logic is scattered in two separate places: in the JUnit test case and in the test web page. Both types of resources need to be kept in sync for the test to succeed.

- *Tests that are difficult to automate*—Automating the execution of the tests is difficult because it involves automatically deploying the web pages on the web server, automatically starting the web server, and then only running the unit tests.

Fortunately, there is an easier solution that consists of using an embedded server. You are testing in Java, so the easiest option would be to use a Java web server that you could embed in the test case class. Such a nice beast exists; it's called Jetty. For the purpose of this book, we will use Jetty to set up stubs. For more information about Jetty in general, visit http://jetty.mortbay.org/jetty/index.html.

Why Jetty? Because it's fast (important when running tests), it's lightweight (a single jar file to put in the classpath), and it can be completely controlled in Java from your test case, which means you can tell it how to behave for the purpose of your tests. Additionally, it is a very good web/servlet container that you can use in production. This is not specifically needed for your tests, but it is always nice to use best-of-breed technology.

Using Jetty allows you to eliminate the drawbacks: The server is started from the JUnit test case, the tests are all written in Java in one location, and automating the test suite is a nonissue. Thanks to Jetty's modularity, the real point of the exercise is only to stub the Jetty handlers and not the whole server from the ground up.

6.2.2 *Using Jetty as an embedded server*

In order to better understand how to set up and control Jetty from your tests, let's implement a simple example that starts Jetty from your Java code. Listing 6.2 shows how to start it from Java and how to define a document root (/) from which to start serving files. Figure 6.3 shows the result when you run the application and open a browser on the URL http://localhost:8080.

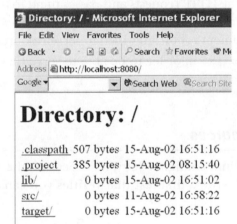

Figure 6.3
Testing the `JettySample` in a browser. These are the results when you run listing 6.2 and open a browser on http://localhost:8080.

Listing 6.2   Starting Jetty in embedded mode—JettySample class

```java
package junitbook.coarse;

import org.mortbay.http.HttpContext;
import org.mortbay.http.HttpServer;
import org.mortbay.http.SocketListener;
import org.mortbay.http.handler.ResourceHandler;

public class JettySample
{
    public static void main(String[] args) throws Exception
```

```
    {
            HttpServer server = new HttpServer();        ❶
            SocketListener listener = new SocketListener();
            listener.setPort(8080);                                    ❷
            server.addListener(listener);

            HttpContext context = new HttpContext();        ❸
            context.setContextPath("/");
            context.setResourceBase("./");
            context.addHandler(new ResourceHandler());  ❹
            server.addContext(context);      ❸
            server.start();           ❺
    }
    }
```

❶ Create the Jetty HttpServer object.

❷ Attach a listener on port 8080 to the HttpServer object so that it can receive HTTP requests.

❸ Create an HttpContext that processes the HTTP requests and passes them to the different handlers. You map the context to the root (/) URL with setContextPath. The setResourceBase method sets the document root from which to serve resources.

❹ Add a resource handler to the HttpContext in order to be able to serve files from the filesystem.

❺ Start the server.

6.3 *Stubbing the web server's resources*

Now that you know how to easily start and configure Jetty, let's focus on the HTTP connection sample unit test. You will write a first test that verifies you can call a valid URL and get its content.

6.3.1 *Setting up the first stub test*

To verify that the WebClient works with a valid URL, you need to start the Jetty server before the test, which you can implement in a setUp method inside a JUnit test case. You can also stop the server in a tearDown method. Listing 6.3 shows the code.

Listing 6.3   Skeleton of the first test to verify that the WebClient works with a valid URL

```
package junitbook.coarse.try1;

import java.net.URL;

import junit.framework.TestCase;

public class TestWebClientSkeleton extends TestCase
{
    protected void setUp()
    {
        // Start Jetty and configure it to return "It works" when
        // the http://localhost:8080/testGetContentOk URL is
        // called.
    }

    protected void tearDown()
    {
        // Stop Jetty.
    }

    public void testGetContentOk() throws Exception
    {
        WebClient client = new WebClient();

        String result = client.getContent(new URL(
            "http://localhost:8080/testGetContentOk"));

        assertEquals ("It works", result);
    }

}
```

In order to implement the setUp and tearDown methods, you have two solutions. You can prepare a static page containing the text *It works* that you put in your document root (controlled by the call to context.setResourceBase(String) in listing 6.2). Alternatively, you can configure Jetty to use your own custom Handler that returns the string directly instead of getting it from a file in the filesystem. This is a much more powerful technique, because it lets you unit-test the case when the remote HTTP server throws an error code at your WebClient client application.

Creating a Jetty handler

Listing 6.4 shows how to create a Jetty Handler that returns *It works*.

Listing 6.4   Create a Jetty Handler that returns *It works* when called

```
private class TestGetContentOkHandler extends AbstractHttpHandler      ❶
{
    public void handle(String pathInContext, String pathParams,
        HttpRequest request, HttpResponse response)
        throws IOException
    {
        OutputStream out = response.getOutputStream();             ❷
        ByteArrayISO8859Writer writer =
            new ByteArrayISO8859Writer();
        writer.write("It works");                    ❸
        writer.flush();
        response.setIntField(HttpFields.__ContentLength,
            writer.size());                                ❹
        writer.writeTo(out);
        out.flush();
        request.setHandled(true);        ❺
    }
}
```

❶ Handlers are easily created by extending the Jetty `AbstractHttpHandler` class, which defines a single `handle` method you need to implement. This method is called by Jetty when the incoming request is forwarded to your handler.

❷ Use the `ByteArrayISO8859Writer` class that Jetty provides to make it easy to send back your string in the HTTP response (❸).

❹ Set the response content length to be the length of the string you wrote to the output stream (this is required by Jetty), and then send the response.

❺ Tell Jetty that the request has been handled and does not need to be passed to any further handler.

Now that this handler is written, you can tell Jetty to use it by calling `context.addHandler(new TestGetContentOkHandler())`.

You are almost ready to run your test. The last issue to solve is the one involving `setUp`/`tearDown` methods. The solution shown in listing 6.3 isn't great, because it means the server will be started and stopped for every single test. Although Jetty is very fast, this process is still not necessary. A better solution is to start the server only once for all the tests. Fortunately, JUnit supports doing this with the notion of `TestSetup`, which lets you wrap a whole suite of tests and have global `setUp` and `tearDown` methods for the suite.

Isolating each test vs. performance considerations

In previous chapters, we went to great lengths to explain why each test should run in a clean environment (even to the extent of using a new classloader instance). However, sometimes there are other considerations to take into account. Performance is a typical one. In the present case, even if starting Jetty takes only 1 second, once you have 300 tests, it will add an overtime of 300 seconds (5 minutes). Test suites that take a long time to execute are a handicap; you will be tempted not to execute them often, which negates the regression feature of unit testing. You must be aware of this tradeoff. Depending on the situation, you may choose to have longer-running tests that execute in a clean environment, or instead tune the tests for performance by reusing some parts of the environment. In the example at hand, you use different handlers for different tests, and you can be pretty confident they will not interfere with one another. Thus, going for faster running tests is probably the best option.

Starting and stopping Jetty once per test suite

Listing 6.5 shows the `TestSetup` with the methods to start and stop Jetty. It also configures Jetty with the `TestGetContentOkHandler` from listing 6.4.

Listing 6.5 Extending TestSetup to configure, start, and stop Jetty once per test suite

```
package junitbook.coarse.try1;

import java.io.IOException;
import java.io.OutputStream;

import org.mortbay.http.HttpContext;
import org.mortbay.http.HttpFields;
import org.mortbay.http.HttpRequest;
import org.mortbay.http.HttpResponse;
import org.mortbay.http.HttpServer;
import org.mortbay.http.SocketListener;
import org.mortbay.http.handler.AbstractHttpHandler;
import org.mortbay.util.ByteArrayISO8859Writer;

import junit.extensions.TestSetup;
import junit.framework.Test;

public class TestWebClientSetup1 extends TestSetup  ❶
{
    protected static HttpServer server;

    public TestWebClientSetup1(Test suite)
    {
        super(suite);
    }

    protected void setUp() throws Exception  ❸
```

❶ Extend TestSetup to provide global setUp and tearDown

❷ Save Jetty server object for use in tearDown

❸ Configure and start Jetty

```
    {
        server = new HttpServer();
        SocketListener listener = new SocketListener();
        listener.setPort(8080);
        server.addListener(listener);

        HttpContext context1 = new HttpContext();
        context1.setContextPath("/testGetContentOk");
        context1.addHandler(new TestGetContentOkHandler());
        server.addContext(context1);

        server.start();
    }

    protected void tearDown() throws Exception        ❹ Stop Jetty
    {
        server.stop();
    }

    private class TestGetContentOkHandler extends        ❺ Implement Jetty
        AbstractHttpHandler                                 Handler as an
    {                                                       inner class
        public void handle(String pathInContext, String pathParams,
            HttpRequest request, HttpResponse response)
            throws IOException
        {
        OutputStream out = response.getOutputStream();
        ByteArrayISO8859Writer writer =
            new ByteArrayISO8859Writer();
        writer.write("It works");
        writer.flush();
        response.setIntField(HttpFields.__ContentLength,
            writer.size());
        writer.writeTo(out);
        out.flush();
        request.setHandled(true);
        }
    }
    }
```

❶ By extending TestSetup, you need to implement a setUp method and a tearDown method. They are called at the beginning of the execution of the test suite and at its end.

❸ In the setUp method, you start Jetty and save a reference to the Jetty HttpServer object (❷) for later use in the tearDown method.

❹ In the tearDown method, you stop the running server.

❺ Implement the content handler that returns *It works* when called as an inner class of TestSetup. (You use an inner class because the handler is strongly linked to the

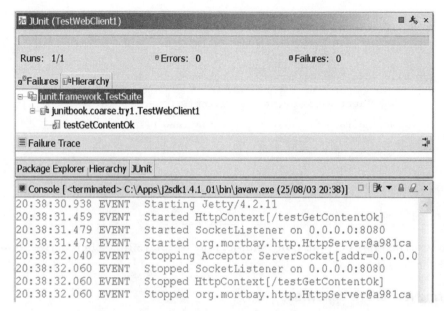

Figure 6.4   Result of the first working test using a Jetty stub. Jetty is automatically started before the test and stopped at the end.

Jetty configuration that is performed in the setUp method. However, you can implement it as a separate class, which may become cleaner should the number of handlers increase dramatically.)

Writing the Test class

The Test class can now be easily written using this TestWebClientSetup1 class, as demonstrated in listing 6.6. When you execute it, you now get the result shown in figure 6.4.

Listing 6.6   Putting it all together

```
package junitbook.coarse.try1;

import java.net.URL;

import junit.framework.Test;
import junit.framework.TestCase;
import junit.framework.TestSuite;

public class TestWebClient1 extends TestCase
{
    public static Test suite()
    {
```

```
        TestSuite suite = new TestSuite();
        suite.addTestSuite(TestWebClient1.class);
        return new TestWebClientSetup1(suite);
    }

    public void testGetContentOk() throws Exception
    {
        WebClient client = new WebClient();

        String result = client.getContent(new URL(
            "http://localhost:8080/testGetContentOk"));

        assertEquals("It works", result);
    }

}
```

The test class has become quite simple, and you have delegated all setup work in
TestWebClientSetup1.

6.3.2 *Testing for failure conditions*

Now that you have the first test working, let's see how to test for server failure conditions. The WebClient.getContent(URL) method returns a null value when a failure happens. You need to test for this possibility, too. With the infrastructure you
have put in place, you simply need to create a new Jetty Handler class that returns
an error code and register it in the TestWebClientSetup1.setUp method.

Let's add a test for an invalid URL—that is, a URL pointing to a file that does
not exist. This case is quite easy, because Jetty already provides a NotFoundHandler
handler class for that purpose. You only need to modify the TestWebClient-
Setup1.setUp method in the following way (changes are in bold):

```
protected void setUp() throws Exception
{
    server = new HttpServer();
    SocketListenerlistener = new SocketListener();
    listener.setPort(8080);
    server.addListener(listener);

    HttpContext context1 = new HttpContext();
    context1.setContextPath("/testGetContentOk");
    context1.addHandler(new TestGetContentOkHandler());
    server.addContext(context1);

    HttpContext context2 = new HttpContext();
    context2.setContextPath("/testGetContentNotFound");
    context2.addHandler(new NotFoundHandler());
    server.addContext(context2);

    server.start();
}
```

Adding a new test in `TestWebClient1` is also a breeze:

```
public void testGetContentNotFound() throws Exception
{
    WebClient client = new WebClient();

    String result = client.getContent(new URL(
        "http://localhost:8080/testGetContentNotFound"));

    assertNull(result);
}
```

In a similar fashion, you can easily add a test to simulate the server having trouble. Returning a 5*XX* HTTP response code indicates this problem. Write a new Jetty `Handler` class, as follows, and register it in `TestWebClientSetup1.setUp`:

```
public class TestGetContentServerErrorHandler extends
    AbstractHttpHandler
{
    public void handle(String pathInContext, String pathParams,
        HttpRequest request, HttpResponse response)
        throws IOException
    {
        response.sendError(HttpResponse.__503_Service_Unavailable);
    }
}
```

Now, that's quite nice. A test like this would be very difficult to perform if you did not choose an embeddable web server.

6.3.3 *Reviewing the first stub test*

You have been able to fully unit-test the `getContent` method in isolation by stubbing the web resource. What have you really tested? What kind of test have you achieved? Actually, you have done something quite powerful: You have unit-tested the method, but at the same time you have executed an integration test. In addition, not only have you tested the code logic, you have also tested the connection part that is outside the code (it uses the JDK's `HttpURLConnection` class).

However, this approach has a few drawbacks. The major one is that it is complex. It took me about four hours from start to finish, including getting enough Jetty knowledge to set it up correctly (I had no prior knowledge of Jetty). In some instances, I also had to debug my stubs to get them to work. There is a very dangerous line that you should not cross: The stub must stay simple and not become a full-fledged application that requires tests and maintenance.

Moreover, in the specific example, you need a web server—but another stub will be different and will need a different setup. Experience helps, but different cases usually require different stubbing solutions.

The example tests are nice because you can both unit-test the code and perform some integration tests at the same time. However, this functionality comes at the cost of complexity. There are more lightweight solutions that focus on unit-testing the code but without performing the integration tests. The rationale is that integration tests are very much needed but could be run in a separate suite of tests or as part of functional tests.

In the next section, we will look at another solution that can still be qualified as stubbing. It is simpler in the sense that it does not require you to stub a whole web server. It brings you one step closer to the mock-object strategy, which is described in the following chapter.

6.4 *Stubbing the connection*

So far, you have stubbed the web server's resources. What about stubbing the HTTP connection, instead? Doing so will prevent you from effectively testing the connection, but that's fine because it isn't your real goal at this point. You are really interested in testing your code logic in isolation. Functional or integration tests will test the connection at a later stage.

When it comes to stubbing the connection without changing your code, you are quite lucky because the JDK's URL and HttpURLConnection classes let you plug in custom protocol handlers to handle any kind of communication protocol. You can have any call to the HttpURLConnection class be redirected to your own test class, which will return whatever is needed for the test.

6.4.1 *Producing a custom URL protocol handler*

To implement a custom URL protocol handler, you need to call the following JDK method and pass it a custom URLStreamHandlerFactory object:

```
java.net.URL.setURLStreamHandlerFactory(
    java.net.URLStreamHandlerFactory);
```

Whenever a URL.openConnection method is called, the URLStreamHandlerFactory class is called to return a URLStreamHandler object. Listing 6.7 shows the code to perform this feat. The idea is to call the static setURLStreamHandlerFactory method in the JUnit setUp method. (A better implementation would use a Test-Setup class, as shown in the previous section, so that it is performed only once during the whole test suite execution.)

Listing 6.7   Providing custom stream handler classes for testing

```java
package junitbook.coarse.try2;

import junit.framework.TestCase;

import java.net.URL;
import java.net.URLStreamHandlerFactory;
import java.net.URLStreamHandler;
import java.net.URLConnection;
import java.io.IOException;

public class TestWebClient extends TestCase
{
    protected void setUp()
    {
        URL.setURLStreamHandlerFactory(
            new StubStreamHandlerFactory());
    }

    private class StubStreamHandlerFactory implements
        URLStreamHandlerFactory
    {
        public URLStreamHandler createURLStreamHandler(
            String protocol)
        {
            return new StubHttpURLStreamHandler();
        }
    }

    private class StubHttpURLStreamHandler extends
        URLStreamHandler
    {
        protected URLConnection openConnection(URL url)
            throws IOException
        {
            return new StubHttpURLConnection(url);
        }
    }

    public void testGetContentOk() throws Exception
    {
        WebClient client = new WebClient();

        String result = client.getContent(
            new URL("http://localhost"));

        assertEquals("It works", result);
    }
}
```

Tell URL class to use factory to handle connections

❶ **Route all connections to HTTP handler**

❷ **Provide handler that returns stubbed HttpURL-Connection class**

Test that exercises WebClient class

You have to use several inner classes (**1** and **2**) to be able to pass the Stub-
HttpURLConnection class. You could also use anonymous inner classes for concise-
ness, but that approach would make the code more complex to read. Note that
you haven't written the StubHttpURLConnection class yet, which is the topic of the
next section.

6.4.2 Creating a JDK HttpURLConnection stub

The last step is to create a stub implementation of the HttpURLConnection class so
you can return any value you want for the test. Listing 6.8 shows a simple implementation that returns the string *It works* as a stream to the caller.

Listing 6.8   Stubbed HttpURLConnection class

```
package junitbook.coarse.try2;

import java.net.HttpURLConnection;
import java.net.ProtocolException;
import java.net.URL;
import java.io.InputStream;
import java.io.IOException;
import java.io.ByteArrayInputStream;

public class StubHttpURLConnection extends HttpURLConnection
{
    private boolean isInput = true;

    protected StubHttpURLConnection(URL url)
    {
        super(url);
    }

    public InputStream getInputStream() throws IOException
    {
        if (!isInput)
        {
            throw new ProtocolException(
                "Cannot read from URLConnection"
                + " if doInput=false (call setDoInput(true))");
        }

        ByteArrayInputStream bais = new ByteArrayInputStream(
            new String("It works").getBytes());

        return bais;
    }

    public void disconnect()
    {
    }
```

*HttpURLConnection
has no interface;
extend it and
override its methods*

*Override getInputStream
method to return a
string*

1 Stub logic

*Return
expected string
as a Stream*

```
        public void connect() throws IOException
        {
        }

        public boolean usingProxy()
        {
            return false;
        }
    }
```

HttpURLConnection does not provide an interface, so you have to extend it and override the methods you want to stub. In this stub, you provide an implementation for the getInputStream method because it is the only method used by your code under test. Should the code to test use more APIs from HttpURLConnection, you would also need to stub these additional methods. This is where the code would become more complex—you would need to completely reproduce the same behavior as the real HttpURLConnection. For example, at ❶, you test that if setDoInput(false) has been called in the code under test, then a call to the getInputStream method returns a ProtocolException. (This is the behavior of HttpURLConnection.) Fortunately, in most cases, you only need to stub a few methods and not the whole API.

6.4.3 *Running the test*

Let's run the TestWebClient test, which uses the StubHttpURLConnection. Figure 6.5 shows the result.

As you can see, it is much easier to stub the connection than to stub the web resource. This approach does not bring the same level of testing (you are not

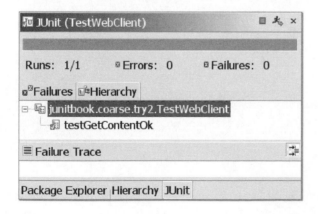

Figure 6.5
Result of executing
TestWebClient **(which uses the**
StubHttpURLConnection**)**

performing integration tests), but it enables you to more easily write a focused unit test for the `WebClient` code logic.

6.5 *Summary*

In this chapter, we have demonstrated how using a stub has helped us unit-test code accessing a remote web server using the JDK's `HttpURLConnection` API. In particular, we have shown how to stub the remote web server by using Jetty. Jetty's embeddable nature lets you concentrate on stubbing only the Jetty HTTP request handler, instead of having to stub the whole container. We also demonstrated a more light-weight stub by writing it for the JDK's `HttpURLConnection` implementation.

The next chapter will demonstrate a technique called *mock objects* that allows fine-grained unit testing, is completely generic, and (best of all) forces you to write good code. Although stubs are very useful in some cases, they're more a vestige of the past, when the general consensus was that tests should be a separate activity and should not modify the code. The new mock-objects strategy not only allows modification of code, it favors it. Using mock objects is a unit-testing strategy, but it is more than that: It is a completely new way of writing code.

Testing in isolation
with mock objects

This chapter covers

- Introducing and demonstrating mock objects
- Performing different refactorings
- Using mock objects to verify API contracts on collaborating classes
- Practicing on an HTTP connection sample application

The secret of success is sincerity. Once you can fake that you've got it made.

—Jean Giraudoux

Unit-testing each method in isolation from the other methods or the environment is certainly a nice goal. But how do you perform this feat? You saw in chapter 6 how the stubbing technique lets you unit-test portions of code by isolating them from the environment (for example, by stubbing a web server, the filesystem, a database, and so on). But what about fine-grained isolation like being able to isolate a method call to another class? Is that possible? Can you achieve this without deploying huge amounts of energy that would negate the benefits of having tests?

The answer is, "Yes! It is possible." The technique is called *mock objects*. Tim Mackinnon, Steve Freeman, and Philip Craig first presented the mock objects concept at XP2000. The mock-objects strategy allows you to unit-test at the finest possible level and develop method by method, while providing you with unit tests for each method.

7.1 *Introducing mock objects*

Testing in isolation offers strong benefits, such as the ability to test code that has not yet been written (as long as you at least have an interface to work with). In addition, testing in isolation helps teams unit-test one part of the code without waiting for all the other parts.

But perhaps the biggest advantage is the ability to write focused tests that test only a single method, without side effects resulting from other objects being called from the method under test. Small is beautiful. Writing small, focused tests is a tremendous help; small tests are easy to understand and do not break when other parts of the code are changed. Remember that one of the benefits of having a suite of unit tests is the courage it gives you to refactor mercilessly—the unit tests act as a safeguard against regression. If you have large tests and your refactoring introduces a bug, several tests will fail; that result will tell you that there is a bug somewhere, but you won't know where. With fine-grained tests, potentially fewer tests will be affected, and they will provide precise messages that pinpoint the exact cause of the breakage.

Mock objects (or *mocks* for short) are perfectly suited for testing a portion of code logic in isolation from the rest of the code. Mocks replace the objects with which your methods under test collaborate, thus offering a layer of isolation. In that sense, they are similar to stubs. However, this is where the similarity ends, because mocks do not implement any logic: They are empty shells that provide methods to let the tests control the behavior of all the business methods of the faked class.

> **DEFINITION** *mock object*—A *mock object* (or *mock* for short) is an object created to stand in for an object that your code will be collaborating with. Your code can call methods on the mock object, which will deliver results as set up by your tests.

We will discuss when to use mock objects in section 7.6 at the end of this chapter, after we show them in action on some examples.

7.2 *Mock tasting: a simple example*

Let's taste our first mock! Imagine a very simple use case where you want to be able to make a bank transfer from one account to another (figure 7.1 and listings 7.1–7.3).

The `AccountService` class offers services related to `Accounts` and uses the `AccountManager` to persist data to the database (using JDBC, for example). The service that interests us is materialized by the `AccountService.transfer` method, which makes the transfer. Without mocks, testing the `AccountService.transfer` behavior would imply setting up a database, presetting it with test data, deploying the code inside the container (J2EE application server, for example), and so forth. Although this process is required to ensure the application works end to end, it is too much work when you want to unit-test only your code logic.

Listing 7.1 presents a very simple `Account` object with two properties: an account ID and a balance.

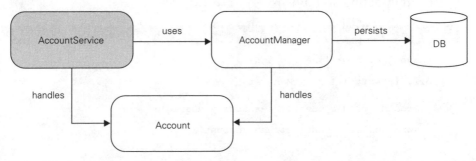

Figure 7.1 In this simple bank account example, you will use a mock object to test an account transfer method.

> **Listing 7.1   Account.java**

```java
package junitbook.fine.tasting;

public class Account
{
    private String accountId;
    private long balance;

    public Account(String accountId, long initialBalance)
    {
        this.accountId = accountId;
        this.balance = initialBalance;
    }

    public void debit(long amount)

    {
        this.balance -= amount;
    }

    public void credit(long amount)

    {
        this.balance += amount;
    }

    public long getBalance()

    {
        return this.balance;
    }
}
```

Listing 7.2 introduces the AccountManager interface, whose goal is to manage the life cycle and persistence of Account objects. (You are limited to finding accounts by ID and updating accounts.)

> **Listing 7.2   AccountManager.java**

```java
package junitbook.fine.tasting;

public interface AccountManager
{
    Account findAccountForUser(String userId);

    void updateAccount(Account account);

}
```

Listing 7.3 shows the `transfer` method for transferring money between two accounts. It uses the `AccountManager` interface you previously defined to find the debit and credit accounts by ID and to update them.

Listing 7.3   AccountService.java

```java
package junitbook.fine.tasting;

public class AccountService
{
    private AccountManager accountManager;

    public void setAccountManager(AccountManager manager)
    {
        this.accountManager = manager;
    }

    public void transfer(String senderId, String beneficiaryId,
        long amount)
    {
        Account sender =
            this.accountManager.findAccountForUser(senderId);
        Account beneficiary =
            this.accountManager.findAccountForUser(beneficiaryId);

        sender.debit(amount);
        beneficiary.credit(amount);

        this.accountManager.updateAccount(sender);
        this.accountManager.updateAccount(beneficiary);
    }
}
```

You want to be able to unit-test the `AccountService.transfer` behavior. For that purpose, you use a mock implementation of the `AccountManager` interface (listing 7.4). You do this because the transfer method is using this interface, and you need to test it in isolation.

Listing 7.4   MockAccountManager.java

```java
package junitbook.fine.tasting;

import java.util.Hashtable;

public class MockAccountManager implements AccountManager
{
    private Hashtable accounts = new Hashtable();

    public void addAccount(String userId, Account account)
    {
```

```
        this.accounts.put(userId, account);
    }
    public Account findAccountForUser(String userId)
    {
        return (Account) this.accounts.get(userId);
    }
    public void updateAccount(Account account)
    {
        // do nothing
    }
}
```

1 The addAccount method uses an instance variable to hold the values to return. Because you have several account objects that you want to be able to return, you store the Account objects to return in a Hashtable. This makes the mock generic and able to support different test cases: One test could set up the mock with one account, another test could set it up with two accounts or more, and so forth.

2 addAccount tells the findAccountForUser method what to return when called.

3 The updateAccount method updates an account but does not return any value. Thus you simply do nothing. When it is called by the transfer method, it will do nothing, as if the account had been correctly updated.

> ### JUnit best practices: don't write business logic in mock objects
>
> The single most important point to consider when writing a mock is that it should not have any business logic. It must be a dumb object that only does what the test tells it to do. In other words, it is purely driven by the tests. This characteristic is exactly the opposite of stubs, which contain all the logic (see chapter 6).
>
> There are two nice corollaries. First, mock objects can be easily generated, as you will see in following chapters. Second, because mock objects are empty shells, they are too simple to break and do not need testing themselves.

You are now ready to write a unit test for AccountService.transfer. Listing 7.5 shows a typical test using a mock.

Listing 7.5   Testing transfer with MockAccountManager

```java
package junitbook.fine.tasting;

import junit.framework.TestCase;

public class TestAccountService extends TestCase
{
    public void testTransferOk()
    {
        MockAccountManager mockAccountManager =
            new MockAccountManager();
        Account senderAccount = new Account("1", 200);
        Account beneficiaryAccount = new Account("2", 100);

        mockAccountManager.addAccount("1", senderAccount);
        mockAccountManager.addAccount("2", beneficiaryAccount);

        AccountService accountService = new AccountService();

        accountService.setAccountManager(mockAccountManager);

        accountService.transfer("1", "2", 50);          ❷

        assertEquals(150, senderAccount.getBalance());
        assertEquals(150, beneficiaryAccount.getBalance());    ❸
    }
}
```

❶

As usual, a test has three steps: the test setup (❶), the test execution (❷), and the verification of the result (❸). During the test setup, you create the MockAccount-Manager object and define what it should return when called for the two accounts you manipulate (the sender and beneficiary accounts). You have succeeded in testing the AccountService code in isolation of the other domain object, Account-Manager, which in this case did not exist, but which in real life could have been implemented using JDBC.

> **JUnit best practices: only test what can possibly break**
>
> You may have noticed that you did not mock the Account class. The reason is that this data-access object class does not need to be mocked—it does not depend on the environment, and it's very simple. Your other tests use the Account object, so they test it indirectly. If it failed to operate correctly, the tests that rely on Account would fail and alert you to the problem.

At this point in the chapter, you should have a reasonably good understanding of what a mock is. In the next section, we will show you that writing unit tests with mocks leads to refactoring your code under test—and that this process is a good thing!

7.3 *Using mock objects as a refactoring technique*

Some people used to say that unit tests should be totally transparent to your code under test, and that you should not change runtime code in order to simplify testing. *This is wrong!* Unit tests are first-class users of the runtime code and deserve the same consideration as any other user. If your code is too inflexible for the tests to use, then you should correct the code.

For example, what do you think of the following piece of code?

```
[...]
import java.util.PropertyResourceBundle;
import java.util.ResourceBundle;

import org.apache.commons.logging.Log;
import org.apache.commons.logging.LogFactory;
[...]

public class DefaultAccountManager implements AccountManager
{
    private static final Log LOGGER =
        LogFactory.getLog(AccountManager.class);                    ❶

    public Account findAccountForUser(String userId)
    {
        LOGGER.debug("Getting account for user [" + userId + "]");
        ResourceBundle bundle =                                     ❷
            PropertyResourceBundle.getBundle("technical");
        String sql = bundle.getString("FIND_ACCOUNT_FOR_USER");

        // Some code logic to load a user account using JDBC
        [...]
    }
    [...]
}
```

❶ You get a `Log` object using a `LogFactory` that creates it.

❷ Use a `PropertyResourceBundle` to retrieve an SQL command.

Does the code look fine to you? We can see two issues, both of which relate to code flexibility and the ability to resist change. The first problem is that it is not possible to decide to use a different `Log` object, as it is created inside the class. For testing, for example, you probably want to use a `Log` that does nothing, but you can't.

As a general rule, a class like this should be able to use whatever `Log` it is given. The goal of this class is not to create loggers but to perform some JDBC logic.

The same remark applies to the use of `PropertyResourceBundle`. It may sound OK right now, but what happens if you decide to use XML to store the configuration? Again, it should not be the goal of this class to decide what implementation to use.

An effective design strategy is to pass to an object any other object that is outside its immediate business logic. The choice of peripheral objects can be controlled by someone higher in the calling chain. Ultimately, as you move up in the calling layers, the decision to use a given logger or configuration should be pushed to the top level. This strategy provides the best possible code flexibility and ability to cope with changes. And, as we all know, change is the only constant.

7.3.1 *Easy refactoring*

Refactoring all code so that domain objects are passed around can be time-consuming. You may not be ready to refactor the whole application just to be able to write a unit test. Fortunately, there is an easy refactoring technique that lets you keep the same interface for your code but allows it to be passed domain objects that it should not create. As a proof, let's see how the refactored `DefaultAccount-Manager` class could look (modifications are shown in bold):

```
public class DefaultAccountManager implements AccountManager
{
    private Log logger;                                    ❶ Log and
    private Configuration configuration;                     Configuration are
                                                             both interfaces
    public DefaultAccountManager()
    {
        this(LogFactory.getLog(DefaultAccountManager.class),
            new DefaultConfiguration("technical"));
    }

    public DefaultAccountManager(Log logger,
        Configuration configuration)
    {
        this.logger = logger;
        this.configuration = configuration;
    }

    public Account findAccountForUser(String userId)
    {
        this.logger.debug("Getting account for user ["
            + userId + "]");
        this.configuration.getSQL("FIND_ACCOUNT_FOR_USER");

        // Some code logic to load a user account using JDBC
        [...]
    }
    [...]
}
```

Notice that at ❶, you swap the `PropertyResourceBundle` class from the previous listing in favor of a new `Configuration` interface. This makes the code more flexible because it introduces an interface (which will be easy to mock), and the implementation of the `Configuration` interface can be anything you want (including using resource bundles). The design is better now because you can use and reuse the `DefaultAccountManager` class with any implementation of the `Log` and `Configuration` interfaces (if you use the constructor that takes two parameters). The class can be controlled from the outside (by its caller). Meanwhile, you have not broken the existing interface, because you have only added a new constructor. You kept the original default constructor that still initializes the `logger` and `configuration` field members with default implementations.

With this refactoring, you have provided a trapdoor for controlling the domain objects from your tests. You retain backward compatibility and pave an easy refactoring path for the future. Calling classes can start using the new constructor at their own pace.

Should you worry about introducing trapdoors to make your code easier to test? Here's how Extreme Programming guru Ron Jeffries explains it:

> *My car has a diagnostic port and an oil dipstick. There is an inspection port on the side of my furnace and on the front of my oven. My pen cartridges are transparent so I can see if there is ink left.*
>
> *And if I find it useful to add a method to a class to enable me to test it, I do so. It happens once in a while, for example in classes with easy interfaces and complex inner function (probably starting to want an Extract Class).*
>
> *I just give the class what I understand of what it wants, and keep an eye on it to see what it wants next.*[1]

7.3.2 *Allowing more flexible code*

What we have described in section 7.3.1 is a well-known pattern called Inversion of Control (IOC). The main idea is to externalize all domain objects from outside the class/method and pass everything to it. Instead of the class creating object instances, the instances are passed to the class (usually through interfaces).

In the example, it means passing `Log` and `Configuration` objects to the `Default-AccountManager` class. `DefaultAccountManager` has no clue what instances are passed to it or how they were constructed. It just knows they implement the `Log` and `Configuration` interfaces.

---

[1] Ron Jeffries, on the TestDrivenDevelopment mailing list: http://groups.yahoo.com/group/testdrivendevelopment/message/3914.

> ### *Design patterns in action: Inversion of Control (IOC)*
>
> Applying the IOC pattern to a class means removing the creation of all object instances for which this class is not directly responsible and passing any needed instances instead. The instances may be passed using a specific constructor, using a setter, or as parameters of the methods needing them. It becomes the responsibility of the calling code to correctly set these domain objects on the called class.[2]

IOC makes unit testing a breeze. To prove the point, let's see how easily you can now write a test for the findAccountByUser method:

```
public void testFindAccountByUser()
{
    MockLog logger = new MockLog();        ❶
    MockConfiguration configuration = new MockConfiguration();    ❷
    configuration.setSQL("SELECT * [...]");

    DefaultAccountManager am =                                    ❸
        new DefaultAccountManager(logger, configuration);

    Account account = am.findAccountForUser("1234");

    // Perform asserts here
    [...]
    }
}
```

❶ Use a mock logger that implements the Log interface but does nothing.

❷ Create a MockConfiguration instance and set it up to return a given SQL query when Configuration.getSQL is called.

❸ Create the instance of DefaultAccountManager that you will test, passing to it the Log and Configuration instances.

You have been able to completely control your logging and configuration behavior from outside the code to test, in the test code. As a result, your code is more flexible and allows for any logging and configuration implementation to be used. You will see more of these code refactorings in this chapter and later ones.

One last point to note is that if you write your test first, you will automatically design your code to be flexible. Flexibility is a key point when writing a unit test. If you test first, you will not incur the cost of refactoring your code for flexibility later.

---

[2] See the Jakarta Avalon framework for a component framework implementing the IOC pattern (http://avalon.apache.org).

7.4 Practicing on an HTTP connection sample

To see how mock objects work in a practical example, let's use a simple application that opens an HTTP connection to a remote server and reads the content of a page. In chapter 6 we tested that application using stubs. Let's now unit-test it using a mock-object approach to simulate the HTTP connection.

In addition, you'll learn how to write mocks for classes that do not have a Java interface (namely, the HttpURLConnection class). We will show a full scenario in which you start with an initial testing implementation, improve the implementation as you go, and modify the original code to make it more flexible. We will also show how to test for error conditions using mocks.

As you dive in, you will keep improving both the test code and the sample application, exactly as you might if you were writing the unit tests for the same application. In the process, you will learn how to reach a simple and elegant testing solution while making your application code more flexible and capable of handling change.

Figure 7.2 introduces the sample HTTP application, which consists of a simple WebClient.getContent method performing an HTTP connection to a web resource executing on a web server. You want to be able to unit-test the get-Content method in isolation from the web resource.

7.4.1 Defining the mock object

Figure 7.3 illustrates the definition of a mock object. The MockURL class stands in for the real URL class, and all calls to the URL class in getContent are directed to the MockURL class. As you can see, the test is the controller: It creates and configures the behavior the mock must have for this test, it (somehow) replaces the real URL class with the MockURL class, and it runs the test.

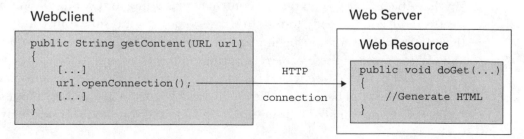

Figure 7.2 The sample HTTP application before introducing the test

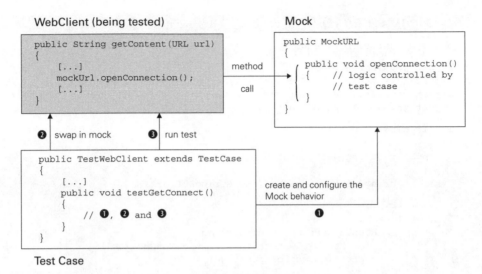

Figure 7.3 The steps involved in a test using mock objects

Figure 7.3 shows an interesting aspect of the mock-objects strategy: the need to be able to swap-in the mock in the production code. The perceptive reader will have noticed that because the URL class is final, it is actually not possible to create a MockURL class that extends it. In the coming sections, we will demonstrate how this feat can be performed in a different way (by mocking at another level). In any case, when using the mock-objects strategy, swapping-in the mock instead of the real class is the hard part. This may be viewed as a negative point for mock objects, because you usually need to modify your code to provide a trapdoor. Ironically, modifying code to encourage flexibility is one of the strongest advantages of using mocks, as explained in section 7.3.1.

7.4.2 Testing a sample method

The example in listing 7.6 demonstrates a code snippet that opens an HTTP connection to a given URL and reads the content found at that URL. Let's imagine that it's one method of a bigger application that you want to unit-test, and let's unit-test that method.

Listing 7.6   Sample method that opens an HTTP connection

```
package junitbook.fine.try1;

import java.net.URL;
import java.net.HttpURLConnection;
import java.io.InputStream;
import java.io.IOException;

public class WebClient
{
    public String getContent(URL url)
    {
        StringBuffer content = new StringBuffer();

        try
        {
            HttpURLConnection connection =                          ❶
                (HttpURLConnection) url.openConnection();
            connection.setDoInput(true);

            InputStream is = connection.getInputStream();  ❷

            byte[] buffer = new byte[2048];                        ❸
            int count;
            while (-1 != (count = is.read(buffer)))
            {
                content.append(new String(buffer, 0, count));
            }
        }
        catch (IOException e)
        {
            return null;
        }

        return content.toString();
    }
}
```

❶ ❷ Open an HTTP connection using the HttpURLConnection class.

❸ Read the content until there is nothing more to read.

If an error occurs, you return null. Admittedly, this is not the best possible error-handling solution, but it is good enough for the moment. (And your tests will give you the courage to refactor later.)

7.4.3   *Try #1: easy method refactoring technique*

The idea is to be able to test the getContent method independently of a real HTTP connection to a web server. If you map the knowledge you acquired in section 7.2, it means writing a mock URL in which the url.openConnection method returns a mock HttpURLConnection. The MockHttpURLConnection class would provide an implementation that lets the test decides what the `getInputStream` method returns. Ideally, you would be able to write the following test:

```
public void testGetContentOk() throws Exception
{
    MockHttpURLConnection mockConnection =                              ❶
        new MockHttpURLConnection();
    mockConnection.setupGetInputStream(
        new ByteArrayInputStream("It works".getBytes()));

    MockURL mockURL = new MockURL();                                   ❷
    mockURL.setupOpenConnection(mockConnection);

    WebClient client = new WebClient();

    String result = client.getContent(mockURL);      ❸

    assertEquals("It works", result);      ❹
}
```

❶ Create a mock `HttpURLConnection` that you set up to return a stream containing *It works* when the `getInputStream` method is called on it.

❷ Do the same for creating a mock `URL` class and set it up to return the `MockURLConnection` when `url.openConnection` is called.

❸ Call the `getContent` method to test, passing to it your `MockURL` instance.

❹ Assert the result.

Unfortunately, this approach does not work! The JDK `URL` class is a final class, and no URL interface is available. So much for extensibility....

You need to find another solution and, potentially, another object to mock. One solution is to stub the `URLStreamHandlerFactory` class. We explored this solution in chapter 6, so let's find a technique that uses mock objects: refactoring the `getContent` method. If you think about it, this method does two things: It gets an `HttpURLConnection` object and then reads the content from it. Refactoring leads to the class shown in listing 7.7 (changes from listing 7.6 are in bold). We have extracted the part that retrieved the `HttpURLConnection` object.

Listing 7.7 Extracting retrieval of the connection object from getContent

```
public class WebClient
{
    public String getContent(URL url)
    {
        StringBuffer content = new StringBuffer();

        try
        {
            HttpURLConnection connection =                              ❶
                createHttpURLConnection(url);
```

```
                    InputStream is = connection.getInputStream();

                    byte[] buffer = new byte[2048];
                    int count;
                    while (-1 != (count = is.read(buffer)))
                    {
                        content.append(new String(buffer, 0, count));
                    }
                }
                catch (IOException e)
                {
                    return null;
                }

                return content.toString();
            }

            protected HttpURLConnection createHttpURLConnection(URL url)     ❶
                throws IOException
            {
                return (HttpURLConnection) url.openConnection();
            }
        }
```

❶ Refactoring. You now call the `createHttpURLConnection` method to create the HTTP connection.

How does this solution let you test `getContent` more effectively? You can now apply a useful trick, which consists of writing a test helper class that extends the `WebClient` class and overrides its `createHttpURLConnection` method, as follows:

```
private class TestableWebClient extends WebClient
{
    private HttpURLConnection connection;

    public void setHttpURLConnection(HttpURLConnection connection)
    {
        this.connection = connection;
    }

    public HttpURLConnection createHttpURLConnection(URL url)
        throws IOException
    {
        return this.connection;
    }
}
```

In the test, you can call the `setHttpURLConnection` method, passing it the mock `HttpURLConnection` object. The test now becomes the following (differences are shown in bold):

```
public void testGetContentOk() throws Exception
{
    MockHttpURLConnection mockConnection =
        new MockHttpURLConnection();
    mockConnection.setupGetInputStream(
        new ByteArrayInputStream("It works".getBytes()));

    TestableWebClient client = new TestableWebClient();
    client.setHttpURLConnection(mockConnection);

    String result = client.getContent(new URL("http://localhost"));

    assertEquals("It works", result);
}
```

❶ Configure `TestableWebClient` so that the `createHttpURLConnection` method returns a mock object.

❷ The `getContent` method accepts a URL as parameter, so you need to pass one. The value is not important, because it will not be used; it will be bypassed by the `MockHttpURLConnection` object.

This is a common refactoring approach called *Method Factory* refactoring, which is especially useful when the class to mock has no interface. The strategy is to extend that class, add some setter methods to control it, and override some of its getter methods to return what you want for the test. In the case at hand, this approach is OK, but it isn't perfect. It's a bit like the Heisenberg Uncertainty Principle: The act of subclassing the class under test changes its behavior, so when you test the subclass, what are you truly testing?

This technique is useful as a means of opening up an object to be more testable, but stopping here means testing something that is similar to (but not exactly) the class you want to test. It isn't as if you're writing tests for a third-party library and can't change the code—you have complete control over the code to test. You can enhance it, and make it more test-friendly in the process.

7.4.4 *Try #2: refactoring by using a class factory*

Let's apply the Inversion of Control (IOC) pattern, which says that any resource you use needs to be passed to the `getContent` method or `WebClient` class. The only resource you use is the `HttpURLConnection` object. You could change the `Web-Client.getContent` signature to

```
public String getContent(URL url, HttpURLConnection connection)
```

This means you are pushing the creation of the `HttpURLConnection` object to the caller of `WebClient`. However, the URL is retrieved from the `HttpURLConnection` class, and the signature does not look very nice. Fortunately, there is a better solution that involves creating a ConnectionFactory interface, as shown in listings 7.8 and 7.9. The role of classes implementing the ConnectionFactory interface is to return an InputStream from a connection, whatever the connection might be (HTTP, TCP/IP, and so on). This refactoring technique is sometimes called a Class Factory refactoring.[3]

Listing 7.8   ConnectionFactory.java

```
package junitbook.fine.try2;

import java.io.InputStream;

public interface ConnectionFactory
{
    InputStream getData() throws Exception;
}
```

The WebClient code then becomes as shown in listing 7.9. (Changes from the initial implementation in listing 7.6 are shown in bold.)

Listing 7.9   Refactored WebClient using ConnectionFactory

```
package junitbook.fine.try2;

import java.io.InputStream;

public class WebClient
{
    public String getContent(ConnectionFactory connectionFactory)
    {
        StringBuffer content = new StringBuffer();

        try
        {
            InputStream is = connectionFactory.getData();

            byte[] buffer = new byte[2048];
            int count;
            while (-1 != (count = is.read(buffer)))
            {
                content.append(new String(buffer, 0, count));
            }
        }
        catch (Exception e)
```

---

[3] J. B. Rainsberger calls it Replace Subclasses with Collaborators: http://www.diasparsoftware.com/articles/refactorings/replaceSubclassWithCollaborator.html.

```
        {
            return null;
        }
        return content.toString();
    }
}
```

This solution is better because you have made the retrieval of the data content independent of the way you get the connection. The first implementation worked only with URLs using the HTTP protocol. The new implementation can work with any standard protocol (file://, http://, ftp://, jar://, and so forth), or even your own custom protocol. For example, listing 7.10 shows the ConnectionFactory implementation for the HTTP protocol.

Listing 7.10   HttpURLConnectionFactory.java

```java
package junitbook.fine.try2;

import java.io.InputStream;

import java.net.HttpURLConnection;
import java.net.URL;

public class HttpURLConnectionFactory.java implements ConnectionFactory
{
    private URL url;

    public HttpURLConnectionFactory(URL url)
    {
        this.url = url;
    }

    public InputStream getData() throws Exception
    {
        HttpURLConnection connection =
            (HttpURLConnection) this.url.openConnection();
        return connection.getInputStream();
    }
}
```

Now you can easily test the getContent method by writing a mock for Connection-Factory (see listing 7.11).

Listing 7.11   MockConnectionFactory.java

```java
package junitbook.fine.try2;

import java.io.InputStream;

public class MockConnectionFactory implements ConnectionFactory
{
    private InputStream inputStream;

    public void setData(InputStream stream)
    {
        this.inputStream = stream;
    }

    public InputStream getData() throws Exception
    {
        return this.inputStream;
    }
}
```

As usual, the mock does not contain any logic and is completely controllable from the outside (by calling the setData method). You can now easily rewrite the test to use MockConnectionFactory as demonstrated in listing 7.12.

Listing 7.12   Refactored WebClient test using MockConnectionFactory

```java
package junitbook.fine.try2;

import java.io.ByteArrayInputStream;

import junit.framework.TestCase;

public class TestWebClient extends TestCase
{
    public void testGetContentOk() throws Exception
    {
        MockConnectionFactory mockConnectionFactory =
            new MockConnectionFactory();

        mockConnectionFactory.setData(
            new ByteArrayInputStream("It works".getBytes()));

        WebClient client = new WebClient();

        String result = client.getContent(mockConnectionFactory);

        assertEquals("It works", result);
    }
}
```

You have achieved your initial goal: to unit-test the code logic of the `WebClient.getContent` method. In the process you had to refactor it for the test, which led to a more extensible implementation that is better able to cope with change.

7.5 *Using mocks as Trojan horses*

Mock objects are Trojan horses, but they are not malicious. Mocks replace real objects from the inside, without the calling classes being aware of it. Mocks have access to internal information about the class, making them quite powerful. In the examples so far, you have only used them to emulate real behaviors, but you haven't mined all the information they can provide.

It is possible to use mocks as probes by letting them monitor the method calls the object under test makes. Let's take the HTTP connection example. One of the interesting calls you could monitor is the `close` method on the `InputStream`. You have not been using a mock object for `InputStream` so far, but you can easily create one and provide a `verify` method to ensure that `close` has been called.

Then, you can call the `verify` method at the end of the test to verify that all methods that should have been called, were called (see listing 7.13). You may also want to verify that `close` has been called exactly once, and raise an exception if it was called more than once or not at all. These kinds of verifications are often called *expectations*.

> **DEFINITION** *expectation*—When we're talking about mock objects, an *expectation* is a feature built into the mock that verifies whether the external class calling this mock has the correct behavior. For example, a database connection mock could verify that the `close` method on the connection is called exactly once during any test that involves code using this mock.

Listing 7.13 Mock InputStream with an expectation on close

```
package junitbook.fine.expectation;

import java.io.IOException;
import java.io.InputStream;

import junit.framework.AssertionFailedError;

public class MockInputStream extends InputStream
{
    private String buffer;                                    ❶
    private int position = 0;
    private int closeCount = 0;                      ❷
```

```java
    public void setBuffer(String buffer)                         ❶
    {
        this.buffer = buffer;
    }

    public int read() throws IOException
    {
        if (position == this.buffer.length())
        {
            return -1;
        }

        return this.buffer.charAt(this.position++);
    }

    public void close() throws IOException
    {
        closeCount++;              ❷
        super.close();
    }

    public void verify() throws AssertionFailedError            ❸
    {
        if (closeCount != 1)
        {
            throw new AssertionFailedError("close() should "
                + "have been called once and once only");
        }
    }
}
```

❶ Tell the mock what the read method should return.

❷ Count the number of times close is called.

❸ Verify that the expectations are met.

In the case of the MockInputStream class, the expectation for close is simple: You always want it to be called once. However, most of the time, the expectation for closeCount depends on the code under test. A mock usually has a method like setExpectedCloseCalls so that the test can tell the mock what to expect.

Let's modify the TestWebClient.testGetContentOk test method to use the new MockInputStream:

```java
package junitbook.fine.expectation;

import junit.framework.TestCase;
import junitbook.fine.try2.MockConnectionFactory;

public class TestWebClient extends TestCase
{
    public void testGetContentOk() throws Exception
```

```
        {
            MockConnectionFactory mockConnectionFactory =
                new MockConnectionFactory();
            MockInputStream mockStream = new MockInputStream();
            mockStream.setBuffer("It works");

            mockConnectionFactory.setData(mockStream);

            WebClient client = new WebClient();

            String result = client.getContent(mockConnectionFactory);

            assertEquals("It works", result);
            mockStream.verify();
        }
    }
```

Instead of using a real `ByteArrayInputStream` as in previous tests, you now use the `MockInputStream`. Note that you call the `verify` method of `MockInputStream` at the end of the test to ensure that all expectations are met. The result of running the test is shown in figure 7.4.

The test fails with the message *close() should have been called once and once only*. Why? Because you have not closed the input stream in the `WebClient.getContent` method. The same error would be raised if you were closing it twice or more, because the test verifies that it is called once and only once. Let's correct the code under test (see listing 7.14). You now get a nice green bar (figure 7.5).

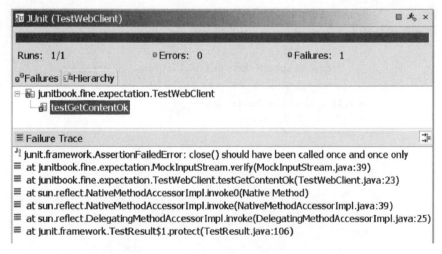

Figure 7.4 Running `TestWebClient` with the new `close` expectation

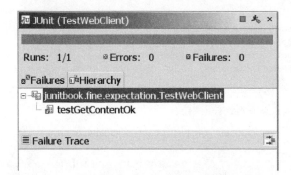

Figure 7.5
Working WebClient **that closes the input stream**

Listing 7.14   WebClient closing the stream

```java
public class WebClient
{
    public String getContent(ConnectionFactory connectionFactory)
        throws IOException
    {
        String result;

        StringBuffer content = new StringBuffer();
        InputStream is = null;
        try
        {
            is = connectionFactory.getData();

            byte[] buffer = new byte[2048];
            int count;
            while (-1 != (count = is.read(buffer)))
            {
                content.append(new String(buffer, 0, count));
            }

            result = content.toString();
        }
        catch (Exception e)
        {
            result = null;
        }

        // Close the stream
        if (is != null)
        {
            try
            {
                is.close();
            }
            catch (IOException e)
            {
```

```
                    result = null;
                }
            }

            return result;
        }
    }
```

1 Close the stream and return null if an error occurs when you're closing it.

There are other handy uses for expectations. For example, if you have a component manager calling different methods of your component life cycle, you might expect them to be called in a given order. Or, you might expect a given value to be passed as a parameter to the mock. The general idea is that, aside from behaving the way you want during a test, your mock can also provide useful feedback on its usage.

> **NOTE**   The MockObjects project (http://www.mockobjects.com) provides some ready-made mock objects for standard JDK APIs. These mocks usually have expectations built in. In addition, the MockObjects project contains some reusable expectation classes that you can use in your own mocks.

7.6 *Deciding when to use mock objects*

You have seen how to create mocks, but we haven't talked about when to use them. For example, in your tests, you have sometimes used the real objects (when you used `ByteArrayInputStream` in listing 7.11, for example) and sometimes mocked them.

Here are some cases in which mocks provide useful advantages over the real objects. (This list can be found on the C2 Wiki at http://c2.com/cgi/wiki?MockObject.) This should help you decide when to use a mock:

- Real object has non-deterministic behavior
- Real object is difficult to set up
- Real object has behavior that is hard to cause (such as a network error)
- Real object is slow
- Real object has (or is) a UI

- Test needs to query the object, but the queries are not available in the real object (for example, "was this callback called?")
- Real object does not yet exist

7.7 Summary

This chapter has described a technique called mock objects that lets you unit-test code in isolation from other domain objects and from the environment. When it comes to writing fine-grained unit tests, one of the main obstacles is to abstract yourself from the executing environment. We have often heard the following remark: "I haven't tested this method because it's too difficult to simulate a real environment." Well, not any longer!

In most cases, writing mock-object tests has a nice side effect: It forces you to rewrite some of the code under test. In practice, code is often not written well. You hard-code unnecessary couplings between the classes and the environment. It's easy to write code that is hard to reuse in a different context, and a little nudge can have a big effect on other classes in the system (similar to the domino effect). With mock objects, you must think differently about the code and apply better design patterns, like Interfaces and Inversion of Control (IOC).

Mock objects should be viewed not only as a unit-testing technique but also as a design technique. A new rising star among methodologies called Test-Driven Development advocates writing tests before writing code. With TDD, you don't have to refactor your code to enable unit testing: The code is already under test! (For a full treatment of the TDD approach, see Kent Beck's book *Test Driven Development*.[4] For a brief introduction, see chapter 4.)

Although writing mock objects is easy, it can become tiresome when you need to mock hundreds of objects. In the following chapters we will present several open source frameworks that automatically generate ready-to-use mocks for your classes, making it a pleasure to use the mock-objects strategy.

---

[4] Kent Beck, *Test Driven Development: By Example* (Boston: Addison-Wesley, 2003).

In-container testing
with Cactus

Good design at good times. Make it run, make it run right.
— Kent Beck, *Test Driven Development: By Example*

Starting with this chapter, we'll study how to unit-test J2EE components. Unit-testing components is more difficult than just testing plain Java classes. The components interact with their container, and the container services are available only when the container is running. JUnit is not designed to run inside a container like a J2EE component. So, how can we unit-test components?

This chapter examines one approach to unit-testing J2EE components: *in-container unit testing*, or *integration unit testing*. (These concepts and terminologies were introduced by the Cactus framework.) More specifically, we'll discuss the pros and cons of running J2EE tests inside the container using the Cactus framework (http://jakarta.apache.org/cactus/). We'll show what can be achieved using the mock-objects approach introduced in chapter 7, where it comes up short, and how the in-container testing approach enables you to write integration unit tests.

8.1 *The problem with unit-testing components*

Imagine you have a web application that uses servlets, and that you wish to unit-test the isAuthenticated method in listing 8.1 from a SampleServlet servlet.

> **Listing 8.1 Sample of a servlet method to unit-test**

```java
package junitbook.container;

import javax.servlet.http.HttpServlet;
import javax.servlet.http.HttpServletRequest;
import javax.servlet.http.HttpSession;

public class SampleServlet extends HttpServlet
{
    public boolean isAuthenticated(HttpServletRequest request)
    {
        HttpSession session = request.getSession(false);

        if (session == null)
        {
            return false;
        }

        String authenticationAttribute =
            (String) session.getAttribute("authenticated");

        return Boolean.valueOf(
            authenticationAttribute).booleanValue();
    }
}
```

In order to be able to test this method, you need to get hold of a valid `HttpServletRequest` object. Unfortunately, it is not possible to call `new HttpServletRequest` to create a usable request. The life cycle of `HttpServletRequest` is managed by the container. JUnit alone is not enough to write a test for the `isAuthenticated` method.

DEFINITION   *component/container*—A component is a piece of code that executes inside a container. A container is a receptacle that offers useful services for the components it is hosting, such as life cycle, security, transaction, distribution, and so forth.

Fortunately, several solutions are available; we'll cover them in the following sections. Overall, we're presenting two core solutions: *outside-the-container testing* with mock objects and *in-container testing* using Cactus.

A variation on these two approaches would be to use a stubbed container, such as the ServletUnit module in HttpUnit (http://httpunit.sourceforge.net/). Unfortunately, we haven't found a full-blown implementation of a stub J2EE container. ServletUnit implements only a portion of the Servlet specification. (For more about stubs, see chapter 6.)

Mock objects and Cactus are both valid approaches. In chapter 7, we discussed the advantages and drawbacks of the mock objects outside-the-container strategy. In this chapter, we focus on the Cactus in-container strategy to show its relative advantages and drawbacks. Chapter 9 turns the focus to unit-testing servlets. In that chapter, we discuss when to use mock objects and when to use Cactus tests when you're testing servlets.

8.2 Testing components using mock objects

Let's try using mock objects to test a servlet and then discuss the benefits and drawbacks of this approach. In chapter 7, you built your own mock objects. Fortunately, several frameworks are available that automate the generation of mock objects. In this chapter you'll use *EasyMock* (http://www.easymock.org/—version 1.0 or above).

EasyMock is one of the best-known mock-object generators today. We'll demonstrate how to use some other generators in later chapters. EasyMock is implemented using Java *dynamic proxies* so that it can transparently generate mock objects at runtime, as shown in the next section.

8.2.1 *Testing the servlet sample using EasyMock*

The solution that comes to mind to unit-test the isAuthenticated method (listing 8.1) is to mock the HttpServletRequest class using the mock objects approach described in chapter 7. This approach would work, but you would need to write quite a few lines of code. The result can be easily achieved using the Easy-Mock framework as demonstrated in listing 8.2.

Listing 8.2   Using EasyMock to unit-test servlet code

```
package junitbook.container;

import javax.servlet.http.HttpServletRequest;
import javax.servlet.http.HttpSession;

import org.easymock.MockControl;

import junit.framework.TestCase;

public class TestSampleServlet extends TestCase
{
    private SampleServlet servlet;

    private MockControl controlHttpServlet;            ❶
    private HttpServletRequest mockHttpServletRequest;

    private MockControl controlHttpSession;
    private HttpSession mockHttpSession;

    protected void setUp()
    {
        servlet = new SampleServlet();

        controlHttpServlet = MockControl.createControl(    ❶
            HttpServletRequest.class);
        mockHttpServletRequest =
            (HttpServletRequest) controlHttpServlet.getMock();

        controlHttpSession = MockControl.createControl(
            HttpSession.class);
        mockHttpSession =
            (HttpSession) controlHttpSession.getMock();
    }

    protected void tearDown()                              ❷
    {
        controlHttpServlet.verify();
        controlHttpSession.verify();
    }

    public void testIsAuthenticatedAuthenticated()
    {
```

```
        mockHttpServletRequest.getSession(false);                        ❸
        controlHttpServlet.setReturnValue(mockHttpSession);

        mockHttpSession.getAttribute("authenticated");                   ❹
        controlHttpSession.setReturnValue("true");

        controlHttpServlet.replay();                                     ❺
        controlHttpSession.replay();

        assertTrue(servlet.isAuthenticated(mockHttpServletRequest));
    }
    public void testIsAuthenticatedNotAuthenticated()
    {
        mockHttpServletRequest.getSession(false);                        ❸
        controlHttpServlet.setReturnValue(mockHttpSession);

        mockHttpSession.getAttribute("authenticated");                   ❻
        controlHttpSession.setReturnValue(null);

        controlHttpServlet.replay();                                     ❺
        controlHttpSession.replay();

        assertFalse(
            servlet.isAuthenticated(mockHttpServletRequest));
    }
    public void testIsAuthenticatedNoSession()
    {
        mockHttpServletRequest.getSession(false);                        ❼
        controlHttpServlet.setReturnValue(null);
        controlHttpServlet.replay();                                     ❺
        controlHttpSession.replay();

        assertFalse(
            servlet.isAuthenticated(mockHttpServletRequest));
    }
}
```

❶ Create two mocks, one of HttpServletRequest and one of HttpSession. EasyMock works by creating a dynamic proxy for the mock, which is controlled through a control object (MockControl).

❷ Tell EasyMock to verify that the calls to the mocked methods have effectively happened. EasyMock reports a failure if you have defined a mocked method that is not called in the test. It also reports a failure if a method for which you have not defined any behavior is called. You do this in JUnit's tearDown method so that the verification is done automatically for all tests. For this factorization to work for all the tests, you have to activate the HttpSession mock in testIsAuthenticatedNoSession, even though you don't use it in that test. With EasyMock, a mock can only be verified if it has been activated.

❸ Using the control object, tell the `HttpServletRequest` mock that when `getSession(false)` is called, the method should return the `HttpSession` mock.

❹ ❻ ❼ Do the same thing as in the previous step, telling the mock how to behave when such-and-such method is called.

❸ ❹ Notice that in order to tell the mocks how to behave, you call their methods and
❻ ❼ then tell the control object what the method should return. This is the EasyMock *training mode*.

❺ Once you activate the mocks here, you step out of the training mode, and calls to the mock methods return the expected results.

The result of executing this `TestSampleServlet TestCase` in Eclipse is shown in figure 8.1. (Of course, other IDEs would yield a similar result.)

8.2.2 *Pros and cons of using mock objects to test components*

The biggest advantage of the mock-object approach is that it does not require a running container in order to execute the tests. The tests can be set up quickly, and they run fast. The main drawback is that the components are not tested in the container in which they will be deployed. You don't get to test the interactions with the container, which is an important part of the code. You're also not testing the interactions between the different components when they are run inside the container.

You still need a way to perform integration testing. Writing and running functional tests could achieve this. The problem with functional tests is that they are coarse-grained and test only a full use case—you lose the benefits of fine-grained

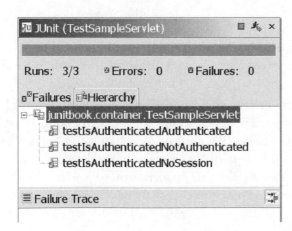

Figure 8.1
**Result of executing the mock
object** `TestCase` **for testing**
`isAuthenticated`

unit testing. You also know that you won't be able to test as many different cases with functional tests as you can with unit tests.

There are also other possible disadvantages of using the mock-objects approach. For example, you may have a lot of mock objects to set up; this may prove to be a non-negligible overhead. Obviously, the cleaner the code is (especially with small and focused methods), the easier tests are to set up.

Another important drawback with the mock-objects approach is that in order to set up the test, you usually must know exactly how the API being mocked behaves. It's easy to know that behavior for your own API, but not so easy for an external API, like the Servlet API.

Even though they all implement the same API, all containers do not behave in the same way. For example, take the following piece of code:

```
public void doGet(HttpServletRequest request,
    HttpServletResponse response)
{
    response.setContentType("text/xml");
}
```

Seems simple enough, but, if you run it in Tomcat 4.x (http://jakarta.apache.org/tomcat/) and in Orion 1.6.0 (http://www.orionserver.com/), you'll notice different behaviors. In Tomcat, the returned content type is text/xml, but in Orion it's text/html.

This may seem like an extreme example, and it is. All servlet containers manage to implement the API in pretty much the same way. But the situation is far worse for the J2EE APIs—especially the EJB APIs. A specification is a document, and sometimes it's possible to interpret a document in different ways. A specification can even be inconsistent, making it impossible to implement it to the letter. (Try talking to servlet container implementers about the Servlet Filters API!) And, of course, containers have bugs. (The example we have shown may be a bug in Orion 1.6.0.) It's an unfortunate fact of life that you have to live with bugs when you're writing an application.

To summarize, the drawbacks of using mock objects for unit-testing J2EE components are that they:

- Do not test interactions with the container or between the components
- Do not test the deployment part of the components
- Need excellent knowledge of the API being called in order to mock it, which can be difficult (especially for external libraries)
- Do not provide confidence that the code will run in the target container

Whereas this section has dwelled on the mock-objects approach, the next section introduces the other approach: integration unit testing.

8.3 *What are integration unit tests?*

Running unit tests inside the container gives you the best of both worlds: all the benefits of unit tests *and* confirmation that your code will run correctly inside its target container. *Integration unit tests* stand between *logic unit tests* (testing individual methods) and *functional tests* (testing interactions between methods). Figure 8.2 depicts the relationship between integration, logic, and functional unit tests.

Viewed from another angle, integration unit-testing is a generalization of logic unit-testing and functional testing. If you set the test-start slider to be in a given method and the test-end slider to be the same method, you get a logic unit test. If you set the start and end sliders to be one of the application entry points, you get a functional test.

The main idea is that nothing is completely white or black. Sometimes you need more flexibility in how you manage your tests, and you would like to perform testing between logic unit tests and functional tests. With integration unit tests, you can decide where the test starts and where it ends. It can begin in a given method, span several method calls, and stop in another method further down the chain. It can begin in a given method and go all the way to the end (up

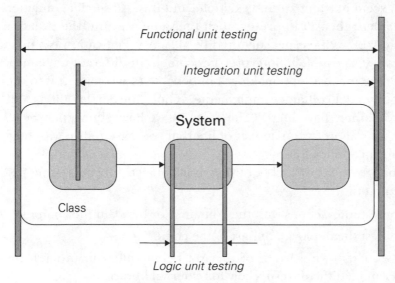

Figure 8.2   Integration unit tests versus logic unit tests versus functional tests

to a database). Or, it can begin at an entry point of the application and stop somewhere in the calling chain (say, by using mock objects or stubs to cut the chain).

In the next section we introduce Jakarta Cactus, a unit-testing framework specializing in integration unit-testing for server-side Java components.

8.4 Introducing Cactus

Cactus is an open source framework (http://jakarta.apache.org/cactus/) for unit-testing server-side Java code (mostly J2EE components in the current version of Cactus). More specifically, it is geared toward integration unit-testing (also called *in-container unit-testing*, a term coined by the Cactus team).

The Cactus vision goes something like this: In the past few years we have seen a move from Java code toward metadata, such as deployment descriptors. Containers offer more services for their components in an increasingly transparent fashion for the component writer. The latest trend is to use Aspect-Oriented Programming (AOP) to decouple programming aspects (security, logging, and so forth) from the business code. The main business code is shrinking, whereas configuration data and metadata are expanding. Integration is becoming more important to verify that an application works. Cactus takes a proactive approach to integration by moving it into the development cycle and providing a solution for fine-grained testing.

Let's see Cactus in action. In later sections, we'll explain in more detail how it works.

8.5 Testing components using Cactus

Let's write unit tests for the isAuthenticated method (listing 8.1). The tests in listing 8.3 are exactly the same tests that you wrote using the mock-objects approach in listing 8.2, but this time you use Cactus.

Listing 8.3 Using Cactus to unit-test servlet code

```
package junitbook.container;

import org.apache.cactus.ServletTestCase;
import org.apache.cactus.WebRequest;

public class TestSampleServletIntegration extends ServletTestCase
{
    private SampleServlet servlet;

    protected void setUp()
    {
```

```
        servlet = new SampleServlet();
    }
    public void testIsAuthenticatedAuthenticated()
    {
        session.setAttribute("authenticated", "true");        ❶
        assertTrue(servlet.isAuthenticated(request));
    }
    public void testIsAuthenticatedNotAuthenticated()
    {
        assertFalse(servlet.isAuthenticated(request));    ❶
    }
    public void beginIsAuthenticatedNoSession(WebRequest request)
    {
        request.setAutomaticSession(false);
    }
    public void testIsAuthenticatedNoSession()
    {
        assertFalse(servlet.isAuthenticated(request));    ❶
    }

}
```

❶ The Cactus framework exposes the container objects (in this case the Http-
ServletRequest and HttpSession objects) to your tests, making it easy and quick
to write unit tests.

8.5.1 *Running Cactus tests*

Let's run the Cactus tests. Doing so is more complex than running a pure JUnit
test, because you need to package your code, deploy it into a container, start the
container, and then start the tests using a JUnit test runner. Fortunately, Cactus
hides much of the complexity and has several runners (a.k.a. *front ends*) that simplify the execution of the tests by automatically performing most, if not all, of
these different steps. We'll demonstrate how to run Cactus tests using the most
advanced runners: Ant integration, the Maven plugin, and Jetty integration.
Figure 8.3 shows the full list (as of this writing) of available Cactus runners. Many
of these are written by the Cactus team: Ant integration, browser integration,
Eclipse plugin, Jetty integration, and the Maven plugin.

8.5.2 *Executing the tests using Cactus/Jetty integration*

Cactus/Jetty integration makes it easy to run the Cactus tests from any IDE, in
much the same way you ran mock objects with Jetty (but this time, the tests will

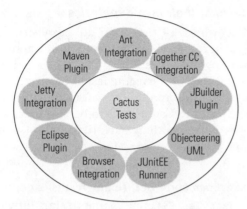

**Figure 8.3
The Cactus runners, which are used
to easily execute Cactus tests**

run inside the container). For these examples, we'll use two of our favorite products, Jetty and Eclipse. (For more about Jetty, see chapter 6. For more about Eclipse, see chapter 5 and appendix B.)

Cactus/Jetty integration yields several benefits: It works with any IDE, it is very fast, and you can set breakpoints for debugging. (Jetty runs in the same JVM as your tests.) As we mentioned in the previous section, Cactus boasts an Eclipse plugin that integrates it even more tightly with Eclipse. However, our goal here is to be tool-agnostic and show you techniques that will work in any IDE.

Figure 8.4 shows what the project looks like in Eclipse. The mock object tests are in `src/test` and the Cactus tests are in `src/test-cactus`.

In order to run a Cactus test with Jetty, you need to create a JUnit test suite containing the tests and wrapped by the special `JettyTestSetup` class provided by Cactus (found in the Cactus jar). `JettyTestSetup` extends the JUnit `TestSetup`

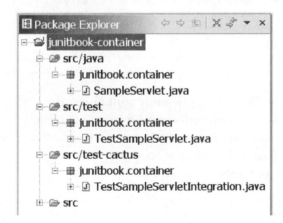

**Figure 8.4
The project structure in Eclipse**

> ### JUnit best practices: put Cactus tests in their own directories
>
> It's a good strategy to put the Cactus tests in their own directory structure, such as in `src/test-cactus`. The main reason is that integration unit tests and pure JUnit tests have different running life cycles: Pure JUnit tests are usually run more often than Cactus tests, because they execute faster. Separate directories allow the build system to perform different build actions on either type of test. Most Cactus test runners expect the Cactus tests to be in a specific directory, because they need a different setup than pure JUnit tests (such as packaging and deploying them in a container, and so forth).

class, which lets you run `setUp` and `tearDown` code before any test is executed and at the end of the test suite execution. `JettyTestSetup` uses that to start Jetty before the suite starts, and it stops Jetty when the suite terminates. Listing 8.4 demonstrates how to create a test suite to run Cactus tests inside the Jetty container.

Listing 8.4   Test suite to run Cactus test inside the Jetty container

```
package junitbook.container;

import org.apache.cactus.extension.jetty.JettyTestSetup;

import junit.framework.Test;
import junit.framework.TestSuite;

public class TestAllWithJetty
{
    public static Test suite()
    {
        System.setProperty("cactus.contextURL",
            "http://localhost:8080/test");                         ❶

        TestSuite suite = new TestSuite("All tests with Jetty");   ❷
        suite.addTestSuite(TestSampleServletIntegration.class);
        return new JettyTestSetup(suite);          ❸
    }
}
```

❶ Define the context under which the web application containing the Cactus tests will run. The `JettyTestSetup` class uses this information to set up a listener on the port defined and to create a context. Because `cactus.contextURL` is a System property, it's also possible to pass it by using a `-Dcactus.contextURL=...` flag when you start the JVM used for the tests.

❷ Create a JUnit test suite and add all the tests found in the `TestSampleServletInt-egration` class.

❸ Wrap the JUnit test suite with the Cactus `JettyTestSetup` so that Jetty will be started and stopped during the execution of the tests.

Now that you have all the required source files, let's see what you need in order to execute the tests with Cactus/Jetty. Cactus requires some jars to be present on your classpath: the Cactus jar, the Commons Logging jar, the Commons HttpClient jar, and the AspectJ runtime jar. You'll be running the Jetty servlet engine, so you also need to have the Jetty jar on your classpath. If you're following the directory structure and the Eclipse projects as defined in appendix A, you should find the jars in the `junitbook/repository` directory, as shown in figure 8.5. Notice that we created an Eclipse project (named `junitbook-repository`) for the `junitbook/repository` directory to make it easier to include these jars on the `junitbook-container` project classpath (but doing so is not mandatory).

Let's now add the required jars to `junitbook-container` project, as shown in figure 8.6. In order to add these jars, right-click your project and select Properties. In the dialog that appears (on the Libraries tab), select Add JARs; then, in the next dialog that appears, open the `junitbook-repository` project and select all the jars you need.

You can now enjoy running the Cactus tests by clicking the Run button in the toolbar. The result is shown in figure 8.7. The console shows that Cactus started Jetty automatically before running the tests. Don't worry if you don't understand how Cactus works at this point. We'll come back to the Cactus mechanism later.

Figure 8.5
The Eclipse project named `junitbook-repository`. It's a placeholder for the jars used in all the other projects.

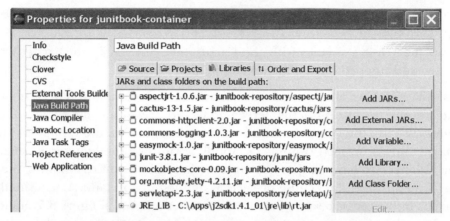

Figure 8.6 Jars required for the `junitbook-container` project in Eclipse

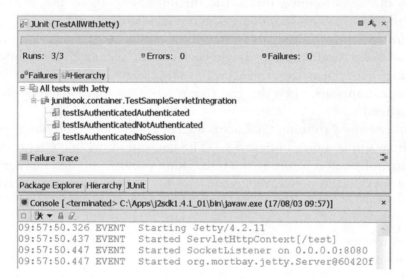

Figure 8.7 Cactus tests running in the Jetty container from inside Eclipse

8.5.3 *Drawbacks of in-container testing*

So far, we've shown you the advantages of in-container unit-testing. However, there are also a few disadvantages.

Specific tools required

A major drawback is that although the concept is generic, the tools that implement in-container unit-testing are very specific to the underlying API being tested. In the J2EE world, the de facto standard is Jakarta Cactus (introduced in the previous section). However, if you wish to write integration unit tests for another component model, chances are that no such framework will exist, and you may have to build one yourself. On the other hand, the mock-objects approach is completely generic and will work for almost any API.

Longer execution time

Another disadvantage is speed of execution. For a test to run in the container, you need to start the container beforehand, and that can take some time. How much time depends on the container: Jetty starts in less than 1 second, Tomcat starts in about 5 seconds, and WebLogic starts in about 30 seconds. The startup lag doesn't end with the container. If your unit tests hit a database or other remote resource, the database must be in a valid state before the test (see chapter 11, which covers database application testing). In terms of execution time, integration unit tests cost more than a mock-objects approach. Consequently, you may not run them as often as logic unit tests.

Complex configuration

The biggest drawback of in-container testing may be the configuration complexity. The tests run inside the container, so you need to package your application (usually as a war or an ear) before you can run the tests, deploy the tests to the server, start the server, and then start the tests.

However, there are some positive counter-arguments. Our favorite is that for production, you need to deploy your application. To do so you must package it, deploy it, and start the server—the same steps required for running a Cactus test! Our belief is that this exercise should be practiced from day one of the project, because it's one of the most complex tasks of a J2EE project. It needs to be done as often as possible and automated as much as possible in order to be able to perform deployments easily. Cactus acts as a triggering element in favor of setting up this process at the beginning of the project; doing so is good and is completely in line with the spirit of *continuous integration*.

The second counter-argument is that the Cactus development team has recognized that it can be a daunting task to set up everything before you can run your first Cactus test. Cactus provides several front ends that hide much (if not all) of the complexity and will run the test for you at the click of a button.

8.6 *How Cactus works*

The following chapters show how to use Cactus to unit-test servlets, filters, JSPs, database code, and EJBs. However, before we rush into the details, you need to understand a bit more about how Cactus works.

The life cycle of a Cactus test is shown in figure 8.8.

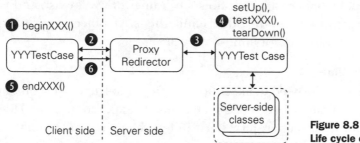

Figure 8.8
Life cycle of a Cactus test

We'll describe the different steps using the `TestSampleServletIntegration` Cactus test from listing 8.3. Say you have already deployed the application in the container, and the container is started. You can submit the Cactus test to a JUnit test runner, and the runner starts the tests.

8.6.1 *Executing client-side and server-side steps*

The life cycle is divided into steps that are executed on the client side and others that are executed on the server side (inside the container JVM). *Client side* refers to the JVM in which you have started the JUnit test runner.

On the client side, the Cactus logic is implemented in the `YYYTestCase` classes that your tests extend (where `YYY` can be `Servlet`, `Jsp`, or `Filter`). More specifically, `YYYTestCase` overrides JUnit `TestCase.runBare`, which is the method called by the JUnit test runner to execute one test. By overriding `runBare`, Cactus can implement its own test logic, as described later.

On the server side, the Cactus logic is implemented in a *proxy redirector* (or *redirector* for short).

8.6.2 *Stepping through a test*

For each test (`testXXX` methods in the `YYYTestCase` classes), the six steps shown in figure 8.8 take place. Let's step through all six.

Step 1: execute beginXXX

If there is a begin*XXX* method, Cactus executes it. The begin*XXX* method lets you pass information to the redirector. The `TestSampleServletIntegration` example extends `ServletTestCase` and connects to the Cactus servlet redirector. The servlet redirector is implemented as a servlet; this is the entry point in the container. The Cactus client side calls the servlet redirector by opening an HTTP connection to it. The begin*XXX* method sets up HTTP-related parameters that are set in the

HTTP request received by the servlet redirector. This method can be used to define HTTP POST/GET parameters, HTTP cookies, HTTP headers, and so forth. For example:

```
public void beginXXX(WebRequest request)
{
    request.addParameter("param1", "value1");
    request.addCookie("cookie1", "value1");
    [...]
}
```

In the `TestSampleServletIntegration` class, we have used the begin*XXX* method to tell the redirector not to create an HTTP session (the default behavior creates one):

```
public void beginIsAuthenticatedNoSession(WebRequest request)
{
    request.setAutomaticSession(false);
}
```

Step 2: open the redirector connection

The `YYYTestCase` opens a connection to its redirector. In this case, the `ServletTest-Case` code opens an HTTP connection to the servlet redirector (which is a servlet).

Step 3: create the server-side TestCase instance

The redirector creates an instance of the `YYYTestCase` class. Note that this is the second instance created by Cactus; a first one has been created on the client side (by the JUnit `TestRunner`). Then, the redirector retrieves container objects and assigns them in the `YYYTestCase` instance by setting class variables.

In the servlet example, the servlet redirector creates an instance of `TestSampleServletIntegration` and sets the following objects as class variables in it: `HttpServletRequest`, `HttpServletResponse`, `HttpSession`, and so forth. The servlet redirector is able to do this because it is a servlet. When it's called by the Cactus client side, it has received a valid `HttpServletRequest`, `HttpServletResponse`, `HttpSession`, and other objects from the container and is passing them to the `YYYTestCase` instance. It acts as a proxy/redirector (hence its name).

The redirector then starts the test (see step 4). Upon returning from the test, it stores the test result in the `ServletConfig` servlet object along with any exception that might have been raised during the test, so the test result can later be retrieved. The redirector needs a place to temporarily store the test result because the full Cactus test is complete only when the end*XXX* method has finished executing (see step 5).

Step 4: call setUp, testXXX, and tearDown on the server side

The redirector calls the JUnit `setUp` method of `YYYTestCase`, if there is one. Then it calls the `testXXX` method. The `testXXX` method calls the class/methods under test, and finally the redirector calls the JUnit `tearDown` method of the `TestCase`, if there is one.

Step 5: execute endXXX

Once the client side has received the response from its connection to the redirector, it calls an `endXXX` method (if it exists). This method is used so that your tests can assert additional results from the code under test. For example, if you're using a `ServletTestCase`, `FilterTestCase`, or `JspTestCase` class, you can assert HTTP cookies, HTTP headers, or the content of the HTTP response:

```
public void endXXX(WebResponse response)
{
    assertEquals("value",
        response.getCookie("cookiename").getValue());
    assertEquals("...", response.getText());
    [...]
}
```

Step 6: Gathering the test result

In step 3, the redirector saves the test result in a variable stored with the `Servlet-Config` object. The Cactus client side now needs to retrieve the test result and tell the JUnit test runner whether the test was successful, so the result can be displayed in the test runner GUI or console. To do this, the `YYYTestCase` opens a second connection to the redirector and asks it for the test result.

This process may look complex at first glance, but this is what it takes to be able to get inside the container and execute the test from there. Fortunately, as users, we are shielded from this complexity by the Cactus framework. You can simply use the provided Cactus front ends to start and set up the tests.

8.7 Summary

When it comes to unit-testing container applications, pure JUnit unit tests come up short. A mock-objects approach (see chapter 7) works fine and should be used. However, it misses a certain number of tests—specifically integration tests, which verify that components can talk to each other, that the components work when run inside the container, and that the components interact properly with the container. In order to perform these tests, an in-container testing strategy is required.

In the realm of J2EE components, the de facto standard framework for in-container unit-testing is Jakarta Cactus.

In this chapter, we ran through some simple tests using both a mock-objects approach and Cactus, in order to get a flavor for how it's done. We also discussed how Cactus works. We're now ready to move to the following chapters, which will let you practice unit-testing J2EE components like web applications and EJBs using both mock objects and Cactus.

Part 3

Testing components

Part 3 lets you practice the the testing knowledge acquired in parts 1 and 2 on J2EE components. You'll see not only how to write unit tests for the whole gamut of J2EE components but also how to set up your projects and how to run and automate the tests with Ant, Maven, and Eclipse.

Chapter 9 focuses on servlets and filters. Chapter 10 will teach you how to test JSPs and taglibs. In chapter 11, you'll learn about an aspect common to almost all applications: unit-testing code that calls the database. Chapter 12 takes you through the journey of EJB unit-testing.

After reading part 3, you'll know how to completely unit-test full J2EE applications. You'll also be familiar with the tradeoffs that exist and when to use one testing strategy over another.

Unit-testing servlets
and filters

This chapter covers

- Demonstrating the Test-Driven Development (TDD) approach
- Writing servlet and filter unit tests with Cactus and mock objects
- Running Cactus tests with Maven
- Choosing when to use Cactus and when to use mock objects

The only time you don't fail is the last time you try anything—and it works.

—William Strong

When you unit-test servlet and filter code, you must test not only these objects, but also any Java class calling the Servlet/Filter API, the JNDI API, or any back-end services. Starting in this chapter, you'll build a real-life sample application that will help demonstrate how to unit-test each of the different kinds of components that make up a full-blown web application. This chapter focuses on unit-testing the servlet and filter parts of that application. Later chapters test the other common components (JSPs, taglibs, and database access).

In this chapter, you'll learn how to unit-test servlets and filters using both the Cactus in-container testing approach and the mock-objects approach with the DynaMock framework from http://www.mockobjects.com/. You'll also learn the pros and cons of each approach and when to use them.

9.1 *Presenting the Administration application*

The goal of this sample Administration application is to let administrators perform database queries on a relational database. Suppose that the application it administers already exists. Administrators can perform queries such as listing all the transactions that took place during a given time interval, listing the transactions that were out of Service Level Agreement (SLA), and so forth. We set up a typical web application architecture (see figure 9.1) to demonstrate how to unit-test each type of component (filter, servlet, JSP, taglib, and database access).

The application first receives from the user an HTTP request containing the SQL query to execute. The request is caught by a security filter that checks

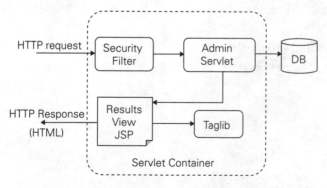

Figure 9.1   The sample Administration application. You'll use it as a base sample in this chapter and following chapters to see how to unit-test servlets, filters, JSPs, taglibs, and database applications.

whether the SQL query is a SELECT query (to prevent modifying the database). If not, the user is redirected to an error page. If the query is a SELECT, the Admin-Servlet servlet is called. The servlet performs the requested database query and forwards the result to a JSP page, which displays the results. The page uses JSP tags to iterate over the returned results and to display them in HTML tables. JSP tags are used for all the presentation logic code. The JSPs contain only layout/style tags (no Java code in scriptlets).

You'll start by unit-testing the AdminServlet servlet. Then, in section 9.4, you'll unit-test your security filter. You'll test the other components of the Administration application in following chapters.

9.2 *Writing servlet tests with Cactus*

In this section, we'll focus on using Cactus to unit-test the AdminServlet servlet (shaded in figure 9.2) from the Administration application.

Let's test AdminServlet by writing the tests before you write the servlet code. This strategy is called Test-Driven Development (TDD) or Test-First, and it's very efficient for designing extensible and flexible code and making sure the unit test suite is as complete as possible. (See chapter 4 for an introduction to TDD.)

Before you begin coding the test, let's review the requirement for AdminServlet. The servlet should extract the needed parameter containing the command to execute from the HTTP request (in this case, the SQL command to run). Then it should fetch the data using the extracted command. Finally, it should pass the control to the JSP page for display, passing the fetched data. Let's call the methods corresponding to these actions getCommand, executeCommand, and callView, respectively.

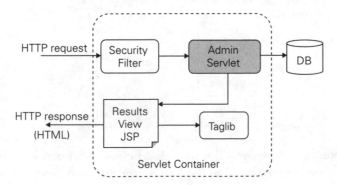

Figure 9.2
Unit-testing AdminServlet of the Administration application

9.2.1 *Designing the first test*

Listing 9.1 shows the unit tests for the getCommand method. Remember that you have not yet written the code under test. The AdminServlet class doesn't exist, and your code doesn't compile (yet).

Listing 9.1 Designing and testing the getCommand method

```
package junitbook.servlets;

import javax.servlet.ServletException;

import org.apache.cactus.ServletTestCase;
import org.apache.cactus.WebRequest;

public class TestAdminServlet extends ServletTestCase
{
    public void beginGetCommandOk(WebRequest request)
    {
        request.addParameter("command", "SELECT...");
    }

    public void testGetCommandOk() throws Exception
    {
        AdminServlet servlet = new AdminServlet();
        String command = servlet.getCommand(request);

        assertEquals("SELECT...", command);
    }

    public void testGetCommandNotDefined
    {
        AdminServlet servlet = new AdminServlet();

        try
        {
            servlet.getCommand(request);
            fail("Command should not have existed");
        }
        catch (ServletException expected)
        {
            assertTrue(true);
        }
    }
}
```

Test valid case: command defined as HTTP parameter

Test invalid case: no command parameter defined

If you've typed this code in Eclipse, you'll notice that Eclipse supports what it calls *Quick Fixes.* Quick Fixes are corrections that the Java editor offers to problems found while you're typing and after compiling. The Quick Fix is visible as a lightbulb in

```
    public void testGetCommandOk() throws Exception
    {
        AdminServlet servlet = new AdminServlet();
        String command = servlet.ge ⊙ Create class 'AdminServlet'     Opens the new class wizard to create the type.
                                      ❶ Create interface 'AdminServlet'
        assertEquals("SELECT...", c                                    Package: junitbook.servlets
    }                                                                  public class AdminServlet {
                                                                       }
    public void testGetCommandNotDe
    {
        AdminServlet servlet = new

        try
        {
            servlet.getCommand(request);
            fail("Command should not have existed");
```

Figure 9.3   Working by intention with Eclipse's Quick Fixes

the left gutter. In figure 9.3, a lightbulb appears on the lines referring to the Admin-
Servlet class (which does not yet exist). Clicking the lightbulb shows the list of
Quick Fixes offered by Eclipse. Here, Eclipse proposes to automatically create the
class for you. The same operation can then be repeated for the getCommand method.
This is very efficient when you're using the TDD approach. (Other IDEs, like IntelliJ
IDEA, also support this feature.)

Listing 9.2 shows the code Eclipse generates for you, to which you have made
some modifications:

- Added the throws ServletException clause. You need it because the
  testGetCommandNotDefined test clearly shows that if the command parameter is not found, the getCommand method should return a ServletException
  exception.

- The request object in TestAdminServlet comes from the ServletTestCase
  class and is of type HttpServletRequestWrapper. This Cactus class transparently wraps an HttpServletRequest object and provides additional features
  that are useful for unit testing. Eclipse thus generated a signature of get-
  Command(HttpServletRequestWrapper request), but what you really want is
  getCommand(HttpServletRequest request).

Listing 9.2   Minimum code to make the TestAdminServlet compile

```
package junitbook.servlets;

import javax.servlet.ServletException;
import javax.servlet.http.HttpServlet;
import javax.servlet.http.HttpServletRequest;

public class AdminServlet extends HttpServlet
{
```

```
    public String getCommand(HttpServletRequest request)
        throws ServletException
    {
        return null;
    }
}
```

This is the minimum code that allows the TestAdminServlet to compile successfully.

Before you continue with the other test cases and implement the minimal application that satisfies your tests, try to run the Cactus test. It should fail, but at least you'll know it does, and that your test correctly reports a failure. Then, when you implement the code under test, the tests should succeed, and you'll know you've accomplished something. It's a good practice to ensure that the tests fail when the code fails.

> ### JUnit best practice: always verify that the test fails when it should fail
>
> It's a good practice to always verify that the tests you're writing work. Be sure a test fails when you expect it to fail. If you're using the Test-Driven Development (TDD) methodology, this failure happens as a matter of course. After you write the test, write a skeleton for the class under test (a class with methods that return null or throw runtime exceptions). If you try to run your test against a skeleton class, it should fail. If it doesn't, fix the test (ironically enough) so that it does fail! Even after the case is fleshed out, you can vet a test by changing an assertion to look for an invalid value that should cause it to fail.

9.2.2   Using Maven to run Cactus tests

In chapter 8, you used the Cactus/Jetty integration to run Cactus tests from an IDE. This time, you'll try to run the tests with Tomcat using the Maven Cactus plugin (http://maven.apache.org/reference/plugins/cactus/). Tomcat is a well-known servlet/JSP engine (it's also the reference implementation for the Servlet/JSP specifications) that can be downloaded at http://jakarta.apache.org/tomcat/. (For a quick reference to Maven, see chapter 5.)

The Maven Cactus plugin is one of the easiest ways to run Cactus tests. Everything is automatic and transparent for the user: *cactification* of your application war file, starting your container, deploying the cactified war, executing the Cactus tests, and stopping your container. (*Cactification* is the automatic addition of the Cactus jars and the addition of Cactus-required entries in your web.xml file.)

Figure 9.4 shows the directory structure. It follows the directory structure conventions introduced in chapters 3 and 8.

By default, the Maven Cactus plugin looks for Cactus tests under the `src/test-cactus` directory, which is where we have put the `TestAdminServlet` Cactus `Servlet-TestCase` class. You place under `src/webapp` all the metadata and resource files needed for your web app. For example, `src/webapp/WEB-INF/web.xml` is the application's `web.xml`. Note that the Maven Cactus plugin automatically adds Cactus-related definitions to `web.xml` during the test, which is why you must provide a `web.xml` file in your directory structure, even if it's empty. The `web.xml` content for the Administration application is as follows:

Figure 9.4   Maven directory structure for running Cactus tests

```xml
<?xml version="1.0" encoding="ISO-8859-1"?>

<!DOCTYPE web-app
    PUBLIC "-//Sun Microsystems, Inc.//DTD Web Application 2.3//EN"
    "http://java.sun.com/dtd/web-app_2_3.dtd">

<web-app>

  <servlet>
    <servlet-name>AdminServlet</servlet-name>
    <servlet-class>junitbook.servlets.AdminServlet</servlet-class>
  </servlet>

  <servlet-mapping>
    <servlet-name>AdminServlet</servlet-name>
    <url-pattern>/AdminServlet</url-pattern>
  </servlet-mapping>

</web-app>
```

You'll be running the Cactus tests with Maven, so you need to provide a valid `project.xml` file, as shown in listing 9.3 (see chapter 5 for details on Maven's `project.xml`).

Listing 9.3 project.xml for running Maven on the junitbook-servlets project

```xml
<?xml version="1.0" encoding="ISO-8859-1"?>

<project>
  <pomVersion>3</pomVersion>
  <id>junitbook-servlets</id>
  <name>JUnit in Action - Unit Testing Servlets and Filters</name>
  <currentVersion>1.0</currentVersion>
  <organization>
    <name>Manning Publications Co.</name>
    <url>http://www.manning.com/</url>
    <logo>http://www.manning.com/front/dance.gif</logo>
  </organization>
  <inceptionYear>2002</inceptionYear>
  <package>junitbook.servlets</package>
  <logo>/images/jia.jpg</logo>

  <description>[...]</description>
  <shortDescription/>[...]</shortDescription>
  <url>http://sourceforge.net/projects/junitbook/servlets</url>
  <developers/>

  <dependencies>

    <dependency>
      <groupId>commons-beanutils</groupId>
      <artifactId>commons-beanutils</artifactId>
      <version>1.6.1</version>
      <properties>
        <war.bundle>true</war.bundle>
      </properties>
    </dependency>

    <dependency>
      <groupId>servletapi</groupId>
      <artifactId>servletapi</artifactId>
      <version>2.3</version>
    </dependency>

    <dependency>
      <groupId>easymock</groupId>
      <artifactId>easymock</artifactId>
      <version>1.0</version>
    </dependency>

    <dependency>
      <groupId>mockobjects</groupId>
      <artifactId>mockobjects-core</artifactId>
      <version>0.09</version>
    </dependency>

  </dependencies>
```

❶ Jars needed in execution classpath

❷ Jar to be included in the war

```
<build>
  <sourceDirectory>src/java</sourceDirectory>
  <unitTestSourceDirectory>src/test</unitTestSourceDirectory>
  <unitTest>                                    ❸  JUnit tests to
    <includes>                                      include/exclude
      <include>**/Test*.java</include>
    </includes>
    <excludes>
      <exclude>**/Test*All.java</exclude>
    </excludes>
  </unitTest>
</build>

<reports>
  <report>maven-cactus-plugin</report>          ❹  Tell Maven to generate
</reports>                                          Cactus report

</project>
```

❶ Define the jars you need when compiling and running the Cactus tests. You don't need to include the Cactus-related jars (the Cactus jars, the Commons HttpClient jar, the Commons Logging jar, and so on), because they are automatically included by the Maven Cactus plugin.

❷ The Maven Cactus plugin uses the war plugin. The `<war.bundle>` element tells Maven to include the Commons BeanUtils jar in the generated production war, which is cactified by the Maven Cactus plugin. Note that you include a dependency on Commons BeanUtils, because you'll use it later in your servlet code.

❸ Include/exclude the pure JUnit tests to match the test you wish to run. These settings only impact the tests found in `src/test` (defined by the `unitTestSourceDirectory` XML element). Thus these include/excludes have no effect on the selection of the Cactus tests (found in `src/test-cactus`). If you wish to precisely define what Cactus tests to include/exclude, you need to define the `cactus.src.includes` and `cactus.src.excludes` properties. The default values for these properties are as follows:

```
# Default Cactus test files to include in the test
cactus.src.includes = **/*Test*.java

# Default Cactus test files to exclude from the test
cactus.src.excludes = **/AllTests.java,**/Test*All.java
```

❹ List the reports to generate. If you don't explicitly define a reports element in your `project.xml`, Maven will generate default reports. However, these reports don't include Cactus tests. To generate a Cactus report as part of the web site generation (maven site), you must explicitly define it.

Before running the Cactus plugin, you need to tell it where Tomcat is installed on your machine, so that it can run the Cactus tests from within that container. Maven reads a project.properties file you put at the same level as your project.xml file. The Cactus plugin needs the following line added to your project.properties:

```
cactus.home.tomcat4x = C:/Apps/jakarta-tomcat-4.1.24
```

C:/Apps/jakarta-tomcat-4.1.24 is the actual path where you have installed Tomcat (you can use any version of Tomcat—we're using 4.1.24 as a sample). If you don't already have it on your system, it's time to download and install it. The installation is as simple as unzipping the file anywhere on your disk.

To start the Cactus tests in Maven, type **maven cactus:test** in project.xml's directory. The result of the run is shown in figure 9.5. As expected, the tests fail, because you have not yet written the code that is tested.

Maven can also generate an HTML report of the Cactus tests (see figure 9.6). By default, the Cactus plugin stops on test failures. To generate the test report, you need to add cactus.halt.on.failure = false to your project.properties (or build.properties) file so the build doesn't stop on test failures. Then, generate the site by typing **maven site**, which generates the web site in the servlets/target/docs directory.

You have executed the Cactus tests using the Tomcat container. However, the Maven Cactus plugin supports lots of other containers you can use to run your Cactus tests. Check the plugin documentation for more details (http://maven.apache.org/reference/plugins/cactus/).

```
cactus:test:
    [cactus] ------------------------------------------------------------
    [cactus] Running tests against Tomcat 4.1.24
    [cactus] ------------------------------------------------------------
    [cactus] Testsuite: junitbook.servlets.TestAdminServlet
    [cactus] Tests run: 2, Failures: 2, Errors: 0, Time elapsed: 1.272 sec
    [cactus]
    [cactus] Testcase: testGetCommandOk(junitbook.servlets.TestAdminServlet):   FAILED
    [cactus] expected:<SELECT...> but was:<null>
    [cactus] junit.framework.ComparisonFailure: expected:<SELECT...> but was:<null>
    [cactus]     at junitbook.servlets.TestAdminServlet.testGetCommandOk(TestAdminServlet.java:20)
    [cactus]     at sun.reflect.NativeMethodAccessorImpl.invoke0(Native Method)
    [cactus]     at sun.reflect.NativeMethodAccessorImpl.invoke(NativeMethodAccessorImpl.java:39)
```

Figure 9.5   Executing the failing Cactus tests using Maven

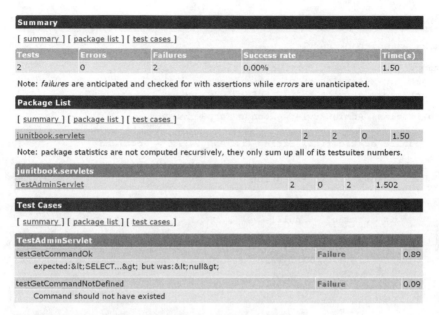

Figure 9.6   Cactus HTML report showing the test results

Let's return to the test. Listing 9.4 shows the code for getCommand. It's a minimal implementation that passes the tests.

> ### JUnit best practice: use TDD to implement The Simplest Thing That Could Possibly Work
>
> *The Simplest Thing That Could Possibly Work* is an Extreme Programming (XP) principle that says over-design should be avoided, because you never know what will be used effectively. XP recommends designing and implementing the minimal working solution and then refactoring mercilessly. This is in contrast to the *monumental methodologies,*[1] which advocated fully designing the solution before starting development.
>
> When you're developing using the TDD approach, the tests are written first— you only have to implement the bare minimum to make the test pass, in order to achieve a fully functional piece of code. The requirements have been fully expressed as test cases, and thus you can let yourself be led by the tests when you're writing the functional code.

---

[1] For more on agile methodologies versus monumental methodologies, read http://www.martinfowler.com/articles/newMethodology.html.

Listing 9.4   Implementation of getCommand that makes the tests pass

```java
package junitbook.servlets;

import javax.servlet.ServletException;
import javax.servlet.http.HttpServlet;
import javax.servlet.http.HttpServletRequest;

public class AdminServlet extends HttpServlet
{
    public static final String COMMAND_PARAM = "command";

    public String getCommand(HttpServletRequest request)
        throws ServletException
    {
        String command = request.getParameter(COMMAND_PARAM);
        if (command == null)
        {
            throw new ServletException("Missing parameter ["
                + COMMAND_PARAM + "]");
        }
        return command;
    }
}
```

Running the tests again by typing **maven cactus:test** yields the result shown in figure 9.7.

```
cactus:test:
   [cactus] -----------------------------------------------------------
   [cactus] Running tests against Tomcat 4.1.24
   [cactus] -----------------------------------------------------------
   [cactus] Testsuite: junitbook.servlets.TestAdminServlet
   [cactus] Tests run: 2, Failures: 0, Errors: 0, Time elapsed: 1.262 sec
   [cactus]
   [cactus] Testcase: testGetCommandOk took 0.671 sec
   [cactus] Testcase: testGetCommandNotDefined took 0.091 sec
BUILD SUCCESSFUL
Total time:  20 seconds
```

Figure 9.7   Execution of successful Cactus tests using Maven

9.2.3   *Finishing the Cactus servlet tests*

At the beginning of section 9.2, we mentioned that you need to write three methods: getCommand, executeCommand, and callView. You implemented getCommand in listing 9.4. The executeCommand method is responsible for obtaining data from the database. We'll defer this implementation until chapter 11, "Unit-testing database applications."

That leaves the `callView` method, along with the servlet `doGet` method, which ties everything together by calling your different methods. One way of designing the application is to store the result of the `executeCommand` method in the HTTP servlet request. The request is passed to the JSP by the `callView` method (via servlet `forward`). The JSP can then access the data to display by getting it from the request (possibly using a `useBean` tag). This is a typical MVC Model 2 pattern used by many applications and frameworks.

> ### Design patterns in action: MVC Model 2 pattern
>
> MVC stands for Model View Controller. This pattern is used to separate the core business logic layer (the Model), the presentation layer (the View), and the presentation logic (the Controller), usually in web applications. In a typical MVC Model 2 design, the Controller is implemented as a servlet and handles all incoming HTTP requests. It's in charge of calling the core business logic services and dynamically choosing the right view (often implemented as a JSP). The Jakarta Struts framework (http://jakarta.apache.org/struts/) is a popular implementation of this pattern.

You still need to define what objects `executeCommand` will return. The `BeanUtils` package in the Jakarta Commons (http://jakarta.apache.org/commons/beanutils/) includes a `DynaBean` class that can expose public properties, like a regular JavaBean, but you don't need to hard-code getters and setters. In a Java class, you access one of the dyna-properties using a map-like accessor:

```
DynaBean employee = ...
String firstName = (String) employee.get("firstName");
employee.set("firstName", "vincent");
```

The `BeanUtils` framework is nice for the current use case because you'll retrieve arbitrary data from the database. You can construct dynamic JavaBeans (or dyna beans) that you'll use to hold database data. The actual mapping of a database to dyna beans is covered in chapter 11.

Testing the callView method

There's enough in place now that you can write the tests for `callView`, as shown in listing 9.5.

Listing 9.5   Unit tests for callView

```java
package junitbook.servlets;
[...]
import java.util.ArrayList;
import java.util.Collection;
import java.util.List;

import org.apache.commons.beanutils.BasicDynaClass;
import org.apache.commons.beanutils.DynaBean;
import org.apache.commons.beanutils.DynaProperty;

public class TestAdminServlet extends ServletTestCase
{
[...]
    private Collection createCommandResult() throws Exception
    {
        List results = new ArrayList();

        DynaProperty[] props = new DynaProperty[] {
            new DynaProperty("id", String.class),
            new DynaProperty("responsetime", Long.class)
        };
        BasicDynaClass dynaClass = new BasicDynaClass("requesttime",
            null, props);

        DynaBean request1 = dynaClass.newInstance();
        request1.set("id", "12345");
        request1.set("responsetime", new Long(500));
        results.add(request1);

        DynaBean request2 = dynaClass.newInstance();
        request1.set("id", "56789");
        request1.set("responsetime", new Long(430));
        results.add(request2);

        return results;
    }

    public void testCallView() throws Exception
    {
        AdminServlet servlet = new AdminServlet();

        // Set the result of the execution of the command in the
        // HTTP request so that the JSP page can get the data to
        // display
        request.setAttribute("result", createCommandResult());

        servlet.callView(request);
    }
}
```

Create objects to be returned by execute-Command

② Set execution results in HTTP requests

To make the test easier to read, you create a `createCommandResult` private method. This utility method creates arbitrary `DynaBean` objects, like those that will be returned by `executeCommand`. In `testCallView`, you place the dyna beans in the HTTP request where the JSP can find them.

There is nothing you can verify in `testCallView`, so you don't perform any asserts there. The call to `callView` forwards to a JSP. However, Cactus supports asserting the result of the execution of a JSP page. So, you can use Cactus to verify that the JSP will be able to display the data that you created in `createCommand-Result`. Because this would be JSP testing, we'll show how it works in chapter 10 ("Unit-testing JSPs and taglibs").

Listing 9.6 shows the simplest code that makes the `testCallView` test pass.

Listing 9.6   Implementation of callView that makes the tests pass

```
package junitbook.servlets;
[...]
public class AdminServlet extends HttpServlet
{
[...]
    public void callView(HttpServletRequest request)
    {
    }
}
```

You don't have a test yet for the returned result, so not returning anything is enough. That will change once you test the JSP.

Testing the doGet method

Let's design the unit test for the `AdminServlet doGet` method. To begin, you need to verify that the test results are put in the servlet request as an attribute. Here's how you can do that:

```
Collection results = (Collection) request.getAttribute("result");
assertNotNull("Failed to get execution results from the request",
    results);
assertEquals(2, results.size());
```

This code leads to storing the command execution result in `doGet`. But where do you get the result? Ultimately, from the execution of `executeCommand`—but it isn't implemented yet. The typical solution to this kind of deadlock is to have an `executeCommand` that does nothing in `AdminServlet`. Then, in your test, you can implement `executeCommand` to return whatever you want:

```
AdminServlet servlet = new AdminServlet()
{
```

```
    public Collection executeCommand(String command)
        throws Exception
    {
        return createCommandResult();
    }
};
```

You can now store the result of the test execution in doGet:

```
public void doGet(HttpServletRequest request,
    HttpServletResponse response) throws ServletException
{
    try
    {
        Collection results = executeCommand(getCommand(request));
        request.setAttribute("result", results);
    }
    catch (Exception e)
    {
        throw new ServletException(
            "Failed to execute command", e);
    }
}
```

Notice that you need the catch block because the Servlet specification says doGet must throw a ServletException. Because executeCommand can throw an exception, you need to wrap it into a ServletException.

If you run this code, you'll find that you have forgotten to set the command to execute in the HTTP request as a parameter. You need a beginDoGet method, such as this:

```
public void beginDoGet(WebRequest request)
{
    request.addParameter("command", "SELECT...");
}
```

The completed unit test is shown in listing 9.7.

Listing 9.7   Unit test for doGet

```
package junitbook.servlets;
[...]
public class TestAdminServlet extends ServletTestCase
{
[...]
    public void beginDoGet(WebRequest request)
    {
        request.addParameter("command", "SELECT...");
    }
```

```
    public void testDoGet() throws Exception
    {
        AdminServlet servlet = new AdminServlet()
        {
            public Collection executeCommand(String command)
                throws Exception
            {
                return createCommandResult();
            }
        };

        servlet.doGet(request, response);

        // Verify that the result of executing the command has been
        // stored in the HTTP request as an attribute that will be
        // passed to the JSP page.
        Collection results =
            (Collection) request.getAttribute("result");
        assertNotNull("Failed to get execution results from the "
            + "request", results);
        assertEquals(2, results.size());
    }
}
```

The doGet code is shown in listing 9.8.

Listing 9.8   Implementation of doGet that makes the tests pass

```
package junitbook.servlets;
[...]
public class AdminServlet extends HttpServlet
{
[...]
    public Collection executeCommand(String command)
        throws Exception
    {
        throw new RuntimeException("not implemented");   ◁──  Throws exception
    }                                                          if called; not
                                                               implemented yet
    public void doGet(HttpServletRequest request,
        HttpServletResponse response) throws ServletException
    {
        try
        {
            Collection results =
                executeCommand(getCommand(request));
            request.setAttribute("result", results);
        }
        catch (Exception e)
        {
```

```
        throw new ServletException(
            "Failed to execute command", e);
    }
  }
}
```

There are two points of note. First, the call to `callView` is not present in `doGet`; the tests don't yet mandate it. (They will, but not until you write the unit tests for your JSP.) Second, you throw a `RuntimeException` object if `executeCommand` is called. You could return null, but throwing an exception is a better practice. An exception clearly states that you have not implemented the method. If the method is called by mistake, there won't be any surprises.

> **JUnit best practice: throw an exception for methods that aren't implemented**
>
> When you're writing code, there are often times when you want to execute the code without having finished implementing all methods. For example, if you're writing a mock object for an interface and the code you're testing uses only one method, you don't need to mock all methods. A very good practice is to throw an exception instead of returning null values (or not returning anything for methods with no return value). There are two good reasons: Doing this states clearly to anyone reading the code that the method is not implemented *and* ensures that if the method is called, it will behave in such a way that you cannot mistake skeletal behavior for real behavior.

9.3 *Testing servlets with mock objects*

You have seen how to write servlet unit tests using Cactus. Let's try to do the same exercise using only a mock-objects approach. We'll then define some rules for deciding when to use the Cactus approach and when to use mock objects.

In chapter 8, you used EasyMock to write mock objects. This time you'll use the DynaMock API, which is part of the MockObjects.com framework (http://www.mockobjects.com/). They both use Dynamic Proxies to generate mock objects at runtime. However, the DynaMock framework has several advantages over EasyMock: Its API is more comprehensive (notably in the definition of the expectations), and it results in more concise code. The downside is that it's slightly more complex to use (at least initially), and it's a less mature framework. (However, we haven't resisted the temptation to show you how to use it, because we think it has a great future.)

EasyMock vs. DynaMock

- DynaMock provides more concise code (about half as much code as EasyMock).

- EasyMock provides strong typing, which is useful for auto-completion and when interfaces change.

- DynaMock has a more comprehensive API (especially for expectations).

- EasyMock is more mature, because it has been around for several years. DynaMock is very new, and its API is not completely stabilized (as of this writing).

9.3.1 Writing a test using DynaMocks and DynaBeans

Listing 9.9 shows the re-implementation of testGetCommandOk and testGet-CommandNotDefined from listing 9.1.

Listing 9.9 Tests for AdminServlet.getCommand using the DynaMock API

```
package junitbook.servlets;
[...]
import com.mockobjects.dynamic.C;
import com.mockobjects.dynamic.Mock;

public class TestAdminServletMO extends TestCase
{
    private Mock mockRequest;
    private HttpServletRequest request;
    private AdminServlet servlet;

    protected void setUp()
    {
        servlet = new AdminServlet();

        mockRequest = new Mock(HttpServletRequest.class);        ❶
        request = (HttpServletRequest) mockRequest.proxy();
    }

    protected void tearDown()
    {                                                            ❷
        mockRequest.verify();
    }

    public void testGetCommandOk() throws Exception
    {
        mockRequest.expectAndReturn("getParameter", "command",   ❸
            "SELECT...");
```

```
            String command = servlet.getCommand(request);
            assertEquals("SELECT...", command);
        }
    public void testGetCommandNotDefined()
    {
        mockRequest.expectAndReturn("getParameter",
            C.isA(String.class), null);

        try
        {
            servlet.getCommand(request);
            fail("Command should not have existed");
        }
        catch (ServletException expected)
        {
            assertTrue(true);
        }
    }
}
```

You're using an `HttpServletRequest` object in the code to test; so, because you aren't running inside a container, you need to create a mock for it. Here you tell the DynaMock API to generate an `HttpServletRequest` mock for you.

Ask your mock to verify the expectations you have set on it and to verify that the methods for which you have defined behaviors have been called.

Tell the mock to return `"SELECT..."` when the `getParameter` method is called with the `"command"` string as parameter.

Tell the mock request to return null when `getParameter` is called with a string parameter passed to it.

9.3.2 *Finishing the DynaMock tests*

Let's finish transforming the other tests from listing 9.1 into DynaMock tests. Listing 9.10 shows the results.

Listing 9.10   Tests for callView and doGet with dynamic mocks

```
package junitbook.servlets;
[...]
public class TestAdminServletMO extends TestCase
{
[...]
    private Mock mockResponse;
    private HttpServletResponse response;
```

```
        protected void setUp()
        {
            servlet = new AdminServlet()
            {
                public Collection executeCommand(String command)
                    throws Exception
                {
                    return createCommandResult();
                }
            };
[...]
            mockResponse = new Mock(HttpServletResponse.class);      ❷
            response = (HttpServletResponse) mockResponse.proxy();
        }
[...]
        private Collection createCommandResult() throws Exception
        {
            // Same as in listing 9.5
        }

        public void testCallView() throws Exception
        {
            servlet.callView(request);
        }

        public void testDoGet() throws Exception
        {
            mockRequest.expectAndReturn("getParameter", "command",    ❷
                "SELECT...");

            // Verify that the result of executing the command has been
            // stored in the HTTP request as an attribute that will be
            // passed to the JSP page.
            mockRequest.expect("setAttribute", C.args(C.eq("result"),  ❷
                C.isA(Collection.class)));

            servlet.doGet(request, response);
        }
    }
```

❶ You need a new mock for the HttpServletResponse class (used in doGet).

❷ Set the behaviors of the mock HttpServletRequest object. You also tell DynaMock to verify that the methods are called and that the parameters they are passed match what is expected. For example, you verify that the setAttribute method call is passed a first parameter matching the "result" string and that the second parameter is a Collection object.

You now have a fully working test suite using mock objects that exercises your servlet code.

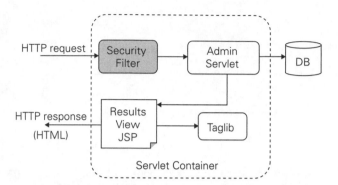

Figure 9.8
Unit-testing the
`SecurityFilter` **of the**
Administration application

9.4 *Writing filter tests with Cactus*

Now that you know how to unit-test servlets, let's change the focus to filters—in particular, the `SecurityFilter` specified by figure 9.8.

The requirement for the `SecurityFilter` is to intercept all HTTP requests and verify that the incoming SQL statement doesn't contain any harmful commands. For now, you'll only check whether the SQL query contains a `SELECT` statement; if it doesn't, you'll forward to an error page (see listing 9.11).

Listing 9.11   SecurityFilter.java

```java
package junitbook.servlets;

import java.io.IOException;

import javax.servlet.Filter;
import javax.servlet.FilterChain;
import javax.servlet.FilterConfig;
import javax.servlet.RequestDispatcher;
import javax.servlet.ServletException;
import javax.servlet.ServletRequest;
import javax.servlet.ServletResponse;

public class SecurityFilter implements Filter
{
    private String securityErrorPage;

    public void init(FilterConfig theConfig) throws ServletException
    {
        this.securityErrorPage =
            theConfig.getInitParameter("securityErrorPage");
    }

    public void doFilter(ServletRequest theRequest,
        ServletResponse theResponse, FilterChain theChain)
        throws IOException, ServletException
```

> Get name
> of error
> page from
> web.xml

```
        {
            String sqlCommand =
                theRequest.getParameter(AdminServlet.COMMAND_PARAM);

            if (!sqlCommand.startsWith("SELECT"))
            {
                // Forward to an error page
                RequestDispatcher dispatcher =            Redirect to
                    theRequest.getRequestDispatcher(      error page
                    this.securityErrorPage);
                dispatcher.forward(theRequest, theResponse);
            }
            else
            {
                theChain.doFilter(theRequest, theResponse);
            }
        }

        public void destroy()
        {
        }
    }
```

Testing this filter with Cactus is very similar to the tests you have already performed on the AdminServlet. The main difference is that the TestCase extends Filter-TestCase instead of ServletTestCase. This change allows the test to get access to the Filter API objects (FilterConfig, Request, Response, and FilterChain).

9.4.1 *Testing the filter with a SELECT query*

Listing 9.12 tests the doFilter method when the SQL query that is passed is a SELECT query.

> **Listing 9.12   TestSecurityFilter.java (testDoFilterAllowedSQL)**

```
package junitbook.servlets;

import java.io.IOException;

import javax.servlet.FilterChain;
import javax.servlet.FilterConfig;
import javax.servlet.ServletException;
import javax.servlet.ServletRequest;
import javax.servlet.ServletResponse;

import org.apache.cactus.FilterTestCase;
import org.apache.cactus.WebRequest;

public class TestSecurityFilter extends FilterTestCase
{
    public void beginDoFilterAllowedSQL(WebRequest request)
```

```
       {
           request.addParameter("command", "SELECT [...]");    ❶
       }
       public void testDoFilterAllowedSQL() throws Exception
       {
           SecurityFilter filter = new SecurityFilter();

           FilterChain mockFilterChain = new FilterChain()
           {
               public void doFilter(ServletRequest theRequest,
                   ServletResponse theResponse) throws IOException,
                   ServletException
               {
               }

               public void init(FilterConfig theConfig)      ❷
               {
               }

               public void destroy()
               {
               }
           };
           filter.doFilter(request, response, mockFilterChain);
       }
   }
```

❶ Use the Cactus begin*XXX* method to add the SQL command to the HTTP request that is processed by your filter. (Note that your SQL query is a SELECT query.)

❷ For this test, you don't want your filter to call the next filter in the chain (or the target JSP/servlet). Thus you create an empty implementation of a FilterChain. You could also let the filter call the next element in the chain. However, a filter is completely independent from other filters or any JSP/servlet that might be called after it in the processing chain. Thus, it makes more sense to test this filter in isolation, especially given that the filter doesn't modify the returned HTTP response.

9.4.2 Testing the filter for other query types

So far, you have tested only one scenario from your filter. You also need to verify that the behavior is correct when the SQL command that is passed is not a SELECT query (see listing 9.13). In that case, the filter behavior should be to redirect the user to an error page. For example, here is the code for securityError.jsp, the JSP error page you're forwarding to in the testDoFilterForbiddenSQL test in listing 9.13:

```
<html>
  <head>
    <title>Security Error Page</title>
  </head>
  <body>
    <p>
      Only SELECT SQL queries are allowed!
    </p>
  </body>
</html>
```

Listing 9.13 TestSecurityFilter.java (testDoFilterForbiddenSQL)

```
package junitbook.servlets;
[...]
public class TestSecurityFilter extends FilterTestCase
{
[...]
    public void beginDoFilterForbiddenSQL(WebRequest request)
    {
        request.addParameter("command", "UPDATE [...]");      ❶
    }

    public void testDoFilterForbiddenSQL() throws Exception
    {
        config.setInitParameter("securityErrorPage",
            "/securityError.jsp");                              ❷
        SecurityFilter filter = new SecurityFilter();
        filter.init(config);                    ❸

        filter.doFilter(request, response, filterChain);
    }

    public void endDoFilterForbiddenSQL(WebResponse response)
    {
        assertTrue("Bad response page",
            response.getText().indexOf(                        ❹
                "<title>Security Error Page</title>") > 0);
    }
}
```

❶ Pass a SQL query that is not a SELECT.

❷ Use a Cactus-specific API (`config.setInitParameter`) to simulate an `init` parameter that represents the name of the security error page. Note that this is the equivalent of defining the `init` parameter in your web application's `web.xml` file, like this:

```
<filter>
    <filter-name>FilterRedirector</filter-name>
    <filter-class>
```

```
            org.apache.cactus.server.FilterTestRedirector
        </filter-class>
        <init-param>
          <param-name>securityErrorPage</param-name>
          <param-value>/securityError.jsp</param-value>
        </init-param>
    </filter>
```

Notice that you add the `init` parameter to the Cactus `FilterRedirector` definition—not to the `SecurityFilter` definition. This is because in the test, you instantiate your `SecurityFilter` class as a plain old Java object (POJO), not as a filter. Cactus, under the hood, calls a Cactus filter redirector that it uses to provide valid filter objects (`Request`, `Response`, `FilterConfig`, `FilterChain`) to your *testXXX* method. However, it's simpler to use the `setInitParameter` method as shown here.

❸ You have instantiated your filter as a POJO, so you need to call its `init(FilterConfig)` method to correctly initialize the filter. (This is what the container would have done internally.)

❹ To verify that the `SecurityFilter` has correctly forwarded you to the error page, check that the returned HTTP response body contains elements that you expect to be present in the error page.

9.4.3 *Running the Cactus filter tests with Maven*

Running your filter tests with Maven is easy. The only prerequisite is to put your sources in the directory structure expected by Maven. Figure 9.9 demonstrates this structure.

The filter code under test is located under `src/java`, the Cactus tests are in `src/test-cactus`, and the web-app resources (`web.xml` and JSPs, for example) are located in `src/webapp`. These are the default locations where Maven expects to find the different sources.

Running the Cactus tests is simply a matter of opening a shell in the `junitbook-servlets` project directory and entering **maven cactus:test**. The Maven `cactus:test` goal automatically calls the Maven war goal, which packages your application in a war file. Then the Cactus plugin repackages this war (by

Figure 9.9 Directory structure for the Cactus filter tests

```
cactus:test:
    [cactus] ----------------------------------------------------------------
    [cactus] Running tests against Tomcat 4.1.24
    [cactus] ----------------------------------------------------------------
    [cactus] Testsuite: junitbook.servlets.TestSecurityFilter
    [cactus] Tests run: 2, Failures: 0, Errors: 0, Time elapsed: 19.218 sec
    [cactus]
    [cactus] Testcase: testDoFilterAllowedSQL took 0.641 sec
    [cactus] Testcase: testDoFilterForbiddenSQL took 18.086 sec
BUILD SUCCESSFUL
Total time:  38 seconds
```

Figure 9.10　Run the Cactus tests using the Maven Cactus plugin.

adding the Cactus jars along with definitions for the Cactus redirectors in the web.xml file), deploys it to your target container, starts the container, runs the tests, and stops the container. Figure 9.10 shows the result.

9.5 *When to use Cactus, and when to use mock objects*

At this point, you must be wondering whether to use Cactus or mock objects to test your servlets and filter. Both approaches have advantages and disadvantages:

- The main difference is that Cactus performs not only unit tests but also integration tests and, to some extent, functional tests. The added benefits come at the cost of added complexity.

- Mock-object tests are usually harder to write, because you need to define the behavior of all calls made to the mocks. For example, if your method under test makes 10 calls to mocks, then you need to define the behavior for these 10 calls as part of the test setup.

- Cactus provides real objects for which you only need to set some initial conditions.

- If the application to unit-test is already written, it usually has to be refactored to support mock-object testing. Extra refactoring is generally not needed with Cactus.

A good strategy is to separate the business-logic code from the integration code (code that interacts with the container), and then:

- Use mock objects to test the business logic.
- Use Cactus to test the integration code.

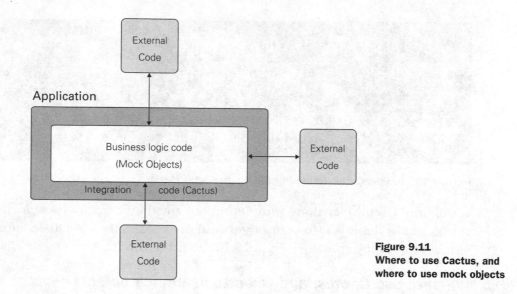

Figure 9.11
Where to use Cactus, and where to use mock objects

Figure 9.11 illustrates this concept. In the example, the business-logic code is the `executeCommand` method; the rest is integration code.

The question is not so much *whether* you should use Cactus *or* mock objects, but rather *where* to use Cactus *and* mock objects. The approaches are not exclusive but complementary. Both can be used to serve the prime objective: increasing overall application quality by discovering as many bugs as early as possible.

9.6 *Summary*

In this chapter, we have demonstrated how to unit-test servlets and filters and, more generally, any code that uses the Servlet/Filters API. You can create and run these kinds of tests using mock objects or Jakarta Cactus. Although the mock-objects approach can unit-test servlet and filter code, the tests cannot achieve the wide range that's possible with Cactus-based tests. In practice, the approaches are complementary. Use mock objects to unit-test business-logic code at a very fine-grained level, and use Cactus to unit-test integration code (code that interacts with the container).

In the next chapter, we'll continue unit-testing the Administration application by moving the focus to unit-testing the JavaServer Pages and Taglib APIs.

Unit-testing JSPs
and taglibs

This chapter covers

- Unit-testing a JSP in isolation with Cactus and mock objects
- Running Cactus JSP tests with Maven
- Unit-testing taglibs with Cactus
- Unit-testing taglibs with mock objects and MockMaker

A test that can't be repeated is worthless.

—Brian Marick

In this chapter, we'll continue with the Administration application we introduced in chapter 9. In chapter 9, we focused on unit-testing the servlet component of the application. In this chapter, we concentrate on the view components—namely the JavaServer Pages (JSPs) and custom tag libraries (taglibs).

We'll cover unit-testing JSPs and taglibs with both Cactus and mock objects. The two techniques are complementary. Mock objects excel at writing focused, fine-grained unit tests against the business logic. Meanwhile, Cactus can perform integration unit tests against the target environment. The integration unit tests are essential in order to ensure that all components work properly when run in their target containers.

10.1 *Revisiting the Administration application*

We'll base our examples on the Administration application (introduced in chapter 9). Its architecture is shown in figure 10.1, which also highlights the parts for which you'll write unit tests (shaded boxes).

You use the application by sending an HTTP request (from your browser) to the AdminServlet. You pass an SQL query to run as an HTTP parameter, which is retrieved by the AdminServlet. The security filter intercepts the HTTP request and verifies that the SQL query is harmless (that is, it's a SELECT query). Then, the servlet executes the query on the database, stores the resulting objects in the HTTP Request object, and calls the Results View page. The JSP takes the results from the Request and displays them, nicely formatted, using custom JSP tags from your tag library.

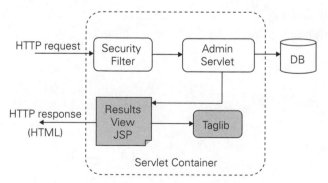

Figure 10.1
Unit-testing the Results View JSP
from the Administration application

10.2 *What is JSP unit testing?*

First, let's remove any doubt: What we call *unit-testing a JSP* is not about unit-testing the servlet that is generated by the compilation of the JSP. We also assume that the JSP is well designed, which means there is no Java code in it. If the page must handle any presentation logic, the logic is encapsulated in a JavaBean or in a taglib. You can perform two kinds of tests to unit-test a JSP: test the JSP page itself in isolation and/or test the JSP's taglibs.

You can isolate the JSP from the back end by simulating the JavaBeans it uses and then verifying that the returned page contains the expected data. We'll use Cactus (see chapter 8) to demonstrate this type of test. Because mock objects (see chapter 7) operate only on Java code, you can't use a pure mock-objects solution to unit-test your JSP in isolation.

You could also write functional tests for the JSP using a framework such as HttpUnit. However, doing so means going all the way to the back end of the application, possibly to the database. With a combination of Cactus and mock objects, you can prevent calling the back end and keep your focus on unit-testing the JSPs themselves.

You can also unit-test the custom tags used in the JSP. You'll do this with both Cactus and mock objects. Both have pros and cons, and they can be used together effectively.

10.3 *Unit-testing a JSP in isolation with Cactus*

The strategy for unit-testing JSPs in isolation with Cactus is defined in figure 10.2.

Here is what happens. The Cactus test case class must extend `ServletTestCase` (or `Jsp-TestCase`):

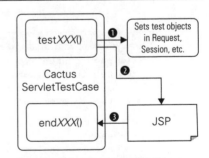

Figure 10.2   Strategy to unit-test JSPs with Cactus

1 In the test*XXX* method (called by Cactus from inside the container), you create the mock objects that will be used by the JSP. The JSP gets its dynamic information either from one container-implicit object (`HttpServletRequest`, `HttpServletResponse`, or `ServletConfig`) or from a taglib. (We handle the taglib case in section 10.4.)

2 Still in test*XXX*, you perform a `forward` to call the JSP under test. The JSP then executes, getting the mock data set up in 1.

③ Cactus calls end*XXX*, passing to it the output from the JSP. This allows you to assert the content of the output and verify that the data you set up found its way to the JSP output, in the correct location on the page.

10.3.1 Executing a JSP with SQL results data

Let's see some action on the Administration application. In chapter 9 ("Unit-testing servlets and filters"), you defined that the results of executing the SQL query would be passed to the JSP by storing them as a collection of DynaBean objects in the HttpServletRequest object. Thanks to the dynamic nature of dyna beans, you can easily write a generic JSP that will display any data contained in the dyna beans. Dyna beans provide metadata about the data they contain. You can create a generic table with columns corresponding to the fields of the dyna beans, as shown in listing 10.1. The result of executing this JSP (using arbitrary SQL results data) is shown in figure 10.3.

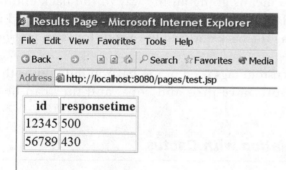

id	responsetime
12345	500
56789	430

Figure 10.3
Result of executing results.jsp
with arbitrary data that comes from
the execution of a SQL query

Listing 10.1   Results View JSP (results.jsp)

```
<%@ page contentType="text/html;charset=UTF-8" language="java" %>
<%@ taglib prefix="c"
    uri="http://jakarta.apache.org/taglibs/core" %>
<%@ taglib prefix="d" uri="/dynabeans" %>

<html>
  <head>
    <title>Results Page</title>
  </head>
  <body bgcolor="white">
    <table border="1">

      <d:properties var="properties"
        item="${requestScope.results[0]}"/>            ❶

      <tr>
        <c:forEach var="property" items="${properties}">
```

```
      <th><c:out value="${property.name}"/></th>
    </c:forEach>
  </tr>

  <c:forEach var="result" items="${requestScope.results}">
    <tr>
      <c:forEach var="property" items="${properties}">
        <td><d:getProperty name="${property.name}"
          item="${result}"/></td>
      </c:forEach>
    </tr>
  </c:forEach>

    </table>
  </body>
</html>
```

You use both JSTL tags and custom taglibs to write the JSP: The JSTL tag library is a standard set of useful and generic tags. It's divided into several categories (core, XML, formatting, and SQL). The category used here is the core, which provides output, management of variables, conditional logic, loops, text imports, and URL manipulation. The JSTL implementation used is the Jakarta Standard 1.0 implementation (http://jakarta.apache.org/taglibs/) of the JSTL specifications (http://java.sun.com/products/jsp/jstl/).

You also write two custom tags (<d:properties> and <d:getProperty>), which are used to extract information from the dyna beans. <d:properties> (**❶**) extracts the name of all properties of a dyna bean, and <d:getProperty> (**❷**) extracts the value of a given dyna bean property.

There are two reasons for writing these custom tags. The primary reason is that it isn't possible to extract dyna bean information without (*ouch!*) embedding Java code in the JSP (at least, not with the current implementation of the JSTL tags and the DynaBean package). The second reason is that it gives you a chance to write and unit-test custom taglibs of your own. (Of course, the Struts 1.1 tags are dynabean-aware, and you could use those, but we decided not to overload this chapter with yet another framework.)

10.3.2 *Writing the Cactus test*

Now let's write a Cactus ServletTestCase for the JSP. In chapter 9, you defined a method named callView from the AdminServlet class. The callView method forwards control to the Results View JSP, as shown in listing 10.2.

Listing 10.2   AdminServlet.callView implementation

```
package junitbook.pages;
[...]
import java.io.IOException;

public class AdminServlet extends HttpServlet
{
    [...]

    public void callView(HttpServletRequest request,
        HttpServletResponse response)
        throws IOException, ServletException
    {
        request.getRequestDispatcher("/results.jsp")
            .forward(request, response);
    }

}
```

Listing 10.3 shows a unit test for `callView` that sets up the `DynaBean` objects in the Request, calls `callView`, and then verifies that the JSP output is what you expect.

Listing 10.3   TestAdminServlet.java: unit tests for results.jsp

```
package junitbook.pages;

import java.util.ArrayList;
import java.util.Collection;
import java.util.List;

import org.apache.cactus.ServletTestCase;
import org.apache.commons.beanutils.BasicDynaClass;
import org.apache.commons.beanutils.DynaBean;
import org.apache.commons.beanutils.DynaProperty;

public class TestAdminServlet extends ServletTestCase
{
    private Collection createCommandResult() throws Exception
    {
        List results = new ArrayList();                          Create test input
                                                                 data for JSP
        DynaProperty[] props = new DynaProperty[] {
            new DynaProperty("id", String.class),
            new DynaProperty("responsetime", Long.class)
        };
        BasicDynaClass dynaClass = new BasicDynaClass("requesttime",
            null, props);

        DynaBean request1 = dynaClass.newInstance();
        request1.set("id", "12345");
        request1.set("responsetime", new Long(500));
```

```
        results.add(request1);                                    ┐
                                                                   │ Create test
        DynaBean request2 = dynaClass.newInstance();               │ input data
        request2.set("id", "56789");                               │ for JSP
        request2.set("responsetime", new Long(430));               │
        results.add(request2);                                     │
                                                                   │
        return results;                                            │
    }                                                             ┘

    public void testCallView() throws Exception
    {
        AdminServlet servlet = new AdminServlet();
        request.setAttribute("results", createCommandResult());  ◁─┘
        servlet.callView(request, response);
    }

    public void endCallView(
        com.meterware.httpunit.WebResponse response)
        throws Exception
    {
        assertTrue(response.isHTML());                            ┐

        assertEquals("tables", 1, response.getTables().length);   │
        assertEquals("columns", 2,                                │
            response.getTables()[0].getColumnCount());            │
        assertEquals("rows", 3,                                   │
            response.getTables()[0].getRowCount());               │ Use
                                                                   │ HttpUnit
        assertEquals("id",                                        │ integration
            response.getTables()[0].getCellAsText(0, 0));         │ for asserting
        assertEquals("responsetime",                              │ HTTP
            response.getTables()[0].getCellAsText(0, 1));         │ response

        assertEquals("12345",                                     │
            response.getTables()[0].getCellAsText(1, 0));         │
        assertEquals("500",                                       │
            response.getTables()[0].getCellAsText(1, 1));         │
        assertEquals("56789",                                     │
            response.getTables()[0].getCellAsText(2, 0));         │
        assertEquals("430",                                       │
            response.getTables()[0].getCellAsText(2, 1));         │
    }                                                             ┘

}
```

You use the Cactus HttpUnit integration in the endCallView method to assert the returned HTML page. When Cactus needs to execute the end*XXX* method, first it looks for an end*XXX*(org.apache.cactus.WebResponse) signature. If this signature is found, Cactus calls it; if it isn't, Cactus looks for an end*XXX*(com.meterware.httpunit.WebResponse) signature and, if it's available, calls it. Using the `org.apache.cactus.WebResponse` object, you can perform asserts on the content of the HTTP response, such as verifying the returned cookies, the returned HTTP headers, or the content. The Cactus `org.apache.cactus.WebResponse` object sports a simple API. The HttpUnit web response API (`com.meterware.http-unit.WebResponse`) is much more comprehensive. With HttpUnit, you can view the returned XML or HTML pages as DOM objects. In listing 10.3, you use the provided HTML DOM to verify that the returned web page contains the expected HTML table.

10.3.3 *Executing Cactus JSP tests with Maven*

Let's run the Cactus tests with the Maven plugin for Cactus (introduced in chapter 9). The Maven directory structure for this chapter is shown in figure 10.4. The figure lists not only the `AdminServlet` and `TestAdminServlet` classes but also tag library classes that you'll develop in section 10.4.

As usual, you put the Java source files in `src/java` (as required by Maven) and the Cactus tests in `src/test-cactus` (as required by the Maven Cactus plugin). Internally, the Maven Cactus plugin calls the Maven war plugin, which requires the web application resource and configuration files to be put in `src/webapp`. The Maven project configuration files (`project.xml` and `project.properties`) are put in the root directory. Table 10.1 describes the different project files.

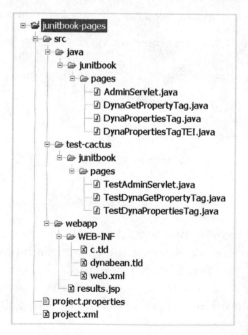

Figure 10.4
Directory structure for the JSP tests showing how to set up a web app for the Maven Cactus plugin

Table 10.1   Source files and directories for the JSP sample project

File and directory locations	Description
`src/java/junitbook/pages/`	Main runtime Java sources
`AdminServlet.java`	Administration servlet that forwards to the `results.jsp` JSP
`Dyna*.java`	Custom taglib implementations described in detail in section 10.4
`src/test-cactus/junitbook/pages/`	Cactus unit tests
`TestAdminServlet.java`	Unit test class for unit-testing the `callView` method of the administration servlet
`TestDyna*.java`	Unit tests for the custom taglibs
`src/webapp/results.jsp`	Results View JSP that you want to unit test
`src/webapp/WEB-INF/`	Web app configuration files
`c.tld`	Configuration file for the JSTL Core taglib
`dynabean.tld`	Configuration file for the custom taglib
`web.xml`	Main web app configuration file containing the taglib mapping between the URIs used in the JSP and the taglib configuration files (`.tld` files)
`project.properties`	Maven configuration file
`project.xml`	Maven project descriptor

> **NOTE**   For conciseness, the `.tld`, `web.xml`, and `project.xml` file contents are not shown here. However, they can be downloaded from the book's web site (see appendix A for details).

Before you execute your tests, you need to tell the Maven Cactus plugin what servlet container to use to execute the Cactus tests. To do so, add a property in your `project.properties` or `build.properties` file. This property defines where the container is installed on the local hard disk. For example, if you want to run the tests in Tomcat 4.1.24, you need to add the following property (assuming you've installed Tomcat in `c:/Apps/jakarta-tomcat-4.1.24`):

```
cactus.home.tomcat4x = C:/Apps/jakarta-tomcat-4.1.24
```

Starting the Maven Cactus plugin is as simple as opening a shell in the `junitbook/pages/` directory and typing **maven cactus:test**. Figure 10.5 shows the result.

```
cactus:test:
    [cactus] ---------------------------------------------------------------
    [cactus] Running tests against Tomcat 4.1.24
    [cactus] ---------------------------------------------------------------
    [cactus] Testsuite: junitbook.pages.TestAdminServlet
    [cactus] Tests run: 1, Failures: 0, Errors: 0, Time elapsed: 5.468 sec
    [cactus]
    [cactus] Testcase: testCallView took 4.997 sec
    [cactus] Testsuite: junitbook.pages.TestDynaGetPropertyTag
    [cactus] Tests run: 1, Failures: 0, Errors: 0, Time elapsed: 2.454 sec
    [cactus]
    [cactus] Testcase: testDoStartTag took 1.963 sec
    [cactus] Testsuite: junitbook.pages.TestDynaPropertiesTag
    [cactus] Tests run: 1, Failures: 0, Errors: 0, Time elapsed: 1.051 sec
    [cactus]
    [cactus] Testcase: testDoStartTag took 0.571 sec
BUILD SUCCESSFUL
Total time:  29 seconds
```

Figure 10.5   Cactus test results for the JSP (`results.jsp`) using the Maven Cactus plugin

10.4 *Unit-testing taglibs with Cactus*

Figure 10.6 depicts how you unit-test a tag from a taglib with Cactus.

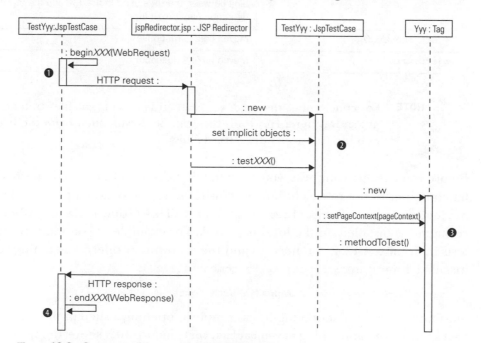

Figure 10.6   Sequence diagram of taglib testing with Cactus

① Cactus instantiates the test class, which must extend `JspTestCase`. You must configure any HTTP parameter needed by the tag you are testing in a begin*XXX* method. For example, if the tag extracts information from an HTTP parameter, you need to define this parameter in begin*XXX*.

② Under the hood, the Cactus `JspTestCase` class calls the Cactus JSP Redirector (which is a JSP). The JSP Redirector is in charge of instantiating the `JspTestCase` class on the server side, passing to it the JSP implicit objects (mainly the `PageContext` object). Then, it calls the test*XXX* test method.

③ In the test*XXX* method, you write code to unit-test the JSP tag. The typical steps for testing a tag are as follows: instantiate the tag by calling new, set the `PageContext` by calling `setPageContext`, call the method to test, and perform server-side assertions. For example, if the tag sets some objects in the HTTP session, you can assert that the object is there.

④ The Cactus JSP Redirector returns the output of the tag to the client side in an HTTP response. You can then assert the tag output by writing an end*XXX* method in the `JspTestCase` class. Cactus provides a tight integration with HttpUnit, which allows very fine-grained assertions on the returned content of the tag.

10.4.1 *Defining a custom tag*

The Administration application displays the query results on a page called the Results View JSP (`results.jsp`). In the Results View JSP, the first tag class you use is `DynaPropertiesTag`. This tag extracts all the properties of a `DynaBean` object into an array. The properties, which are `DynaProperty` objects, are stored in the `PageContext` under a name passed to the tag. Here's how the tag is used:

```
<d:properties var="properties" item="${dynaBean}"/>
```

where `properties` is the variable name to use for the array of `DynaProperty` objects and `dynaBean` is the `DynaBean` instance from which to extract your properties.

The `DynaPropertiesTag` code is shown in listing 10.4.

Listing 10.4   DynaPropertiesTag.java

```java
package junitbook.pages;

import org.apache.commons.beanutils.DynaBean;
import org.apache.taglibs.standard.lang.support.
→      ExpressionEvaluatorManager;

import javax.servlet.jsp.tagext.TagSupport;
import javax.servlet.jsp.JspException;

public class DynaPropertiesTag extends TagSupport
{
```

```java
    private String varName;
    private String item;

    public void setVar(String varName)
    {
        this.varName = varName;
    }

    public String getVar()
    {
        return this.varName;
    }

    public void setItem(String item)
    {
        this.item = item;
    }

    public String getItem()
    {
        return this.item;
    }

    public int doStartTag() throws JspException
    {
        // Evaluate the item attribute (an EL expression) which
        // must result in a DynaBean object.
        DynaBean bean =
            (DynaBean) ExpressionEvaluatorManager.evaluate(
            "item", getItem(), DynaBean.class, this,
            this.pageContext);

        // Get the DynaBean meta-properties and store them in the
        // variable pointed to by the "var" attribute.
        this.pageContext.setAttribute(getVar(),
            bean.getDynaClass().getDynaProperties());
        return SKIP_BODY;
    }

    public int doEndTag() throws JspException
    {
        return EVAL_PAGE;
    }
}
```

To be consistent with the JSTL library (http://java.sun.com/products/jsp/jstl/), you implement the content of the item attribute as an Expression Language (EL) expression. EL is the expression language used in the JSTL tags. It's very convenient for passing variables from one JSP tag to another. For example, in the tag shown before listing 10.4, you pass the dynaBean variable (${dynaBean}) to the

<d:properties> tag. This is a very simple usage of EL, but you can use any valid EL expression in this item attribute. The beauty of it is that you need only one line of code to implement this functionality (as shown in the doStartTag method).

10.4.2 *Testing the custom tag*

Your next challenge is to unit-test this custom tag. What do you need to test? Well, you need to verify whether this tag correctly stores the properties of the DynaBean object passed in PageContext scope. See the testDoStartTag method in listing 10.5 for this example.

Listing 10.5   Unit tests for DynaPropertiesTag

```
package junitbook.pages;

import org.apache.cactus.JspTestCase;
import org.apache.commons.beanutils.DynaProperty;
import org.apache.commons.beanutils.BasicDynaClass;
import org.apache.commons.beanutils.DynaBean;

import javax.servlet.jsp.tagext.Tag;

public class TestDynaPropertiesTag extends JspTestCase
{
    private DynaBean createDynaBean() throws Exception
    {
        DynaProperty[] props = new DynaProperty[] {
            new DynaProperty("id", String.class),
            new DynaProperty("responsetime", Long.class)
        };
        BasicDynaClass dynaClass = new BasicDynaClass("requesttime",
            null, props);

        DynaBean bean = dynaClass.newInstance();
        bean.set("id", "12345");
        bean.set("responsetime", new Long(500));

        return bean;
    }

    public void testDoStartTag() throws Exception
    {
        DynaPropertiesTag tag = new DynaPropertiesTag();

        tag.setPageContext(pageContext);

        pageContext.setAttribute("item", createDynaBean());
        tag.setItem("${item}");
        tag.setVar("var");

        int result = tag.doStartTag();
```

Create instance of tag to test — points to `DynaPropertiesTag tag = new DynaPropertiesTag();`

Set PageContext to initialize tag — points to `tag.setPageContext(pageContext);`

Set environmental parameters for tag — points to the `pageContext.setAttribute` / `tag.setItem` / `tag.setVar` block

```
        assertEquals(Tag.SKIP_BODY, result);
        assertTrue(pageContext.getAttribute("var")          Assert server-side
            instanceof DynaProperty[]);                      environment after
                                                             execution
        DynaProperty[] props = (DynaProperty[])
            pageContext.getAttribute("var");
        assertEquals(props.length, 2);
    }

}
```

The tag is simple and implements a single life cycle `doStartTag` method. The full life
cycle of a simple tag (a tag that does not need to manipulate its body) is as follows:

```
ATag t = new ATag();
t.setPageContext(...);
t.setParent(...);
t.setProperty1(value1);
[...]
t.setPropertyN(valueN);
t.doStartTag();
t.doEndTag();
t.release();
```

In the example (listing 10.5), you instantiate the tag, call `setPageContent`, set the
needed properties, and call `doStartTag`. Because the tag isn't a nested tag, you
don't call `setParent`, because you don't need to fetch anything from a superclass.
(For more about collaborating tags, see section 10.4.4.) You also don't implement
`release`. If you did, you'd write tests for it the same way you wrote a unit test for
the `doStartTag` method. The `doEndTag` method implementation is "too simple to
break" (see listing 10.4), so you don't even need to test it!

10.4.3 *Unit-testing tags with a body*

So far, we've demonstrated how to unit-test simple tags (tags without a body).
Let's see now how you can unit-test a tag with a body. A *body tag* is a tag that
encloses content, which can be text or other tags. Let's take the example of a
`<sortHtmlTable>` tag, which sorts column elements in an HTML table:

```
<table>

  <d:sortHtmlTable order="ascending" column="1">
    <c:forEach items="${customers}" var="customer">
      <tr>
        <td><c:out value="${customer.getLastName()}"/></td>
        <td><c:out value="${customer.getFirstName()}"/></td>
      </tr>
    </c:forEach>
  </d:sortHtmlTable>

</table>
```

A quick implementation that skips the details of the sorting algorithm is shown in listing 10.6.

Listing 10.6   Skeleton for SortHtmlTableTag (leaves out the sort algorithm)

```java
package junitbook.pages;

import javax.servlet.jsp.JspException;
import javax.servlet.jsp.tagext.BodyContent;
import javax.servlet.jsp.tagext.BodyTagSupport;

public class SortHtmlTableTag extends BodyTagSupport
{
    private String sortOrder = "ascending";
    private int sortColumn = 1;

    public void setOrder(String sortOrder)
    {
        this.sortOrder = sortOrder;
    }

    public void setColumn(int sortColumn)
    {
        this.sortColumn = sortColumn;
    }

    public int doAfterBody() throws JspException
    {
        // The body content has been evaluated, now we need to
        // parse it and sort the table lines.
        BodyContent body = getBodyContent();              Retrieve body
        String content = body.getString();                content as a String
        body.clearBody();           Clear body content to replace
                                    it with transformed content
        try
        {
            getPreviousOut().print(sortHtmlTable(content));    Output new
        }                                                       modified body
        catch (Exception e)                                     content
        {
            throw new JspException("Failed to sort body content ["
                + content + "]", e);
        }

        return SKIP_BODY;
    }

    private String sortHtmlTable(String content)
    {
        // Algorithm skipped :-)
        return content;
    }
}
```

You have two options to test this: reproduce some parts of the container life cycle and write a focused unit test that exercises the doAfterBody method, or use a Cactus helper class called JspTagLifecycle that reproduces the full container life cycle for you. The latter solution provides more coarse-grained tests. All the tag life cycle methods (doStartTag, doInitBody, and so forth) are called in sequence. You can perform assertions only once all the methods have been called.

Testing a tag life cycle method

In order to write focused tests for a given method of the tag life cycle, you have to understand what you need to set up prior to calling that method. Thus, you need to understand the *body tag container* life cycle (the order in which the container calls the different tag methods):

```
ATag t = new ATag();
t.doStartTag();
out = pageContext.pushBody();
t.setBodyContent(out);
// perform any initialization needed after body content is set
t.doInitBody();
t.doAfterBody();
// while doAfterBody returns EVAL_BODY_BUFFERED we
// iterate body evaluation
[...]
t.doAfterBody();
t.doEndTag();
t.pageContext.popBody();
t.release();
```

In the SortHtmlTableTag example, you only needed a doAfterBody method. Reading the previous life cycle, you need to instantiate the tag, call pageContext.push-Body to create a BodyContent object, assign the body content to the tag object, put some content in the BodyContent object by calling one of its print methods, and call the doAfterBody method. To send back the generated output in the HTTP response, you must also be sure to call pageContext.popBody when you're finished. Listing 10.7 integrates all these steps into a test case.

Listing 10.7   Cactus tests for SortHtmlTableTag using a fine-grained approach

```
package junitbook.pages;

import javax.servlet.jsp.tagext.BodyContent;
import javax.servlet.jsp.tagext.Tag;

import org.apache.cactus.JspTestCase;
import org.apache.cactus.WebResponse;
```

```
public class TestSortHtmlTableTag extends JspTestCase
{
    private SortHtmlTableTag sortTag;
    private BodyContent bodyContent;

    protected void setUp()
    {
        sortTag = new SortHtmlTableTag();
        sortTag.setPageContext(pageContext);              ❶
        bodyContent = pageContext.pushBody();
        sortTag.setBodyContent(bodyContent);
    }

    protected void tearDown()
    {
        pageContext.popBody();             ❶
    }

    public void testDoAfterBody() throws Exception
    {
        bodyContent.print("<tr><td>Vincent</td></tr>"    ❷
            + "<tr><td>Ted</td></tr>");

        int result = sortTag.doAfterBody();

        assertEquals(Tag.SKIP_BODY, result);
    }

    public void endDoAfterBody(WebResponse response)
    {
        String expectedString = "<tr><td>Ted</td></tr>"
            + "<tr><td>Vincent</td></tr>";               ❸

        assertEquals(expectedString, response.getText());
    }

    // Other tests to write to be complete: empty body content,
    // already ordered list, only one line in table to order,
    // bad content (i.e. not a table).
}
```

❶ Factorize the tag life cycle methods common to all tests in `setUp` and `tearDown`.

❷ Define the input data you will feed to the tag.

❸ Verify that the result is sorted. Of course, because you have not yet implemented the sorting algorithm (the implementation in listing 10.6 simply returns the content, untouched), the test will fail. To make it work, you need to either implement the sorting algorithm or modify the `expectedString` to put *Vincent* before *Ted*.

Testing all the life cycle methods at once

Cactus provides a helper class called `JspTagLifecycle` that automatically performs all the initialization steps—like setting the page context and creating body content—and calls the different life cycle methods in the right order. It also provides some expectation methods to verify whether the tag body was evaluated, and so forth.

Rewriting the previous example (`TestSortHtmlTableTag`) leads to listing 10.8 (changes from listing 10.7 are shown in bold).

Listing 10.8   Cactus tests for SortHtmlTableTag using the JspTagLifecycle approach

```
package junitbook.pages;

import org.apache.cactus.JspTestCase;
import org.apache.cactus.WebResponse;
import org.apache.cactus.extension.jsp.JspTagLifecycle;

public class TestSortHtmlTableTag2 extends JspTestCase
{
    private SortHtmlTableTag sortTag;
    private JspTagLifecycle lifecycle;

    protected void setUp()
    {
        sortTag = new SortHtmlTableTag();
        lifecycle = new JspTagLifecycle(pageContext, sortTag);     ❶
    }

    public void testDoAfterBody() throws Exception
    {
        lifecycle.addNestedText("<tr><td>Vincent</td></tr>"        ❷
            + "<tr><td>Ted</td></tr>");
        lifecycle.expectBodyEvaluated();     ❸
        lifecycle.invoke();     ❹
    }

    public void endDoAfterBody(WebResponse response)
    {
        String expectedString = "<tr><td>Ted</td></tr>"
            + "<tr><td>Vincent</td></tr>";

        assertEquals(expectedString, response.getText());
    }

    // Other tests to write to be complete: empty body content,
    // already ordered list, only one line in table to order,
    // bad content (i.e. not a table).
}
```

❶ Create the `JspTagLifecycle` helper, passing to it the `PageContext` object and the tag instance you're testing.

❷ ❸ Configure the `JspTagLifecycle` object and tell it what to expect. In **❷**, you tell it that the tag contains some nested text; in **❸**, you tell it that you expect the tag body to be evaluated once (the `doAfterBody` tag method is called once and only once).

❹ When you call `JspTagLifecycle.invoke`, the `JspTagLifecycle` object executes the standard tag life cycle, calling the life cycle methods one after another. It also verifies that the expectations are met.

The advantage of this approach is that there is minimal setup in the test and the full tag life cycle is executed. However, you still benefit from the unit-test approach because you can perform server-side assertions after you have called `lifecycle.invoke`, such as verifying that an attribute the tag is supposed to set is effectively set, and so forth.

10.4.4 *Unit-testing collaboration tags*

A *collaboration tag* is nested within another tag and needs to communicate with the parent tag in order to retrieve some value. Unit-testing a collaboration tag requires that you call `setParent` on the tag in your test case. Once this is done, the tag will correctly work when it invokes `findAncestorWithClass` or `getParent` to find the parent tag.

For example, you could write the following in the `JspTestCase` class:

```
MyParentTag parentTag = new MyParentTag();
parentTag.setXXX(value);
MyChildTag childTag = new MyChildTag();
childTag.setParent(parentTag);
[...]
```

10.5 *Unit-testing taglibs with mock objects*

You have seen that it isn't possible to unit-test a JSP purely with the mock-objects approach because a JSP isn't Java code. On the other hand, tag libraries (taglibs) are pure Java code, which should make them easy to test with mock objects. However, it isn't that easy.... You need a mock object for `PageContext`, which is an *abstract* Java class.

In chapters 8 and 9, you learned that it's easy to use mock objects when they are generated on the fly by frameworks such as EasyMock and DynaMock. However, these frameworks use the JDK 1.3+ Dynamic Proxy feature, which can only generate proxies for *interfaces*. It doesn't work for classes.

You'll hit the same limitation if you're stuck with a JDK older than version 1.3. You can always write mock objects by hand (tedious, but not so bad). However, there is a better solution: Use a mock-objects generation framework, like Mock-Maker, that generates mocks from classes.

10.5.1 *Introducing MockMaker and installing its Eclipse plugin*

MockMaker (http://mockmaker.org/) is a *build-time* (as opposed to runtime) mock-object generation tool. It generates source files that need to be added to your project's test source files before compilation. Under the hood, MockMaker uses the MockObjects.com framework, so the mocks it generates use that syntax and those conventions.

You can run MockMaker three ways: by running it as a Java application on the command line, by using the provided Ant task, or by using its Eclipse plugin. This section demonstrates how to run it as an Eclipse plugin, because that's probably the easiest way to use MockMaker (at least, if you're already using Eclipse!).

Installing the Eclipse plugin is easy: Get it from http://mockmaker.org/ and unzip the plugin in your ECLIPSE_HOME/plugins directory. (ECLIPSE_HOME is the directory where you have installed Eclipse.)

10.5.2 *Using MockMaker to generate mocks from classes*

In this section, you'll use MockMaker to generate a mock implementation of PageContext. In order to generate the PageContext mock using the Eclipse plugin (see figure 10.7), you need to select the class to mock first (PageContext). Then, right-click and choose MockMaker→Select Package to identify the output directory where MockMaker will generate the mock. Select the junitbook-pages/src/test/junitbook/pages output directory. MockMaker generates a mock class named PageContext in that directory.

> **NOTE**   The current version of MockMaker (v1.12) doesn't generate the Java imports needed by the generated mocks, so you'll have to perform this step manually.

Let's now write a mock-objects test for the DynaPropertiesTag class (see listing 10.9).

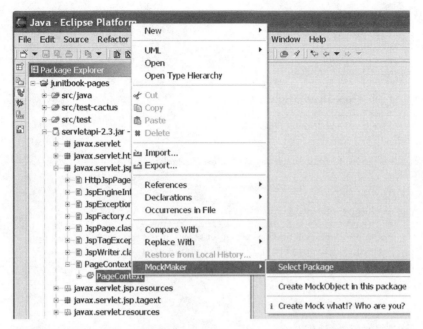

Figure 10.7 Generating the `PageContext` mock using the MockMaker Eclipse plugin

---

Listing 10.9   Mock-objects test for DynaPropertiesTag

```
package junitbook.pages;

import junit.framework.TestCase;
import org.apache.commons.beanutils.DynaBean;
import org.apache.commons.beanutils.DynaProperty;
import org.apache.commons.beanutils.BasicDynaClass;

import javax.servlet.jsp.tagext.Tag;

public class TestDynaPropertiesMO extends TestCase
{
    private DynaPropertiesTag tag;
    private MockPageContext mockPageContext;

    private DynaBean createDynaBean() throws Exception
    {
        DynaProperty[] props = new DynaProperty[] {
            new DynaProperty("id", String.class),
            new DynaProperty("responsetime", Long.class)
        };
        BasicDynaClass dynaClass = new BasicDynaClass("requesttime",
            null, props);

        DynaBean bean = dynaClass.newInstance();
        bean.set("id", "12345");
```

```
        bean.set("responsetime", new Long(500));

        return bean;
    }

    protected void setUp()
    {
        tag = new DynaPropertiesTag();
        mockPageContext = new MockPageContext();
        tag.setPageContext(mockPageContext);
    }

    public void testDoStartTag() throws Exception
    {
        DynaBean bean = createDynaBean();

        mockPageContext.setupFindAttribute(bean);                    ❶
        mockPageContext.addExpectedFindAttributeValues("item");      ❷
        mockPageContext.addExpectedSetAttributeStringObjectValues(
            "var", bean.getDynaClass().getDynaProperties());         ❸

        tag.setItem("${item}");
        tag.setVar("var");

        int result = tag.doStartTag();

        assertEquals(Tag.SKIP_BODY, result);
    }

    protected void tearDown()
    {
        mockPageContext.verify();                    ❹
    }
}
```

As with all mock-objects tests, you need to go over all the mock-object methods that will be called and tell the mocks how to behave. In this simple case, only one mock method is called: `PageContext.findAttribute` (❶). The second typical step with mock objects is to tell the mocks what values they should expect (❷ and ❸), so you can verify that the mocks methods were actually called with the expected values (❹).

If you're observant, you may have noticed a slight difference between the Cactus test implementation and the mock-objects implementation. Mocks usually need a deeper knowledge of the implementation than the Cactus tests. In ❶, you have to tell the mock that `PageContext.findAttribute` will be called and that it should return `item`. However, you aren't calling `findAttribute` anywhere in the implementation of `DynaPropertiesTag`! That's because you're calling `Expression-EvaluatorManager.evaluate("item", ..., pageContext, ...)`. `ExpressionEvaluatorManager` is a utility class from the JSTL library. It uses the passed `PageContext` to search for an `item` attribute in the page, request, session (if valid), or application scope(s).

10.6   *When to use mock objects and when to use Cactus*

One good rule is to always separate, as much as possible, integration code from business logic code. If you're coding a tag that retrieves a list of users from a database, you should implement the process with two Java classes. One class can handle the business logic and avoid dependencies on the Taglib API. A second class can implement the actual tag.

The *separation of concerns* strategy permits reuse of classes in more than one context *and* simplifies testing. You can test the business logic class with JUnit and mock objects, in the usual way. The integration code method that implements the tag can be handled separately, using Cactus.

Cactus requires more setup than mock objects but is well worth the effort. You may not run the Cactus tests as often, but they can confirm that your tags will work in the target environment the way you expect them to.

Sometimes, you may be tempted to skip testing the taglib components. "After all," someone might say, "they will eventually be tested as a side effect of the application's general functional tests, won't they?" We recommend that you fight this temptation. Taglib components deserve the benefits of unit testing as much as any other components. These benefits include:

- Fine-grained tests that can be run over and over and that tell you whether something has broken and exactly where it broke. Integration code is at least as complex as business logic code, and it should also be exercised with unit tests. Cactus provides an easy way of doing so.

- Ability to fully test your taglibs, not only for the successful cases but for failure cases as well. Given the example of a tag accessing a database, you should confirm that the tag behaves well when the connection with the database is broken (for example). Something like this is hard to test in automated functional tests, but easy to test when you combine Cactus and mock objects.

10.7   *Summary*

Cactus provides a unique ability to unit-test JSPs by allowing the interception of the JSP calls on the server side, thus providing a hook to set up objects in the HTTP request, HTTP session, or the JSP page context. Cactus enables unit-testing of JSPs in isolation. Cactus provides a `JspTestCase` class—an extension to the JUnit `TestCase` class—that allows unit-testing of taglibs.

In this chapter, we also demonstrated how to automate unit-testing of JSPs and taglibs using Maven and how to unit-test taglibs using mock objects. You used MockMaker to generate a `PageContext` mock, even though `PageContext` is a class and not an interface. (The JDK 1.3 Dynamic Proxy feature only works with interfaces.) Taglibs need more than a Java class to run. Taglibs also require deployment descriptors (`web.xml` and `.tld` files). This point is where Cactus shows all its strength. Cactus can quickly build automated JSP and taglibs test suites that not only verify the code at the unit level but also verify that the deployment descriptors are correct, and that the code runs correctly in the target container.

11

Unit-testing
database applications

Dependency is the key problem in software development at all scales.... [E]liminating duplication in programs eliminates dependency.

—Kent Beck, *Test-Driven Development: By Example*

For the combined 22 years that we have been writing business applications, we can't recall a single project that did not use a database of some sort! How do people unit-test code that calls a database? Most of them don't. Many developers deem the database problem to be too complex and rely solely on functional tests.

Our goal in this chapter is to show you not only that unit-testing database access code is possible, but also that you can use several different solutions. After we explore the approaches for unit-testing databases, we'll provide some guidelines for deciding which one to use for your particular application.

11.1 *Introduction to unit-testing databases*

We'll use the simple Administration application that we started in chapter 9 (see figure 11.1) to demonstrate how to unit-test database applications. By the end of this chapter, we will have completely covered the unit-testing of the Administration application.

The Administration application is a typical web app. A SQL query is contained in the HTTP request. A security filter verifies that the query found in the request is safe to execute. The processing logic is in the `AdminServlet`. The servlet receives the request (if it passes the filter), extracts the SQL query, calls the database using JDBC, and forwards to a JSP to display the result. The JSP uses tags to help render the dynamic data as HTML.

In chapters 9 and 10, we covered how to unit-test the servlet, filter, and JSP components of this application. Here, we'll focus on showing you how to unit-test the JDBC component (the shaded part in figure 11.1).

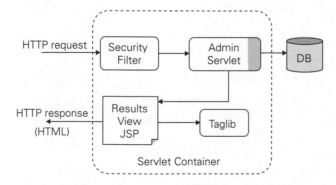

Figure 11.1
Unit-testing the database access part of the Administration application

Suppose your database access code has been cleanly separated from your business logic code. Separation of concerns is a good practice here, because it lets you change the persistence strategy without changing the rest of the application, and it simplifies unit testing.

You can write different types of tests involving database access (see figure 11.2):

- *Logic unit tests*—The goal of these tests is to unit-test business logic code in isolation of database access code (called *persistence code* in figure 11.2). The strategy is to mock database access code using a mock-objects approach.

- *Database access unit tests*—The database access code uses a persistence API (the JDBC API in this example) to access your database. The goal of this type of test is to validate that you're correctly using the persistence API. Using a mock-objects strategy, you can mock the persistence API, allowing you to run these tests without being connected to a database and without running inside a container.

- *Database integration unit tests*—These types of tests check the database functionality: connectivity, queries, stored procedures, triggers, constraints, and referential integrity. These tests must be run from within the container in order to test the code in the same context from which it will be run. This approach allows you to use the same mechanism to get a `DataSource` (connection pooling) and test transactions. Cactus provides a solution for

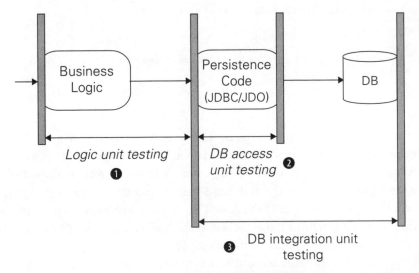

Figure 11.2 Different types of unit tests involving database access: logic unit tests, database access unit tests, and database integration unit tests

in-container testing, and DbUnit (as you'll see) offers a way to preload the database with test data.

In this chapter, we'll demonstrate how to perform each type of database unit test. We'll begin with testing the application's business logic.

11.2　Testing business logic in isolation from the database

The goal here is to unit-test the business logic code without involving the database access code. Although this type of test isn't a database test per se, it's a good strategy to test the business logic in isolation of harder-to-test database code. Fortunately, this task is easy if you separate the database access layer from the business logic layer. Let's see what this means on the Administration application. The AdminServlet class has the following signatures:

```
public class AdminServlet extends HttpServlet
{
    public void doGet(HttpServletRequest request,
        HttpServletResponse response) throws ServletException
    {
    }

    public String getCommand(HttpServletRequest request)
        throws ServletException
    {
    }

    public void callView(HttpServletRequest request)
    {
    }

    public Collection executeCommand(String command)
        throws Exception
    {
    }
}
```

The execution flow of the different methods is described in figure 11.3. The doGet method is the main entry point. It receives the HTTP requests (❶) and calls the getCommand method to extract the SQL query from it (❷). It then calls executeCommand (❸) to execute the database call (using the extracted SQL query) and return the results as a Collection. The results are then put in the HTTP request (as a request attribute) and, at last, doGet calls callView (❹) to invoke the JSP page that presents the results to the user (❺).

　The challenge is to be able to unit-test doGet, getCommand, and callView without executing the database access code that is run by executeCommand. The easiest

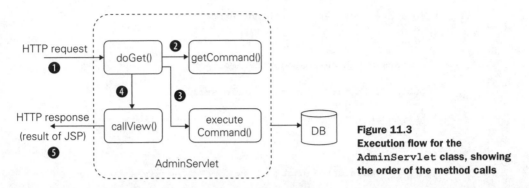

Figure 11.3
Execution flow for the
`AdminServlet` **class, showing**
the order of the method calls

and most generic solution is to create a database access layer that handles all database access. (In this case, it's a single class.) The trick is then to create an interface for the database access layer. Given an interface, you can unit-test database access using the mock-objects strategy (see chapter 7).

11.2.1 *Implementing a database access layer interface*

Let's call this interface `DataAccessManager` (listing 11.1) and the implementation `JdbcDataAccessManager`.

Listing 11.1   Isolating the database access layer: DataAccessManager.java

```
package junitbook.database;

import java.util.Collection;

public interface DataAccessManager
{
    Collection execute(String sql) throws Exception;
}
```

Now that you have a data access interface, you need to refactor the `AdminServlet` class to use that interface and to instantiate the `JdbcDataAccessManager` implementation of `DataAccessManager`. Listing 11.2 demonstrates this refactoring.

Listing 11.2   Isolating the database access layer: AdminServlet.java

```
package junitbook.database;

import java.util.Collection;

import javax.naming.NamingException;
import javax.servlet.ServletException;
import javax.servlet.http.HttpServlet;
```

```
public class AdminServlet extends HttpServlet
{
    // [...]

    private DataAccessManager dataManager;

    public void init() throws ServletException
    {
        super.init();

        try
        {
            this.dataManager = new JdbcDataAccessManager();
        }
        catch (NamingException e)
        {
            throw new ServletException(e);
        }
    }

    public Collection executeCommand(String command)
        throws Exception
    {
        return this.dataManager.execute(command);
    }
}
```

Writing a unit test for a method of the AdminServlet class is now easy. All you need to do is create a mock-object implementation of DataAccessManager. The only tricky part is deciding how to pass the mock instance to the AdminServlet class so that it uses the mock instead of the real JdbcDataAccessManager implementation.

11.2.2 *Setting up a mock database interface layer*

There are several strategies you could use to pass a DataAccessManager mock object to AdminServlet:

- Create a constructor that accepts the DataAccessManager interface as a parameter.

- Create a setter method (setDataAccessManager(DataAccessManager manager)).

- Extend AdminServlet to override the executeCommand method and return the result of calling the mock's executeCommand method.

- Make the data access manager implementation a parameter of your application by defining the class name in the web.xml as an AdminServlet initialization parameter.

The challenge is to use the most natural solution—either the one that makes the class more flexible and extensible *or* the one that requires the fewest changes. The constructor solution is really not natural in this case, because the class is a servlet and a servlet must only have a default constructor. Extending AdminServlet sounds nice, because it doesn't involve modifying the AdminServlet class; but this approach has the drawback that the test won't exercise AdminServlet but rather the class that extends it. The web.xml solution sounds even nicer; but then you have to make the DataAccessManager implementation class an application parameter, which may not be your intent. (In this case, it isn't.)

In this case, the setter solution sounds most natural. Listing 11.3 shows the implementation. The refactoring performed is shown in bold; all you do is add a setDataAccessManager method.

Listing 11.3   Setter approach to introduce DataAccessManager mock

```java
package junitbook.database;

import java.util.Collection;

import javax.naming.NamingException;
import javax.servlet.ServletException;
import javax.servlet.http.HttpServlet;

public class AdminServlet extends HttpServlet
{
    // [...]

    private DataAccessManager dataManager;

    public void setDataAccessManager(DataAccessManager manager)
    {
        this.dataManager = manager;
    }

    public void init() throws ServletException
    {
        super.init();

        try
        {
            setDataAccessManager(new JdbcDataAccessManager());
        }
        catch (NamingException e)
        {
            throw new ServletException(e);
        }
    }

    public Collection executeCommand(String command)
        throws Exception
```

```
        {
            return this.dataManager.execute(command);
        }
    }
```

11.2.3 *Mocking the database interface layer*

Listing 11.4 is a test case template that demonstrates how to create and use a mock `DataAccessManager` class for unit-testing the `AdminServlet` class. You can now write any mock object unit test using this canvas. The listing demonstrates writing mocks using the DynaMock API (see chapter 9). However, the strategy will also work with any other mock-object framework (EasyMock, for example).

Listing 11.4   Canvas for mocking the database layer using the DynaMock API

```
package junitbook.database;

import java.util.ArrayList;

import com.mockobjects.dynamic.Mock;
import com.mockobjects.dynamic.C;

import junit.framework.TestCase;

public class TestAdminServletDynaMock extends TestCase
{
    public void testSomething() throws Exception
    {
        Mock mockManager = new Mock(DataAccessManager.class);
        DataAccessManager manager =
            (DataAccessManager) mockManager.proxy();

        mockManager.expectAndReturn("execute", C.ANY_ARGS,
            new ArrayList());

        AdminServlet servlet = new AdminServlet();
        servlet.setDataAccessManager(manager);

        // Call the method to test here. For example:
        // manager.doGet(request, response)

        // [...]
    }
}
```

You start by creating a `DataAccessManager` mock using the DynaMock API. Next, you tell the mock object to return an empty `ArrayList` when the execute method is called. Then, you set up the mock manager using the `setDataAccessManager` method introduced in listing 11.3.

11.3 *Testing persistence code in isolation from the database*

You saw in the previous section that separating the database access layer from the business layer is a good practice. This strategy allows you to use mock objects to easily test the business logic in isolation from the database access code. However, that still leaves you with some untested code: the database access logic code itself.

How do you test database access logic code? Is it desirable to test it at all? The "how" is relatively easy, because the JDBC API is well designed and uses Java interfaces. JDBC lends itself very well to the mock-objects strategy. We will answer the "why" question later, in section 11.7, "Overall database unit-testing strategy."

Let's implement database access unit tests using the MockObjects.com JDBC API. (See the `com.mockobjects.sql` package.) You could use the DynaMock API instead; it yields test code of about the same complexity as the conventional Mock-Objects.com API, but in a few more lines of code. The advantage of the conventional SQL mock objects from MockObjects.com is that they don't need to be created dynamically (because they already exist), and they are tuned for unit-testing JDBC code.

Let's see what the code to test looks like. Listing 11.5 shows the first implementation of `JdbcDataAccessManager.java`.

Listing 11.5   JdbcDataAccessManager.java

```java
package junitbook.database;

import java.sql.Connection;
import java.sql.ResultSet;
import java.sql.SQLException;
import java.util.Collection;

import javax.naming.InitialContext;
import javax.naming.NamingException;
import javax.sql.DataSource;

import org.apache.commons.beanutils.RowSetDynaClass;

public class JdbcDataAccessManager implements DataAccessManager
{
    private DataSource dataSource;

    public JdbcDataAccessManager() throws NamingException
    {
        this.dataSource = getDataSource();
```

```
    }

    protected DataSource getDataSource() throws NamingException
    {
        InitialContext context = new InitialContext();
        DataSource dataSource =
            (DataSource) context.lookup("java:/DefaultDS");
        return dataSource;
    }

    protected Connection getConnection() throws SQLException
    {
        return this.dataSource.getConnection();
    }

    public Collection execute(String sql) throws Exception
    {
        Connection connection = getConnection();

        // For simplicity, we'll assume the SQL is a SELECT query
        ResultSet resultSet =
            connection.createStatement().executeQuery(sql);

        RowSetDynaClass rsdc = new RowSetDynaClass(resultSet);

        resultSet.close();
        connection.close();

        return rsdc.getRows();
    }
}
```

Get Data-
Source
from JNDI

Execute SQL
query

Wrap ResultSet in RowSetDynaClass
dyna bean for easy retrieval of data

Return a collection of dyna
beans, one for each result
set row

As you can see, the execute method is simple and generic. The simplicity stems from use of the BeanUtils package. BeanUtils provides a RowSetDynaClass that wraps a ResultSet and maps database columns to bean properties. You can then use the DynaBean API to access the columns as properties.

The RowSetDynaClass class automatically copies the ResultSet columns to dyna bean properties, allowing you to close the database connection as soon as you have instantiated a RowSetDynaClass object.

11.3.1 *Testing the execute method*

Let's write unit tests for the execute method. The idea is to provide mocks for all calls to the JDBC API. Listing 11.5 shows that you need to mock the Connection object. The mocked Connection can then return other mocks (mock ResultSet, mock Statement, and so forth). Thus, the first question you need to ask is how to pass a mock Connection object to the JdbcDataAccessManager class.

Passing the mock Connection object

You could pass the mock Connection object as a parameter to the execute method. However, in this example, you want to keep the creation of the Connection object contained within the JdbcDataAccessManager class. There are two other valid solutions:

- *Create a new component class*—You can create a new DataSourceComponent class with a getConnection method and then add a JdbcDataAccessManager(DataSourceComponent) constructor.

- *Create a wrapper class*—You can mark getConnection as protected (instead of private) and then create a TestableJdbcDataAccessManager class that extends JdbcDataAccessManager and adds a setConnection(Connection) method. You can set the mock Connection by bypassing the use of the DataSource to get the connection.

The first solution sounds too complex for the simple needs of this example. Listing 11.6 demonstrates the wrapper-class solution.

Listing 11.6   Wrapper to make JdbcDataAccessManager testable

```java
package junitbook.database;

import java.sql.Connection;
import java.sql.SQLException;

import javax.naming.NamingException;
import javax.sql.DataSource;

public class TestableJdbcDataAccessManager
    extends JdbcDataAccessManager
{
    private Connection connection;

    public TestableJdbcDataAccessManager() throws NamingException
    {
        super();
    }

    public void setConnection(Connection connection)
    {
        this.connection = connection;
    }

    protected Connection getConnection() throws SQLException
    {
        return this.connection;
    }

    protected DataSource getDataSource() throws NamingException
    {
```

```
        return null;
    }
}
```

You now have your way in the execute method, so you can begin writing the first unit test for it. As with any test using mock objects, the hard part is finding what methods you need to mock. In other words, you need to understand exactly what methods of your mocked API are being called, in order to provide mocked responses. Often, trial and error is enough to get you started. Begin with the minimum mocks, run the tests (which usually fail), and then refactor, one step at a time.

Creating a first test

To demonstrate, listing 11.7 shows the first test implementation for the execute method.

Listing 11.7   First try at unit-testing JdbcDataAccessManager.execute

```java
package junitbook.database;

import java.util.Collection;
import java.util.Iterator;

import org.apache.commons.beanutils.DynaBean;

import com.mockobjects.sql.MockConnection2;
import com.mockobjects.sql.MockStatement;

import junit.framework.TestCase;

public class TestJdbcDataAccessManagerMO1 extends TestCase
{
    private MockStatement statement;
    private MockConnection2 connection;
    private TestableJdbcDataAccessManager manager;

    protected void setUp() throws Exception
    {
        statement = new MockStatement();                    ❶
        connection = new MockConnection2();
        connection.setupStatement(statement);               ❷

        manager = new TestableJdbcDataAccessManager();      ❸
        manager.setConnection(connection);
    }

    public void testExecuteOk() throws Exception
    {
        String sql = "SELECT * FROM CUSTOMER";

        Collection result = manager.execute(sql);           ❹
```

```
            Iterator beans = result.iterator();
            assertTrue(beans.hasNext());
            DynaBean bean1 = (DynaBean) beans.next();
            assertEquals("John", bean1.get("firstname"));
            assertEquals("Doe", bean1.get("lastname"));
            assertTrue(!beans.hasNext());
        }
    }
```

① Create the `Statement` and `Connection` mocks.

② Have the `Connection` mock return the mock `Statement` object.

③ Instantiate the wrapper class (wrapping the class to test) and call the `setConnection` method (added in listing 11.6) to pass the mock `Connection` object.

④ Call the method to unit-test.

⑤ Assert the results by browsing the returned `Collection`.

Obviously, this test isn't finished. For example, you haven't told the mock `Statement` what to return when the `executeQuery` method is called (see listing 11.5). Let's run the test and see what happens (figure 11.4).

As expected, you get an error, because you haven't told the mock `Statement` what to return when `executeQuery` is called. (The stack trace indicates that line 68 of `CommonMockStatement` is trying to return a `ResultSet`, but it hasn't been told what to return.)

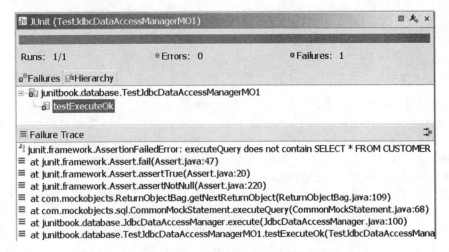

Figure 11.4   Result of running an incomplete mock-object test

Refining the test

Let's now add the mock ResultSet (see listing 11.8; additions are in bold).

Listing 11.8   Second try at unit-testing JdbcDataAccessManager.execute

```
package junitbook.database;
[...]
import com.mockobjects.sql.MockSingleRowResultSet;
[...]
public class TestJdbcDataAccessManagerMO2 extends TestCase
{
    private MockSingleRowResultSet resultSet;
[...]
    protected void setUp() throws Exception
    {
        resultSet = new MockSingleRowResultSet();

        statement = new MockStatement();
[...]
    }

    public void testExecuteOk() throws Exception
    {
        String sql = "SELECT * FROM CUSTOMER";
        statement.addExpectedExecuteQuery(sql, resultSet);

        String[] columnsLowercase =
            new String[] {"firstname", "lastname"};
        resultSet.addExpectedNamedValues(columnsLowercase,
            new Object[] {"John", "Doe"});

        Collection result = manager.execute(sql);
[...]
    }
}
```

Note that you use the MockSingleRowResultSet implementation. Mock-Objects.com provides two implementations: MockSingleRowResultSet and Mock-MultiRowResultSet. As their names indicate, the first implementation is used to simulate a result set with one row, and the second implementation is used to simulate a result set with several rows.

Running the test still fails (see figure 11.5), but you have made some progress—even if it isn't yet apparent! The error means that ResultSet.getMetaData is called somewhere in the flow of the test. But, you don't call getMetaData anywhere in the test class or in the class under test. Thus, it must be called by another package you're using. As the stack trace shows, the org.apache.commons.beanutils.Row-SetDynaClass.introspect method calls MockResultSet.getMetaData. Further

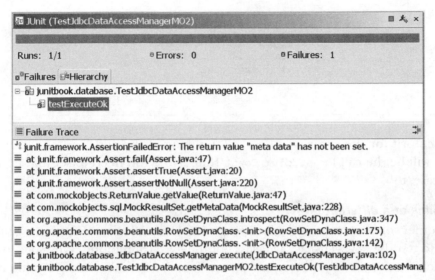

Figure 11.5 The test still fails after you add a mock `ResultSet`.

investigation shows that `introspect` is called when the `RowSetDynaClass` class is instantiated.

Tracing this error illustrates one of the potential issues with using mock objects: You often need intimate knowledge of the implementation of classes calling your mocks. You can discover indirect calls to your mocks through trial and error, as we just demonstrated. There are two other solutions: get access to the source code, or mock at a different level.

Discovering indirect calls in source code

Getting the source code isn't always possible and may be time consuming.[1] In this specific case, the Commons BeanUtils is an open source project. The relevant portion of the code is shown in listing 11.9.

Listing 11.9 Code from RowSetDynaClass highlighting the call to getMetaData

```
343 protected void introspect(ResultSet resultSet)
        throws SQLException {
344
345        // Accumulate an ordered list of DynaProperties
346        ArrayList list = new ArrayList();
347        ResultSetMetaData metadata = resultSet.getMetaData();
348        int n = metadata.getColumnCount();
```

---

[1] A nice decompiler plugin for Eclipse called JadClipse allows you to see code for which you don't have the source. Be aware that doing this may be illegal in some cases.

```
349         for (int i = 1; i <= n; i++) { // JDBC is one-relative!
350             DynaProperty dynaProperty =
                    createDynaProperty(metadata, i);
351             if (dynaProperty != null) {
352                 list.add(dynaProperty);
353             }
354         }
```

The culprit for the error is at line 347. Looking at the code, note that the next issue will be the call to getColumnCount (line 348). You need to set that up in the test case, too.

Mocking at a different level

The other solution, mocking at a different level, can be very useful. Your goal here isn't to test the RowSetDynaClass class but the execute method. One solution is to create a mock RowSetDynaClass and pass it (somehow) to the execute method.

In the case at hand, it seems easier to set up two additional methods (getMetaData and getColumnCount). However, mocking at a different level is often the solution to follow when the fixture for a given test becomes long and complex.

> ### JUnit best practices: refactor long setups when using mock objects
>
> When you're using mock objects, if the amount of setup you need to perform before being able to call the method under test is becoming excessive, you should consider refactoring. A long setup usually means one of two things: either the method under test does too much, so it's difficult to set up its environment, or the mocks you're using are not the correct ones. This happens if you're mocking too deep. In that case, you should introduce new mocks that are directly used by the method under test.
>
> The following illustration demonstrates that mocking at the wrong level forces you to create more mocks:
>
>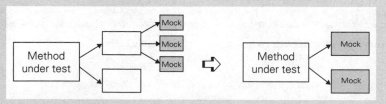
>
> The more mocks you have, the more setup you need.

Fixing the test

Let's modify the test case to support the calls to getMetaData and getColumnCount. Listing 11.10 show the additions in bold.

Listing 11.10 Adding a ResultSetMetaData mock

```java
package junitbook.database;
[...]
import com.mockobjects.sql.MockResultSetMetaData;
[...]
public class TestJdbcDataAccessManagerMO3 extends TestCase
{
[...]
    private MockResultSetMetaData resultSetMetaData;

    protected void setUp() throws Exception
    {
        resultSetMetaData = new MockResultSetMetaData();

        resultSet = new MockSingleRowResultSet();
        resultSet.setupMetaData(resultSetMetaData);
[...]
    }

    public void testExecuteOk() throws Exception
    {
        String sql = "SELECT * FROM CUSTOMER";
        statement.addExpectedExecuteQuery(sql, resultSet);

        String[] columnsLowercase =
            new String[] {"firstname", "lastname"};
        String[] columnsUppercase = new String[] {"FIRSTNAME",
            "LASTNAME"};
        String[] columnClasseNames = new String[] {
            String.class.getName(), String.class.getName()};

        resultSetMetaData.setupAddColumnNames(columnsUppercase);
        resultSetMetaData.setupAddColumnClassNames(
            columnClasseNames);
        resultSetMetaData.setupGetColumnCount(2);

        resultSet.addExpectedNamedValues(columnsLowercase,
            new Object[] {"John", "Doe"});

        Collection result = manager.execute(sql);
[...]
    }
}
```

The test now succeeds (see figure 11.6).

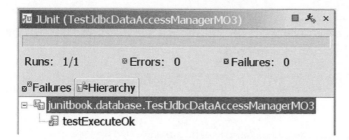

Figure 11.6 Successful test for unit-testing the `JdbcDataAccessManager`'s `execute` method in isolation from the database, by using MockObjects.com JDBC mocks

11.3.2 Using expectations to verify state

Although the test was successful, there are still assertions that you may want to verify as part of the test. For example, you may want to verify that the database connection was closed correctly (and only once), that the query string executed was the one you passed during the test, that a `PreparedStatement` was created only once, and so forth. These kinds of verifications are called *expectations* in MockObjects.com terminology. (See section 7.5 in chapter 7 for more about expectations.) Almost all mock objects from MockObjects.com expose an Expectation API in the form of `addExpectedXXX` or `setExpectedXXX` methods. The expectations are confirmed by calling the `verify` method on the respective mocks. Some of the MockObjects.com mocks perform default verifications. For example, when you write `statement.addExpectedExecuteQuery(sql, resultSet)`, the MockObjects code verifies at the end of the test that the `ResultSet` was accessed and the SQL executed was the query passed as parameter. Otherwise, the mock raises an `AssertionFailedError`.

Adding expectations

Let's modify listing 11.10 to add some expectations. The result is shown in listing 11.11 (changes are in bold).

Listing 11.11 Adding expectations to the testExecuteOk method

```
public void testExecuteOk() throws Exception
{
    String sql = "SELECT * FROM CUSTOMER";
    statement.addExpectedExecuteQuery(sql, resultSet);    ❶

    String[] columnsUppercase = new String[] {"FIRSTNAME",
        "LASTNAME"};
    String[] columnsLowercase = new String[] {"firstname",
        "lastname"};
```

```
            String[] columnClasseNames = new String[] {
                String.class.getName(), String.class.getName()};

            resultSetMetaData.setupAddColumnNames(columnsUppercase);
            resultSetMetaData.setupAddColumnClassNames(
                columnClasseNames);
            resultSetMetaData.setupGetColumnCount(2);

            resultSet.addExpectedNamedValues(columnsLowercase,
                new Object[] {"John", "Doe"});

            connection.setExpectedCreateStatementCalls(1);      ❷
            connection.setExpectedCloseCalls(1);           ❸

            Collection result = manager.execute(sql);
    [...]
        }

        protected void tearDown()             ❹
        {
            connection.verify();
            statement.verify();
            resultSet.verify();
        }
```

❶ Add an expectation to verify that the SQL string executed is the one passed by the test, unmodified. This expectation isn't new; you've used it since listing 11.8. It was needed earlier because the call to addExpectedExecuteQuery performs two actions: It sets what SQL query the mock Statement should simulate and verifies that the SQL query that is executed is the one expected. However, because you were not calling the verify method on your Statement mock, the expectation wasn't verified.

❷ Verify that only one Statement is created.

❸ Verify that the close method is called and that it's called only once.

❹ Verify the expectations set on mocks in ❶, ❷, and ❸.

So far, you have only tested a valid execution of the execute method. Obviously this isn't enough for a real-world test class. Alternate execution paths are a leading source of bugs in software. It's extremely important to unit-test exception paths. Put yourself in Murphy's shoes: Ask yourself what could possibly go wrong, and then write a test for that possibility.

Testing for errors
Here is a non-exhaustive list of things that can go wrong in your code and that therefore deserve a test case:

- The getConnection may fail with a SQLException. (There may be no connections left in the pool, the database may be offline, and so forth.)
- The creation of the Statement may fail.
- The execution of the query may fail.

These types of errors are easy to discover. However, there are always other errors that aren't so obvious. The subtle, unexpected errors can only be exposed through experience (and bug reports).

In the database application realm, there is a well-known error that can happen: The database connection may not be closed when an exception is raised. This is a common error, so let's write a test for it (see listing 11.12).

Listing 11.12   Verifying that the connection is closed even when an exception is raised

```
public void testExecuteCloseConnectionOnException()
    throws Exception
{
    String sql = "SELECT * FROM CUSTOMER";

    statement.setupThrowExceptionOnExecute(            ❶
        new SQLException("sql error"));

    connection.setExpectedCloseCalls(1);        ❷

    try
    {
        manager.execute(sql);
        fail("Should have thrown a SQLException");
    }
    catch (SQLException expected)
    {
        assertEquals("sql error", expected.getMessage());
    }
}
```

---

❶ To verify that the database connection is correctly closed when a database exception is raised, tell the MockStatement to throw a SQLException when it's executed.

❷ Add an expectation to verify that a close call on the mock Connection happens once and only once.

If you try to run the test now, it fails as shown in figure 11.7. (Flip back to listing 11.5, where you implemented the execute method, and you may see why.) You can easily fix the code by wrapping it in a try/finally block:

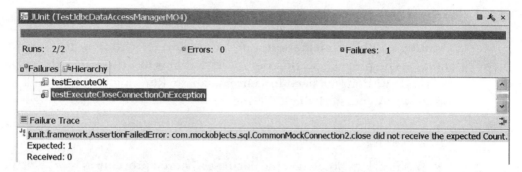

Figure 11.7 Failure to close the connection when a database exception is raised

```java
public Collection execute(String sql) throws Exception
{
    ResultSet resultSet = null;
    Connection connection = null;
    Collection result = null;

    try
    {
        connection = getConnection();

        resultSet =
            connection.createStatement().executeQuery(sql);

        RowSetDynaClass rsdc = new RowSetDynaClass(resultSet);

        result = rsdc.getRows();
    }
    finally
    {
        if (resultSet != null)
        {
            resultSet.close();
        }
        if (connection != null)
        {
            connection.close();
        }
    }

    return result;
}
```

That's much better. You can now be confident that the database access code performs as expected. But there is more to database access than SQL code. For example, are you sure the connection pool is set up correctly? Do you have to wait for functional tests to discover that something else doesn't work? The focus of the next section is the third type of test: database integration unit testing.

11.4 *Writing database integration unit tests*

Executing database integration unit tests means executing unit tests with a live database. The previous section demonstrated how to write unit tests for database access code without the need for a live database. Running unit tests on a live database allows you to check the following:

- Integration issues, such as verifying that the connection with the database is working
- Business logic located in the database as stored procedures is working properly
- Database triggers are set up correctly
- Database constraints work as intended
- Referential integrity is properly set up in the database

You may find that writing both unit tests in isolation from the database and database integration unit tests is redundant and time-consuming—and you would be right. It's important to define an overall unit-testing strategy that prevents you from having to write too many tests, thus making the process fastidious. In the next section, we look at choosing an appropriate strategy.

11.4.1 *Filling the requirements for database integration tests*

Say you need to write integration unit tests. In order to run integration unit tests, you require two features from the testing framework:

- The ability to preset the database with test data.
- The ability to start the test from within the running container. This step verifies that the component can talk with the database.

You can use two frameworks for this task: Cactus and DbUnit (http://www.dbunit.org/). Cactus allows you to start the test inside the container. (See chapter 8.)DbUnit is a database unit-testing framework that provides two main features: the ability to easily preload the database with test data, and the ability to compare the content of the database after the test with reference data.

Because you want to run the tests in a container, let's pick a J2EE container and a database for the Administration application example. Two free open source tools that are very easy to use are JBoss and Hypersonic SQL. Better yet, JBoss comes preconfigured with Hypersonic SQL. This pair is a particularly good choice because this chapter isn't about how to set up a database—it's about testing a database. Be assured that everything demonstrated here should work with any J2EE container and with any database.

As for the build tool, you'll run the full scenario using the well-known Ant (see chapter 5). You'll start Cactus from Ant and use the Cactus/Ant integration module.

Moreover, in this section you'll continue to use the Administration application. You'll also write integration unit tests for the JdbcDataAccessManager execute method that you have already unit-tested using mock objects (see section 11.3), but this time you'll use Cactus.

11.4.2 *Presetting database data*

You could preset the database data using JDBC Java code, as part of the test code—in a setUp method, for example. This way, you would keep the test code and data in a single place (the Java class). However, there are some drawbacks:

- The database data cannot easily be shared among several test cases. It requires the creation of helper classes.

- Java code isn't the best place to write database queries. You would need to find a framework that lets you easily send SQL code. DbUnit doesn't support creating the dataset from Java. (Its preferred strategy is to use an external file containing the data.)

- The database data cannot be shared between different types of tests: integration unit tests, functional tests, and stress tests. (More information is provided in section 11.7, "Overall database unit-testing strategy.")

In the rest of this section, we'll demonstrate how to preset the database with data defined in an XML file that you load using DbUnit. Listing 11.13 shows a Cactus test that exercises the JdbcDataAccessManager's execute method.`

Listing 11.13   Cactus test case for testing the execute method

```
package junitbook.database;

import java.util.Collection;
import java.util.Iterator;

import org.apache.cactus.ServletTestCase;
import org.apache.commons.beanutils.DynaBean;

public class TestJdbcDataAccessManagerIC extends ServletTestCase    ❶
{
    public void testExecuteOk() throws Exception
    {
        JdbcDataAccessManager manager =                      ❷
            new JdbcDataAccessManager();

        Collection result =
            manager.execute("SELECT * FROM CUSTOMER");
```

```
        Iterator beans = result.iterator();

        assertTrue(beans.hasNext());
        DynaBean bean1 = (DynaBean) beans.next();
        assertEquals("John", bean1.get("firstname"));
        assertEquals("Doe", bean1.get("lastname"));

        assertTrue(!beans.hasNext());
    }
}
```

❶ Run the test from the context of a servlet by extending the Cactus `ServletTest-Case` class.

❷ The main difference from the previous mock tests is that you're not mocking the `DataAccessManager` interface anymore; you're using the real implementation that goes to the database.

Connecting to the database

The `JdbcDataAccessManager` implementation uses a `DataSource` to connect to the database, as shown in listing 11.14 (new code in bold).

Listing 11.14 DataSource implementation in JdbcDataAccessManager

```
package junitbook.database;

import java.sql.Connection;
import java.sql.ResultSet;
import java.sql.SQLException;
import java.util.Collection;

import javax.naming.InitialContext;
import javax.naming.NamingException;
import javax.sql.DataSource;

import org.apache.commons.beanutils.RowSetDynaClass;

public class JdbcDataAccessManager implements DataAccessManager
{
    private DataSource dataSource;

    public JdbcDataAccessManager() throws NamingException
    {
        this.dataSource = getDataSource();
    }

    protected DataSource getDataSource() throws NamingException
    {
        InitialContext context = new InitialContext();
        DataSource dataSource =
            (DataSource) context.lookup("java:/DefaultDS");
```

```
        return dataSource;
    }

    protected Connection getConnection() throws SQLException
    {
        return this.dataSource.getConnection();
    }

    public Collection execute(String sql) throws Exception
    {
[...]
    }
}
```

When you execute new JdbcDataAccessManager() in the TestJdbcDataAccess-ManagerIC class (listing 11.13), the DataSource is looked up with JNDI. Note that you're looking up the DataSource using the java:/DefaultDS JNDI key. By default, JBoss defines a Hypersonic DataSource at this location.

If you run this test as is, it will fail because you haven't preset the database with the correct data. Let's do this next.

Setting up the database with data

Listing 11.15 shows how to use DbUnit to preset the database with the correct data. You use DbUnit in your TestCase's setUp method so that the data will be preset before each test.

Listing 11.15 Presetting database data in the setUp method

```
package junitbook.database;
[...]
import org.dbunit.database.DatabaseDataSourceConnection;
import org.dbunit.database.IDatabaseConnection;
import org.dbunit.dataset.IDataSet;
import org.dbunit.dataset.xml.FlatXmlDataSet;
import org.dbunit.operation.DatabaseOperation;

public class TestJdbcDataAccessManagerIC extends ServletTestCase
{
    protected void setUp() throws Exception
    {
        IDatabaseConnection connection =                       ❶
            new DatabaseDataSourceConnection(new InitialContext(),
            "java:/DefaultDS");

        IDataSet dataSet = new FlatXmlDataSet(                 ❷
            this.getClass().getResource(
            "/junitbook/database/data.xml"));
```

```
        try
        {
            DatabaseOperation.CLEAN_INSERT.execute(connection,    ③
                dataSet);
        }
        finally
        {
            connection.close();        ④
        }
    }

    public void testExecuteOk() throws Exception
    {
        [...]
    }
}
```

❶ Create a database connection using the `DataSource` bound with the `java:/DefaultDS` JNDI name.

❷ Load the XML data file.

❸ Apply its content to the database by using the `CLEAN_INSERT` strategy. This strategy ensures that the content of the database is exactly the same as what you have in the `data.xml` file.

❹ Remember to close the connection!

You're putting the XML data file next to the `TestCase` in the directory structure. (See section 11.5.1 on the project directory structure for more.) This is why you load it as a Java resource. Its content is very simple for this test, because you need only to fill the `CUSTOMER` table with one record for John Doe to make the test pass (listing 11.16).

Listing 11.16   Data.xml containing a single record

```
<dataset>
    <CUSTOMER FIRSTNAME="John" LASTNAME="Doe"/>
</dataset>
```

DbUnit supports several XML file formats, but the simplest is the Flat XML format used in listing 11.16. Each XML element represents a record. The element name is the name of the table where this record applies, the attributes are column names, and the attribute values are the record values.

11.5 Running the Cactus test using Ant

Let's run the Cactus test using Ant. But first, let's review the project directory structure.

11.5.1 Reviewing the project structure

Figure 11.8 shows the project directory structure for the Cactus testing. You cleanly separate the main classes (in src/java) from the Cactus test classes (in src/test-cactus). Plain JUnit test classes would go in src/test to separate them from the other type of classes. Of course, you're free to use whatever directory structure you like. The one we show here is a commonly used structure that we consider a best practice.

Table 11.1 describes the files for the project. The last files in table 11.1 are new to the project, so let's discuss what they do.

Figure 11.8   Project directory structure for the database integration unit-testing project

Table 11.1   The project directory for the database unit tests using Cactus and Ant contains seven files.

File	Description
JdbcDataAccessManager.java	The class you're testing
TestJdbcDataAccessManagerIC.java	The Cactus test case class
data.xml	The data to preset in the database, read by the TestDataAccessManagerIC class
data.sql	Used to create the database schema; contains the commands to create the CUSTOMER table
web.xml	The web application descriptor
build.xml	The Ant build file
build.properties	The properties file for the build, which contains Ant properties that are environment dependent

The `conf/data.sql` file creates the database schema. Although DbUnit sets up the data in the database tables, it doesn't create the schema. Happily, you can get Ant to create the schema using the Ant `sql` task. To get you started, `data.sql` needs only a single SQL command:

```
CREATE TABLE CUSTOMER (lastname varchar primary key,
    firstname varchar);
```

If you execute the `data.sql` file a second time, you need to remove the table before creating it again, or you'll get an error. To remove the table first, you can insert another SQL command:

```
DROP TABLE CUSTOMER;
CREATE TABLE CUSTOMER (lastname varchar primary key,
    firstname varchar);
```

You'll use the Ant war task to create the web application. Unsurprisingly, the Ant war task requires a `web.xml` file. For this example, you can leave the file empty:

```
<?xml version="1.0" encoding="ISO-8859-1"?>

<!DOCTYPE web-app
    PUBLIC "-//Sun Microsystems, Inc.//DTD Web Application 2.3//EN"
    "http://java.sun.com/dtd/web-app_2_3.dtd">

<web-app>
</web-app>
```

In production, the `web.xml` file would register the servlets (like the `AdminServlet`) and taglibs, among other things.

11.5.2 *Introducing the Cactus/Ant integration module*

The Cactus/Ant integration module is a jar containing a set of Ant tasks that you can use in your own Ant buildfiles to run Cactus tests. It provides the following tasks:

- `cactifywar`—Transforms an ordinary war file into a Cactus-ready war. This means adding all Cactus-required jars to the original war, adding the Cactus tests, and modifying the `web.xml` descriptor to add the definition for the Cactus redirectors and other miscellaneous entries. This process is called *cactification.*

- `cactus`—Executes Cactus tests. The `cactus` task performs several actions: It configures the container in which running you're the Cactus tests, deploys a *cactified* war into the container, starts the container, runs the tests, and stops the running container. The `cactus` task is an extension of the Ant `junit` task used to automatically run Cactus tests.

You can obtain the Cactus/Ant integration jar by downloading the `jakarta-cactus-13-<version>.zip` file from the Cactus web site (http://jakarta.apache.org/cactus/). The *13* stands for the J2EE API 1.3, which you are using here. The zip contains a `cactus-ant-<version>.jar` file with the Ant tasks we discussed. You can use these tasks directly in your Ant buildfile via the Ant `taskdef` syntax. For more about the Cactus/Ant integration module, see http://jakarta.apache.org/cactus/integration/ant/index.html.

11.5.3 *Creating the Ant build file step by step*

Let's create the Ant buildfile step by step. Because the Cactus/Ant integration module does 99% of the work for you, the steps are neither long nor complex:

1. Create the database schema.
2. Create the web application war.
3. Compile the Cactus tests.
4. Run the Cactus tests.

Creating the database schema

Ant's `sql` task makes this step easy, because it can execute arbitrary SQL commands. The Ant target shown in listing 11.17 reads the SQL from the `data.sql` file and executes it against the Hypersonic SQL database defined by the `${database}` property.

Listing 11.17   Ant target to create the database schema

```
<?xml version="1.0"?>

<project name="Database" default="createdb" basedir=".">

  <property file="build.properties"/>
  <property name="conf.dir" location="conf"/>

  <target name="createdb">
    <sql driver="org.hsqldb.jdbcDriver"
        url="jdbc:hsqldb:${database}"
        userid="sa"
        password="">
      <fileset dir="${conf.dir}">
        <include name="data.sql" />
      </fileset>
      <classpath>
        <pathelement location="${hsqldb.jar}"/>
```

```
        </classpath>
      </sql>
    </target>

</project>
```

To set this up, you use the `build.properties` file to define two Ant properties: `${database}` (location of the Hypersonic database) and `${hsqldb.jar}` (location of the Hypersonic jar):

```
cactus.home.jboss3x = C:/Apps/jboss-3.2.1
hsqldb.jar = ${cactus.home.jboss3x}/server/default/lib/hsqldb.jar
database =
  ${cactus.home.jboss3x}/server/default/data/hypersonic/default
```

You use the Hypersonic default database, located in the JBoss directory hierarchy. You also use the Hypersonic jar (`hsqldb.jar`) located in the JBoss directory hierarchy.

If you open a command shell and run the `createdb` target by entering **ant createdb**, you get the result shown in figure 11.9.

Creating the web application war

This is a web application. So, you need a target to create a war to deploy the application. You don't need to include anything related to Cactus in the war, because you'll use the Cactus Ant integration `cactifywar` task to Cactus-enable the war.

To create the war, you need to compile the sources first. Thus you create two targets: `compile` and `war`, shown in listing 11.18.

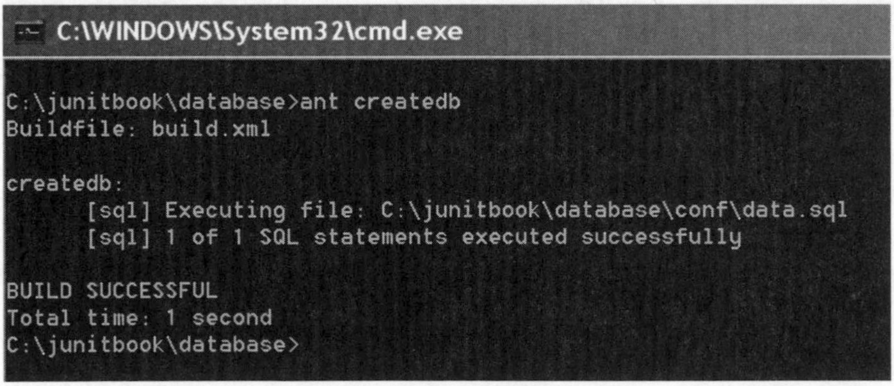

```
C:\WINDOWS\System32\cmd.exe

C:\junitbook\database>ant createdb
Buildfile: build.xml

createdb:
    [sql] Executing file: C:\junitbook\database\conf\data.sql
    [sql] 1 of 1 SQL statements executed successfully

BUILD SUCCESSFUL
Total time: 1 second
C:\junitbook\database>
```

Figure 11.9   Result of executing the `createdb` Ant target

Listing 11.18   Ant targets to create the application war

```xml
<?xml version="1.0"?>

<project name="Database" default="war" basedir=".">

[...]

  <target name="compile">
    <mkdir dir="target/classes"/>
    <javac destdir="target/classes" srcdir="src/java">
      <classpath>
        <pathelement location="${beanutils.jar}"/>
        <pathelement location="${servlet.jar}"/>
      </classpath>
    </javac>
  </target>

  <target name="war" depends="compile">
    <war destfile="target/database.war"
        webxml="src/webapp/WEB-INF/web.xml">
      <classes dir="target/classes"/>
      <lib file="${beanutils.jar}"/>
      <lib file="${collections.jar}"/>
    </war>
  </target>

</project>
```

To set this up, you define three Ant properties in the build.properties file—
${beanutils.jar}, ${servlet.jar}, and ${lib.dir} (the location of the jars):

```
lib.dir = ../repository

beanutils.jar =
→     ${lib.dir}/commons-beanutils/jars/commons-beanutils-1.6.1.jar
collections.jar =
→     ${lib.dir}/commons-collections/jars/commons-collections-2.1.jar
servlet.jar = ${lib.dir}/servletapi/jars/servletapi-2.3.jar
```

Compiling the Cactus tests

Before you can run the Cactus tests, you need to add a target to compile them,
like the one shown here:

```xml
<target name="compile.cactustest">
  <mkdir dir="target/cactus-test-classes"/>
  <javac destdir="target/cactus-test-classes"
      srcdir="src/test-cactus">
    <classpath>
      <pathelement location="target/classes"/>
      <pathelement location="${beanutils.jar}"/>
```

```
            <pathelement location="${dbunit.jar}"/>
            <pathelement location="${cactus.jar}"/>
        </classpath>
    </javac>
    <copy todir="target/cactus-test-classes">
        <fileset dir="src/test-cactus">
        <include name="**/*.xml"/>
        </fileset>
    </copy>
</target>
```

❶ You need to add the jars for DbUnit and Cactus to the compilation classpath, because classes from these jars are used in the test cases. So, you define two more properties in the build.properties file, ${dbunit.jar} and ${cactus.jar}:

```
cactus.jar = ${lib.dir}/cactus/jars/cactus-13-1.5.jar
dbunit.jar = ${lib.dir}/dbunit/jars/dbunit-1.5.5.jar
```

❷ Back in listing 11.15, you loaded the data.xml file as a Java resource. This means it has to be in the test classpath when you execute the tests. So, here you copy any XML file in the test source directory structure (src/test-cactus) to the target compilation directory (where the compiled test classes are put).

Running the Cactus tests

You're almost ready to execute the tests using the cactus Ant task from the Cactus/Ant integration module. However, you need to pass a cactified war to the cactus task. The cactifywar Ant task can handle this for you. Before you can use the Cactus/Ant integration tasks, you need to define them in your buildfile as follows:

```
<target name="test" depends="war,compile.cactustest">

    <taskdef resource="cactus.tasks">
        <classpath>
            <pathelement location="${cactus.ant.jar}"/>
            <pathelement location="${cactus.jar}"/>
            <pathelement location="${logging.jar}"/>
            <pathelement location="${aspectjrt.jar}"/>
            <pathelement location="${httpclient.jar}"/>
        </classpath>
    </taskdef>
```

You have added all the Cactus jars to the classpath of the taskdef. This classpath will be used by both cactifywar and cactus. The cactifywar task puts the Cactus jars in the cactified war, and the cactus task puts the Cactus jars in the test execution classpath.

As usual, you create Ant properties to hold the path to your jars in the build.properties file:

```
cactus.ant.jar = ${lib.dir}/cactus/jars/cactus-ant-13-1.5.jar
aspectjrt.jar = ${lib.dir}/aspectj/jars/aspectjrt-1.0.6.jar
logging.jar =
→      ${lib.dir}/commons-logging/jars/commons-logging-1.0.3.jar
httpclient.jar =
→      ${lib.dir}/commons-httpclient/jars/commons-httpclient-2.0.jar
```

Writing the cactification task is easy:

```
<target name="test" depends="war,compile.cactustest">

  <taskdef resource="cactus.tasks">
[...]
  </taskdef>

  <cactifywar srcfile="target/database.war"
      destfile="target/test.war">
    <classes dir="target/cactus-test-classes"/>
    <lib file="${dbunit.jar}"/>
    <lib file="${exml.jar}"/>
  </cactifywar>
```

The `cactifywar` task transforms the `target/database.war` war into a Cactus-enabled `target/test.war` war. This task adds all the jars you have defined in the `taskdef` to the war. Here, you use the nested `lib` element to add the `${dbunit.jar}` and `${exml.jar}` jars.

DbUnit needs the Electric XML jar (`exml.jar`) at runtime. So, you add it to the `build.properties` file:

```
exml.jar = ${lib.dir}/dbunit/jars/exml-dbunit-1.5.5.jar
```

The content of the resulting `test.war` is shown in figure 11.10.

The last step is to execute the Cactus tests by using the `cactus` task:

```
<target name="test" depends="war,compile.cactustest">

  <taskdef resource="cactus.tasks">
[...]
  </taskdef>

  <cactifywar srcfile="target/database.war"
[...]
  </cactifywar>

  <cactus warfile="target/test.war" fork="yes" printsummary="yes"
      haltonerror="true" haltonfailure="true">
    <containerset>
      <jboss3x dir="${cactus.home.jboss3x}"
          output="target/jbossresult.txt"/>
    </containerset>
    <formatter type="brief" usefile="false"/>
    <batchtest>
```

```
        <fileset dir="src/test-cactus">
          <include name="**/TestJdbcDataAccessManagerIC.java"/>
        </fileset>
      </batchtest>
      <classpath>
        <pathelement location="target/classes"/>
        <pathelement location="target/cactus-test-classes"/>
        <pathelement location="${dbunit.jar}"/>
      </classpath>
    </cactus>

  </target>
```

The cactus task extends the junit Ant task. Thus, all attributes available to the junit task are also directly available to the cactus task. For example, you use the fork, printsummary, haltonerror, and haltonfailure attributes from the junit task. You also use the formatter, batchtest, and classpath elements from the junit task.

You need to tell the cactus task what container you wish to run the tests with. In this case, you're using JBoss 3.2.1; hence the jboss3x element. The cactus task supports several other containers, such as Tomcat (3.x, 4.x, 5.x),

Name	Path ▲
jspRedirector.jsp	
MANIFEST.MF	META-INF\
web.xml	WEB-INF\
AdminServlet.class	WEB-INF\classes\junitbook\database\
data.xml	WEB-INF\classes\junitbook\database\
DataAccessManager.class	WEB-INF\classes\junitbook\database\
JdbcDataAccessManager.class	WEB-INF\classes\junitbook\database\
TestJdbcDataAccessManagerIC.class	WEB-INF\classes\junitbook\database\
aspectjrt-1.0.6.jar	WEB-INF\lib\
cactus-13-1.5.jar	WEB-INF\lib\
commons-beanutils-1.6.1.jar	WEB-INF\lib\
commons-collections-2.1.jar	WEB-INF\lib\
commons-httpclient-2.0.jar	WEB-INF\lib\
commons-logging-1.0.3.jar	WEB-INF\lib\
dbunit-1.5.5.jar	WEB-INF\lib\
exml-dbunit-1.5.5.jar	WEB-INF\lib\
junit.jar	WEB-INF\lib\

Figure 11.10   Content of the cactified war. The jspRedirector.jsp **file, the test classes, and the Cactus-related jars have been added by the cactification. In addition, the** web.xml **file has been modified to include the Cactus redirector definitions and mappings.**

Orion (1.x, 2.x), Resin (2.x), and WebLogic (7.x), to name a few. (See the Cactus web site for full information.)

The output attribute of the jboss3x element redirects all container output to the target/jbossresult.txt file. This keeps stdout from becoming cluttered.

The cactus task automatically adds the jars you have defined in the taskdef to the execution classpath (the classpath of the JVM where the JUnit test runner executes). You need to explicitly add the DbUnit jar because it's referenced from your Cactus TestJdbcDataAccessManagerIC test case class.

The full listing of the test target is shown in listing 11.19.

Listing 11.19 Ant target that calls the Cactus/Ant integration module to run the tests

```xml
<?xml version="1.0"?>

<project name="Database" default="test" basedir=".">

[...]

  <target name="test" depends="war,compile.cactustest">

    <taskdef resource="cactus.tasks">
      <classpath>
        <pathelement location="${cactus.ant.jar}"/>
        <pathelement location="${cactus.jar}"/>
        <pathelement location="${logging.jar}"/>
        <pathelement location="${aspectjrt.jar}"/>
        <pathelement location="${httpclient.jar}"/>
      </classpath>
    </taskdef>

    <cactifywar srcfile="target/database.war"
        destfile="target/test.war">
      <classes dir="target/cactus-test-classes"/>
      <lib file="${dbunit.jar}"/>
      <lib file="${exml.jar}"/>
    </cactifywar>

    <cactus warfile="target/test.war" fork="yes" printsummary="yes"
        haltonerror="true" haltonfailure="true">
      <containerset>
        <jboss3x dir="${cactus.home.jboss3x}"
            output="target/jbossresult.txt"/>
      </containerset>
      <formatter type="brief" usefile="false"/>
      <batchtest>
        <fileset dir="src/test-cactus">
          <include name="**/TestJdbcDataAccessManagerIC.java"/>
        </fileset>
      </batchtest>
      <classpath>
```

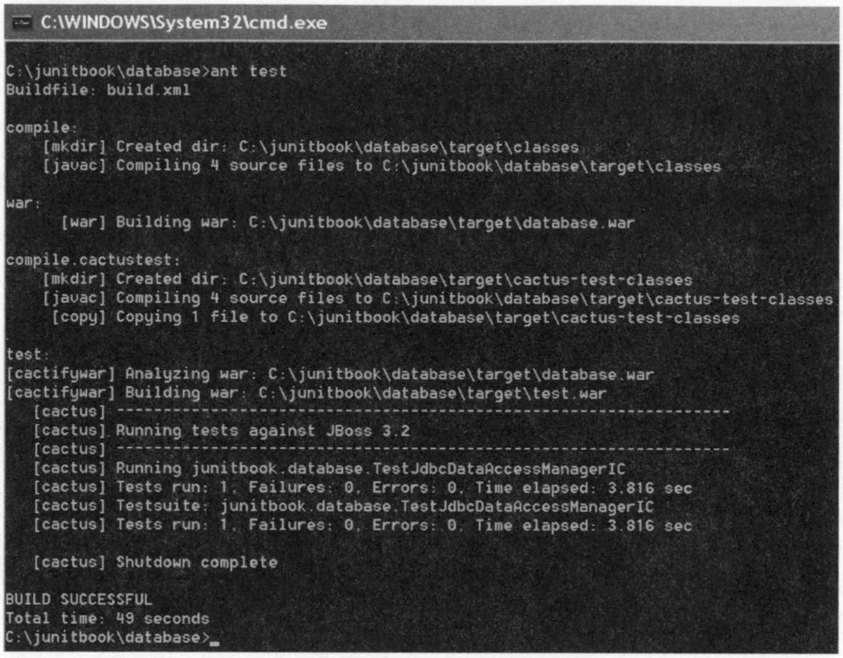

Figure 11.11   Result of executing Cactus tests automatically using Ant against JBoss 3.2.1

```
        <pathelement location="target/classes"/>
        <pathelement location="target/cactus-test-classes"/>
        <pathelement location="${dbunit.jar}"/>
      </classpath>
    </cactus>

  </target>

</project>
```

This example needs only a few of the many features available through the Cactus/
Ant integration module. To learn more, visit the Cactus web site (http://
jakarta.apache.org/cactus/).

11.5.4 *Executing the Cactus tests*

You now have a full-fledged build system that automatically executes the Cactus
tests. Let's run it by entering **ant test** from a command shell. The result is shown
in figure 11.11. You can now run the database integration unit tests automatically
from Ant whenever you like.

11.6 *Tuning for build performance*

This example includes only a single integration test. The test takes 49 seconds to run, so you'll probably run it as often as needed. But in a production application with hundreds of test cases, the total time of execution becomes significant. If the tests take too long to run, you may not run them as often as you should.

Several strategies can help tune test execution performance:

- Factor out read-only data.
- Group tests in functional test suites.
- Use an in-memory database.

11.6.1 *Factoring out read-only data*

Some of the data in a database is only read and never modified by the application. Instead of initializing this data in the setUp method (which is called once for every test), a better solution is to preset it in a TestSuite setUp method (which is executed once per test suite run).

For example, the execute method in the JdbcDataAccessManager class only reads data and doesn't perform any deletes or updates. You can refactor TestJdbcDataAccessManagerIC (from listing 11.15) and move the database initialization into a JUnit TestSetup class, as shown by listing 11.20.

Listing 11.20   Factorizing read-only database data in a JUnit TestSetup class

```
package junitbook.database;

import javax.naming.InitialContext;

import junit.extensions.TestSetup;
import junit.framework.Test;

import org.dbunit.database.DatabaseDataSourceConnection;
import org.dbunit.database.IDatabaseConnection;
import org.dbunit.dataset.IDataSet;
import org.dbunit.dataset.xml.FlatXmlDataSet;
import org.dbunit.operation.DatabaseOperation;

public class DatabaseTestSetup extends TestSetup
{
    public DatabaseTestSetup(Test suite)
    {
        super(suite);
    }

    protected void setUp() throws Exception
    {
```

```
IDatabaseConnection connection =
    new DatabaseDataSourceConnection(new InitialContext(),
    "java:/DefaultDS");

IDataSet dataSet = new FlatXmlDataSet(
    this.getClass().getResource(
    "/junitbook/database/data.xml"));

try
{
    DatabaseOperation.CLEAN_INSERT.execute(connection,
        dataSet);
}
finally
{
    connection.close();
}
}
}
```

Now that you have factored the common database setup into a DatabaseTestSetup class, you can call it from the TestJdbcDataAccessManagerIC test case class, as shown in listing 11.21.

Listing 11.21 TestJdbcDataAccessManager using the DatabaseTestSetup class

```
package junitbook.database;

import junit.framework.Test;
import junit.framework.TestSuite;

import org.apache.cactus.ServletTestCase;

public class TestJdbcDataAccessManagerIC2 extends ServletTestCase
{
    public static Test suite()
    {
        TestSuite suite = new TestSuite();
        suite.addTestSuite(TestJdbcDataAccessManagerIC2.class);
        return new DatabaseTestSetup(suite);
    }

    protected void setUp() throws Exception
    {
        // Database initialization for data that need to be
        // reset before each test.
    }

    public void testExecute1() throws Exception
    {
        [...]
```

```
    }

    public void testExecute2() throws Exception
    {
        [...]
    }

    public void testExecute3() throws Exception
    {
        [...]
    }
}
```

Although listing 11.21 includes three tests, the database will be initialized only once with the read-only data. The `suite` method is executed only once by the JUnit test runner.

11.6.2 Grouping tests in functional test suites

In practice, test cases often use similar sets of database data or perform a common set of operations. If you group these tests together, they can share resources, including the overhead of establishing the resources. For example, imagine you have several classes that are used to implement customer-related services (get customer details, get customer accounts, add new customers, and so forth). Instead of having one XML data file for each test case, you can have only one that you execute once before all the customer tests. If you have use cases that modify data, you can create several customers in the XML file so that one test will work on one customer and other tests can work on other customer records.

Listing 11.22 shows a class that is used only to group together test cases.

Listing 11.22   Grouping all customer-related test cases

```
package junitbook.database;

import junit.framework.Test;
import junit.framework.TestSuite;

public class TestCustomerAll
{
    public static Test suite()
    {
        TestSuite suite = new TestSuite(
            "Customer Related Tests");

        // Add tests from Customer related test cases
        suite.addTestSuite(TestCustomer1.class);
        suite.addTestSuite(TestCustomer2.class);
```

```
[...]
        suite.addTestSuite(TestCustomerN.class);

        return suite;
    }
}
```

11.6.3 *Using an in-memory database*

Most applications spend most of their time waiting for the database. The same is true for the database integration unit tests. If the test can access the database more quickly, the test will also run more quickly.

For running tests, an in-memory database can be accessed much more quickly (by several orders of magnitude) than a conventional database. As a result, your tests also run faster, by several orders of magnitude. Hypersonic SQL, among others, has an in-memory mode that is ideal for running tests.

Unfortunately, using a different database isn't a viable option for many applications. Often, the SQL is optimized for the target database. Several common needs are not standardized by SQL. For example, to return pages of data, Oracle has a rowid feature; but other databases implement this feature differently. Different vendors implement other commonly used database features, like triggers and referential integrity, differently. However, if your application uses SQL that can be used with an in-memory database as well as your target database, this can be an excellent optimization.

11.7 *Overall database unit-testing strategy*

You have seen two main approaches to testing database applications. One uses mock objects to perform unit tests in isolation. Another uses in-container testing (with a tool like Cactus) and preset database data (created with a tool like DbUnit) to perform integration tests.

At this point, you're probably wondering whether you need to write both types of tests. Is it enough to write only mock-object tests? Can Cactus tests be replaced by functional tests? Let's address these crucial questions.

11.7.1 *Choosing an approach*

There are two valid approaches:

- *Mock objects / functional testing*—Write mock-objects-style unit tests for the business logic (by separating the business logic from the database access layer). Also write mock-objects-style unit tests for the database access layer code. Finally, write functional tests to ensure the whole thing works when it's running in the deployed environment.

- *Mock objects / database integration unit tests / functional tests*—Write mock-objects-style unit tests for the business logic, as shown in section 11.6, by separating the business logic from the database access layer. Don't write mock-object unit tests for the database access layer code. Instead, write Cactus integration unit tests (possibly using some mocks to test failure conditions). Also write functional tests (as in the previous approach) for end-to-end testing.

The difference between the two approaches is that in the second, you use Cactus to perform integration unit tests. This approach provides better test coverage but requires more setup, because you need a database (or private dataspace) installed for each developer. You also need to think about builds and deployment from day one (but that can be a *good* thing).

11.7.2 *Applying continuous integration*

The Cactus approach pushes the integration issues into the development realm. This is helpful, because too often integration comes as a second phase in the project life cycle. In some projects, integration is treated almost as an afterthought!

Integration is when the real problems start to happen: Architectural decisions are changed, leading to rewriting of a portion of the application; deployment teams have not been trained beforehand and begin discovering how the application works—and of course the project becomes late. The cost of dealing with integration issues in a J2EE project is extremely high.

Our recommendation is to begin practicing packaging and deployment from day one (maybe after a first exploratory iteration) and improve the process continuously as the project progresses, by automating more and more. As you do this, you'll find that you gain increasing control over the configuration of your container, and that it takes less time to put a release into production. On a recent project, a complex system took two hours flat to deploy from development to pre-production, and we could put our system into production at any point in time.

The second approach using Cactus, discussed in the previous section, takes longer in execution time, but that shouldn't be an issue. We usually execute all the pure JUnit and mock-objects tests continuously from our development IDE and only execute the integration unit tests from time to time. For large projects, we always have a continuous build system located on a dedicated machine that runs continuously and executes all the tests all the time; it sends us an email if there is a build failure. This way, we benefit from the best of both worlds.

11.8 Summary

Most developers feel that it's difficult to unit-test applications that access a database. In this chapter, we've shown three types of simple unit tests that can test the data-access code calling the real database: *business logic unit tests* that test the business code in isolation from the database, *data access unit tests* that test the data-access code in isolation from the database, and *integration unit tests*.

Business logic tests and data access unit tests are easy to run as ordinary JUnit tests, with some help from mock objects. The MockObjects.com framework is especially useful, because it provides prewritten mocks for the SQL packages.

For integration unit tests, we have demonstrated the powerful Cactus/DbUnit combo. Not only have we succeeded in running database tests from inside the container, but we have also automated the execution of the tests using Ant. This combo paves the way for practicing *continuous integration*.

In chapter 9, we started down a path to completely unit-test a web application, including its servlets, filters, taglibs, JSPs, and database access. In this chapter, we completed that path by showing how easy it can be to unit-test database access. In the next chapter, we will introduce an EJB application that demonstrates unit-testing of EJBs.

12 Unit-testing EJBs

This chapter covers

- Unit-testing all types of EJBs: session beans, entity beans, and message-driven beans
- Using mock objects, pure JUnit, and Cactus
- Automating packaging, deployment, and container start/stop using Ant

"The time has come," the Walrus said, "To talk of many things: Of shoes—and ships—and sealing-wax—Of cabbages—and kings—And why the sea is boiling hot—And whether pigs have wings."

—Lewis Carroll, Through the Looking Glass

Testing EJBs has a reputation of being a difficult task. One of the main reasons is that EJBs are components that run inside a container. Thus, you either need to abstract out the container services used by your code or perform in-container unit testing. In this chapter, we'll demonstrate different techniques that can help you write EJB unit tests. We'll also provide guidelines and hints for helping you choose when to select one strategy over another.

12.1 *Defining a sample EJB application*

In previous chapters, we used a sample Administration application to demonstrate how to unit-test web components (servlets, filters, taglibs, JSPs) and database access code. In order to demonstrate the different EJB unit-testing techniques, we've chosen a simple order-processing application, which you'll implement using different types of EJBs components.

The inspiration for this example comes from the xPetstore application (http://xpetstore.sf.net/). xPetstore is an XDoclet version of the standard Java Pet Store demonstration application (http://developer.java.sun.com/developer/releases/petstore/). We've simplified the original xPetstore to focus on our topic of unit-testing different types of EJBs, as shown in figure 12.1.

As you can see from the figure, the sample Order application includes a message-driven bean (MDB), a remote stateless session bean (remote SLSB), and a local container-managed persistence (CMP) entity bean (local CMP EB). This chapter focuses on demonstrating how to unit-test each type of EJB. The example doesn't include stateful session beans (SFSB) because they are unit-tested in the same manner as SLSBs. In addition, we aren't covering bean-managed persistence (BMP) entity beans (BMP EB); they're the same as CMP EBs for which the

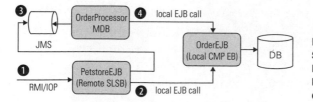

Figure 12.1
Sample Order application made of three EJBs: a remote stateless session bean, a local CMP entity bean, and a message-driven bean

persistence is performed manually, and we covered unit-testing database code in chapter 11.

The sample Order application has the following use case:

❶ The client application (whatever that is: another EJB, a Java Swing application, a servlet, and so on) calls the `PetstoreEJB` and calls its `createOrder` method.

❷ ❸ `PetStoreEJB`'s `createOrder` method creates an `OrderEJB` order and then sends a JMS message containing the Order ID to a JMS queue. With JMS you can process the different orders coming into the system asynchronously. It allows an immediate reply to the client application, indicating that the order is being processed.

❹ The JMS message is processed by the `OrderProcessorMDB` MDB, which extracts the order ID from the message in the queue, finds the corresponding `OrderEJB` EJB, and performs some business operation (you don't need to know the details of this business operation for the purpose of this chapter). In a production application, the `OrderProcessorMDB` could also send an email to the customer to tell them that their order has been processed.

We believe that the best way to demonstrate how to use the different techniques is by showing the code of this sample application as you would have written it without thinking about unit testing (or as it would have been written had it been a legacy application for which you were asked to write unit tests). Then, we'll show how the code needs to be refactored (or not refactored) to be testable, using different techniques.EJB:defining sample applications

12.2 *Using a façade strategy*

The *façade strategy* is an architectural decision that has the nice side effect of making your application more testable. This is the approach of designing for testability that we have recommended throughout this book.

Using this strategy, you consider EJBs as plumbing and move all code logic outside the EJBs. More specifically, you keep session beans or MDBs as a façade to the outside world and move all the business code into POJOs (plain old Java objects), for which you can then write unit tests easily. Yes, this is a strong architectural decision. For example, you won't use EJBs for persisting your data. Moreover, you'll need to cleanly separate any access to the container API (such as looking up objects in JNDI for obtaining data sources, JMS factories, mail sessions, and so on).

You must realize that this technique won't provide any means for unit-testing the container-related code you have separated. That code will be tested only during integration and functional tests.

This strategy will not work in the following cases:

- The application is a legacy application using EJBs that call each other (as in the `PetstoreEJB` SLSB calling the `OrderEJB` EB). Because the application is already written, it doesn't seem worthwhile to redesign it completely using a different architecture (POJOs).

- It has been decided that the application architecture has EJBs calling other EJBs.

- The application needs to access objects published in JNDI, such as data sources, JMS factories, mail sessions, EJB homes, and so on.

For all these cases, using this façade strategy won't help. For example, in the Order application, you would have to rewrite the `OrderEJB` EJB by transforming it into a class using JDBC (for example) in order to support this façade technique. But even then, you would still use JNDI to send the order ID in a JMS message. Thus, in this case, the façade technique isn't appropriate and would require too many changes.

To summarize, the façade strategy isn't a strategy to unit-test EJBs but rather a strategy to bypass testing of EJBs. You'll often read on the Web or in other books that unit-testing EJBs is a false problem and that EJBs should only be used as a pure façade, thus eliminating the need to unit-test them. Our belief is that EJBs are very useful in lots of situations and that there are several easy unit-testing techniques for exercising them, as demonstrated in the following sections.

12.3 *Unit-testing JNDI code using mock objects*

In this section and those that follow, we'll demonstrate how to use different mock-objects techniques to test session beans. We have chosen to use the DynaMock API from MockObjects.com to illustrate these techniques (see chapter 9 for an introduction to DynaMock).

Unit-testing EJB code that uses JNDI is the most difficult case to address in EJB unit testing. One reason is that the EJB homes are usually cached in static variables to enhance performance. Thus, the code to create a session bean instance usually consists of static methods.

Another complication is that you access JNDI objects by creating an `Initial-Context` (`new InitialContext()`). In other words, the JNDI API doesn't follow the Inversion Of Control (IOC) pattern. Thus, it isn't easy to pass a mock `Initial-Context` instead of the real one. However, as you'll see in one of the possible techniques, thanks to the Factory pattern followed by the JNDI API, it's possible to pass a mock `InitialContext` with a minimal amount of code.

We will now demonstrate three refactoring techniques you can use to unit-test JNDI code and, more specifically, to unit-test code that looks up EJBs (that is, that calls `InitialContext.lookup`):

- *Factory method*—Isolates the creation of domain objects in separate methods that can be overridden to return the mock instances
- *Factory class*—Isolates the creation of domain objects in factory classes, introduces setters for these factories, and provides mock factories for your tests
- *Mock JNDI implementation*—Sets up a mock JNDI implementation that returns mock objects whenever the `lookup` method is called

12.4 *Unit-testing session beans*

Let's follow the use case flow (see figure 12.1) and start by unit-testing the `Pet-storeEJB` SLSB. You'll try each of the approaches listed in the previous section. The `PetstoreEJB` code, which is the bean implementation of the `Petstore` EJB, is shown in listing 12.1.

Listing 12.1   Initial PetstoreEJB.java

```
package junitbook.ejb.service;

import java.rmi.RemoteException;
import java.util.Date;

import javax.ejb.CreateException;
import javax.ejb.EJBException;
import javax.ejb.SessionBean;
import javax.ejb.SessionContext;

import junitbook.ejb.domain.OrderLocal;
import junitbook.ejb.domain.OrderUtil;
import junitbook.ejb.util.JMSUtil;
import junitbook.ejb.util.JNDINames;

public class PetstoreEJB implements SessionBean
{
    public int createOrder(Date orderDate, String orderItem)      ❶
        throws RemoteException
    {
        OrderLocal order = OrderUtil.createOrder(orderDate,       ❷
            orderItem);

        try
        {
```

```
                    JMSUtil.sendToJMSQueue(JNDINames.QUEUE_ORDER,
                        order.getOrderId(), false);
            }
            catch (Exception e)
            {
                throw new EJBException(e);
            }
            return order.getOrderId().intValue();
        }

        public void setSessionContext(SessionContext sessionContext)
            throws EJBException, RemoteException {}
        public void ejbRemove()
            throws EJBException, RemoteException {}
        public void ejbActivate()
            throws EJBException, RemoteException {}
        public void ejbPassivate()
            throws EJBException, RemoteException {}
}
```

3

1 For simplicity, you have only one method to unit-test in `PetStoreEJB`: `createOrder`.
2 **3** As you can see from the code, this method calls two static methods—
`OrderUtil.createOrder` and `JMSUtil.sendToJMSQueue`—which, respectively, create
an `OrderEJB` EB instance and send the order ID to a JMS queue (for later processing by the `OrderProcessorMDB`, as shown in figure 12.1).

Listing 12.2 shows the code for the `OrderUtil` helper class.

Listing 12.2   Initial OrderUtil.java

```java
package junitbook.ejb.domain;

import java.util.Date;

import javax.ejb.CreateException;
import javax.ejb.FinderException;
import javax.rmi.PortableRemoteObject;

import junitbook.ejb.util.JNDINames;
import junitbook.ejb.util.JNDIUtil;

public class OrderUtil
{
    private static OrderLocalHome orderLocalHome;

    protected static OrderLocalHome getOrderHome()        1
    {
        if (orderLocalHome == null)
        {
            Object obj =
```

```
                    JNDIUtil.lookup(JNDINames.ORDER_LOCALHOME);
            orderLocalHome =
                (OrderLocalHome) PortableRemoteObject.narrow(
                    obj, OrderLocalHome.class);
        }
        return orderLocalHome;
    }

    public static OrderLocal createOrder(Date orderDate,       ❷
        String orderItem)
    {
        try
        {
            return getOrderHome().create(orderDate, orderItem);
        }
        catch (CreateException e)
        {
            throw new RuntimeException("Failed to create ["
                + OrderLocal.class.getName() + "]. Reason ["
                + e.getMessage() + "]");
        }
    }

    public static OrderLocal getOrder(Integer orderId)          ❸
    {
        try
        {
            return getOrderHome().findByPrimaryKey(orderId);
        }
        catch (FinderException e)
        {
            throw new RuntimeException("Failed to find Order "
                + "bean for id [" + orderId + "]");
        }
    }
}
```

The OrderUtil class provides two public and static helper methods: createOrder (❷) and getOrder (❶). The createOrder method creates an instance of the Order EJB, whereas getOrder retrieves an Order EJB instance by its order ID. The getOrderHome (❶) method is protected and only used internally by the other two methods introduced; it is used to retrieve the Order EJB home instance.

In this section, the challenge is to be able to unit-test the Petstore EJB's createOrder method (listing 12.1). The main issue you'll have to overcome is replacing the JNDI lookup calls to return mock objects instead of the real objects. The static methods in listing 12.2 will be the main hurdle.

Listing 12.3 shows the code for the JMSUtil helper class.

Listing 12.3   Initial JMSUtil.java

```java
package junitbook.ejb.util;

import java.io.Serializable;
import javax.jms.JMSException;
import javax.jms.ObjectMessage;
import javax.jms.Queue;
import javax.jms.QueueConnection;
import javax.jms.QueueConnectionFactory;
import javax.jms.QueueSender;
import javax.jms.QueueSession;
import javax.naming.InitialContext;
import javax.naming.NamingException;

public class JMSUtil
{
    public static void sendToJMSQueue(String queueName,          ❶
        Serializable obj, boolean transacted)
        throws NamingException, JMSException
    {
        InitialContext ic = null;
        QueueConnection cnn = null;
        QueueSender sender = null;
        QueueSession session = null;

        try
        {
            ic = new InitialContext();

            Queue queue = (Queue) ic.lookup(queueName);

            QueueConnectionFactory factory =
                (QueueConnectionFactory) ic.lookup(
                JNDINames.QUEUE_CONNECTION_FACTORY);
            cnn = factory.createQueueConnection();
            session = cnn.createQueueSession(transacted,
                QueueSession.AUTO_ACKNOWLEDGE);

            ObjectMessage msg = session.createObjectMessage(obj);

            sender = session.createSender(queue);
            sender.send(msg);
        }
        finally
        {
            if (sender != null)
            {
                sender.close();
            }
            if (session != null)
            {
                session.close();
```

```
        }
        if (cnn != null)
        {
            cnn.close();
        }
        if (ic != null)
        {
            ic.close();
        }
    }
  }
}
```

❶ The `JMSUtil` class only defines a single static `sendToJMSQueue`, which sends a given object to a queue.

12.4.1 *Using the factory method strategy*

This is one of the easiest possible refactorings because it lets you introduce the mock objects by only impacting the class under test and not any of the dependent classes it calls. In the example at hand, it impacts only the `PetstoreEJB` class.

The strategy consists of finding all the places where your method to test creates domain objects. For each of these, you introduce a factory method that returns the domain object. See figure 12.2 for an example.

```
public class SomeClass
{
    public void someMethod()
    {
        DomainObject object = new DomainObject();
        object.someOtherMethod();
    }
}
```

refactored to ⬇

```
public class SomeClass
{
    public void someMethod()
    {
        getDomainObject().someOtherMothod();
    }

    public DomainObject getDomainObject()
    {
        return new DomainObject();
    }
}
```

Figure 12.2 Performing a factory method refactoring to decouple the creation of a domain object from the method using that object, in order to replace it later with a mock object

Note that depending on the use case, you can also write a variation where the new `DomainObject` happens only once and the resulting instance is saved in a private class variable.

Refactoring the PetstoreEJB class

For the sample Order application, this means transforming the `PetstoreEJB` class into the one shown in listing 12.4 (the changes have been marked in bold).

Listing 12.4   PetstoreEJB.java after a factory method refactoring

```java
package junitbook.ejb.service;
[...]
public abstract class PetstoreEJB implements SessionBean
{
    public int createOrder(Date orderDate, String orderItem)
    {
        OrderLocal order = createOrderHelper(orderDate, orderItem);

        try
        {
            sendToJMSQueueHelper(JNDINames.QUEUE_ORDER,
                order.getOrderId(), false);
        }
        catch (Exception e)
        {
            throw new EJBException(e);
        }
        return order.getOrderId().intValue();
    }

    protected OrderLocal createOrderHelper(Date orderDate,
        String orderItem)
    {
        return OrderUtil.createOrder(orderDate, orderItem);
    }

    protected void sendToJMSQueueHelper(String queueName,
        Serializable object, boolean transacted)
        throws NamingException, JMSException
    {
        JMSUtil.sendToJMSQueue(queueName, object, transacted);
    }
[...]
```

You can now easily write a unit test for the `createOrder` method by creating a class that extends `PetstoreEJB` and overrides the `createOrderHelper` and `sendToJMS-QueueHelper` methods.

Mocking factory methods

The behavior of the overridden methods is controlled by the unit test in exactly the same spirit as mock objects. Let's call `TestablePetstoreEJB` the extended class (see listing 12.5). Said differently, the `TestablePetstore` mocks the factory methods you have introduced.

Listing 12.5   TestablePetstoreEJB (mocks the factory methods)

```
package junitbook.ejb.service;

import java.io.Serializable;
import java.util.Date;

import javax.jms.JMSException;
import javax.naming.NamingException;

import junitbook.ejb.domain.OrderLocal;

public class TestablePetstoreEJB extends PetstoreEJB
{
    private OrderLocal orderLocal;
    private JMSException jmsExceptionToThrow;
    private NamingException namingExceptionToThrow;

    public void setupCreateOrderHelper(OrderLocal orderLocal)
    {
        this.orderLocal = orderLocal;
    }

    protected OrderLocal createOrderHelper(Date orderDate,
        String orderItem)
    {
        return this.orderLocal;
    }

    public void setupThrowOnSendToJMSQueueHelper(
        JMSException exception)
    {
        this.jmsExceptionToThrow = exception;
    }

    public void setupThrowOnSendToJMSQueueHelper(
        NamingException exception)
    {
        this.namingExceptionToThrow = exception;
    }

    protected void sendToJMSQueueHelper(String queueName,
        Serializable object, boolean transacted)
        throws NamingException, JMSException
    {
        if (this.jmsExceptionToThrow != null)
        {
```

Defines what create-OrderBean method should throw when called

Defines what exception sendOrder method should throw when called

```
                    throw this.jmsExceptionToThrow;
            }
            if (this.namingExceptionToThrow != null)
            {
                    throw this.namingExceptionToThrow;
            }
        }

    }
```

Writing the unit tests

You now have all the parts you need to write the unit tests (see listing 12.6).

Listing 12.6 TestPetstoreEJB using the factory method strategy

```
package junitbook.ejb.service;
[...]
public class TestPetstoreEJB extends TestCase
{
    private TestablePetstoreEJB petstore;
    private Mock mockOrderLocal;
    private OrderLocal orderLocal;

    protected void setUp()
    {
        petstore = new TestablePetstoreEJB();              ❶

        mockOrderLocal = new Mock(OrderLocal.class);       ❷
        orderLocal = (OrderLocal) mockOrderLocal.proxy();

        petstore.setupCreateOrderHelper(orderLocal);

        mockOrderLocal.matchAndReturn("getOrderId",        ❸
            new Integer(1234));
    }

    protected void tearDown()
    {
        mockOrderLocal.verify();                           ❹
    }

    public void testCreateOrderOk() throws Exception       ❺
    {
        int orderId = petstore.createOrder(new Date(), "item1");
        assertEquals(1234, orderId);
    }

    public void testCreateOrderJMSException() throws Exception  ❻
    {
        petstore.setupThrowOnSendToJMSQueueHelper(         ❼
            new JMSException("error"));
```

```
        try
        {
            petstore.createOrder(new Date(), "item1");
            fail("Should have thrown an EJBException");
        }
        catch (EJBException e)
        {
            assertEquals("error",
                e.getCausedByException().getMessage());
        }
    }
}
```

❶ Instantiate the `TestablePetstoreEJB` class instead of `PetstoreEJB` as you would normally do for a standard test case.

❷ Create a mock `OrderLocal` bean and set up `TestablePetstoreEJB` to return it when its `createOrderHelper` method is called.

❸ Tell the `OrderLocal` mock to return the 1234 `Integer` whenever its `getOrderId` method is called. Note that if you used `expectAndReturn` instead of `matchAnd-Return`, you would need to write the following two same lines (because `expect*` calls are expected, whereas `match*` calls return the specified return value whenever they match the call):

```
mockOrderLocal.matchAndReturn("getOrderId", new Integer(1234));
mockOrderLocal.matchAndReturn("getOrderId", new Integer(1234));
```

❹ In the `tearDown` method, you tell the `OrderLocal` mock to verify the expectations set on it (all the `expect*` calls you have set up).

❺ Write the first test, which verifies that the `createOrder` method works fine when you pass valid parameters to it.

❻ Verify that the `createOrder` method correctly throws an `EJBException` when a `JMSException` is thrown when sending the JMS order message.

❼ Use the mock to simulate the `JMSException`.

12.4.2 Using the factory class strategy

The general idea for this strategy is to add setter methods to introduce all the domain objects used by the methods to test. This then allows you to call these setters, passing them mock objects from the test case classes. Namely, this means introducing protected `setOrderUtil(OrderUtil)` and `setJMSUtil(JMSUtil)` methods in the `PetstoreEJB` class.

The following refactoring tasks are involved to transform the initial Pet-storeEJB, OrderUtil, and JMSUtil classes:

- Create new OrderUtil and JMSUtil interfaces.
- Add two static private variables to PetstoreEJB.
- Add two methods to set the OrderFactory and JMSUtil domain objects.

Making the interfaces

First, you make OrderUtil and JMSUtil interfaces and rename the old OrderUtil and JMSUtil classes DefaultOrderUtil and DefaultJMSUtil. In addition, during this refactoring it becomes clear that the OrderUtil interface and Default-OrderUtil class would be better named OrderFactory and DefaultOrderFactory. This renaming illustrates that performing refactorings also make you think about what you're doing and usually lets you enhance the code with small improvements. Of course, in the renaming case, you have to be careful not to break public APIs unintentionally. The refactoring yields the following for the OrderFactory class:

```
public interface OrderFactory
{
    OrderLocal createOrder(Date orderDate, String orderItem);
    OrderLocal getOrder(Integer orderId);
}

public class DefaultOrderFactory implements OrderFactory
{
    private static OrderLocalHome orderLocalHome;

    protected OrderLocalHome getOrderHome()
    {
        [...]
    }

    public OrderLocal createOrder(Date orderDate, String orderItem)
    {
        [...]
    }

    public OrderLocal getOrder(Integer orderId)
    {
        [...]
    }
}
```

Note that you drop the static modifiers on methods (see the initial listing 12.2) because you have moved from a unique OrderUtil static class to a normal Default-OrderFactory class, allowing several instances to be created (especially a mock one).

The refactoring for the JMSUtil class gives the following:

```
public interface JMSUtil
{
    void sendToJMSQueue(String queueName, Serializable obj,
    boolean transacted) throws NamingException, JMSException;
}

public class DefaultJMSUtil implements JMSUtil
{
    public void sendToJMSQueue(String queueName, Serializable obj,
        boolean transacted) throws NamingException, JMSException
    {
        [...]
    }
}
```

Adding static private variables

Next, you add two static private variables to PetstoreEJB. These variables will hold the default OrderFactory and JMSUtil domain objects to be used by the create-Order method:

```
public abstract class PetstoreEJB implements SessionBean
{
    private static OrderFactory orderFactory =
        new DefaultOrderFactory();
    private static JMSUtil jmsUtil = new DefaultJMSUtil();
[...]
```

Adding methods to set the domain objects

Finally, add two methods to set OrderFactory and JMSUtil domain objects different from the default ones:

```
[...]
    protected void setOrderFactory(OrderFactory factory)
    {
        orderFactory = factory;
    }

    protected void setJMSUtil(JMSUtil util)
    {
        jmsUtil = util;
    }
```

Creating the test case

You can now use a standard mock-objects approach to create the TestCase, as shown in listing 12.7.

Listing 12.7   TestPetstoreEJB using the factory class strategy

```
package junitbook.ejb.service;
[...]
public class TestPetstoreEJB extends TestCase
{
    private PetstoreEJB petstore;
    private Mock mockOrderFactory;
    private Mock mockJMSUtil;
    private OrderFactory orderFactory;
    private JMSUtil jmsUtil;

    private Mock mockOrderLocal;
    private OrderLocal orderLocal;

    protected void setUp()
    {
        petstore = new PetstoreEJB() {};

        mockOrderLocal = new Mock(OrderLocal.class);
        orderLocal = (OrderLocal) mockOrderLocal.proxy();

        mockOrderFactory = new Mock(OrderFactory.class);        ❶
        orderFactory = (OrderFactory) mockOrderFactory.proxy();

        mockJMSUtil = new Mock(JMSUtil.class);
        jmsUtil = (JMSUtil) mockJMSUtil.proxy();

        petstore.setOrderFactory(orderFactory);               ❷
        petstore.setJMSUtil(jmsUtil);

        mockOrderFactory.expectAndReturn("createOrder",        ❸
            C.args(C.IS_ANYTHING, C.IS_ANYTHING), orderLocal);
        mockOrderLocal.matchAndReturn("getOrderId",
            new Integer(1234));
    }

    protected void tearDown()
    {
        mockJMSUtil.verify();
        mockOrderFactory.verify();
        mockOrderLocal.verify();
    }

    public void testCreateOrderOk() throws Exception
    {
        mockJMSUtil.expect("sendToJMSQueue",                   ❸
            C.args(C.IS_ANYTHING, C.eq(new Integer(1234)),
                C.IS_ANYTHING));

        int orderId = petstore.createOrder(new Date(), "item1");

        assertEquals(1234, orderId);
```

```
    }
    public void testCreateOrderJMSException() throws Exception
    {
        mockJMSUtil.expectAndThrow("sendToJMSQueue",                    ❸
            C.args(C.IS_ANYTHING, C.eq(new Integer(1234)),
                C.IS_ANYTHING), new JMSException("error"));

        try
        {
            petstore.createOrder(new Date(), "item1");
            fail("Should have thrown an EJBException");
        }
        catch (EJBException expected)
        {
            assertEquals("error",
                expected.getCausedByException().getMessage());
        }

    }
}
```

❶ Now that you have `OrderFactory` and `JMSUtil` interfaces, you can create mock objects for them.

❷ Call the newly introduced setter methods (`setOrderFactory` and `setJMSUtil`) to set the mock objects on the `PetstoreEJB` class.

❸ Then, as usual, tell the mocks how to behave for the different tests.

Let's now see the third strategy to introduce mock objects for unit-testing the `PetstoreEJB` `createOrder` method: the mock JNDI implementation strategy.

12.4.3 *Using the mock JNDI implementation strategy*

This is a very logical strategy that consists of mocking the JNDI implementation. It lets you write unit tests without impacting the code under test, which can be quite nice if you're writing unit tests for a legacy application, for example.

This is possible because the JNDI API offers the possibility to easily plug any JNDI implementation. You can do this several ways (using a System property, using a `jndi.properties` file, and so on); but the best way in this case is to use the `NamingManager.setInitialContextFactoryBuilder` API, which lets you set up an initial context factory. Once it has been set, every call to `new InitialContext` will call this factory.

Mocking the JNDI implementation

Here is a compact solution (using inner classes) that returns a mock Context whenever new InitialContext is called:

```
NamingManager.setInitialContextFactoryBuilder(
    new InitialContextFactoryBuilder()
    {
        public InitialContextFactory createInitialContextFactory(
            Hashtable environment) throws NamingException
        {
            return new InitialContextFactory() {
                public Context getInitialContext(Hashtable env)
                    throws NamingException
                {
                    // Return the mock context here
                    return context;
                }
            };
        }
    }
);
```

The only limitation is that the setInitialContextFactoryBuilder method can be called only once during the JVM lifetime (otherwise it will throw an IllegalState-Exception). Thus you need to wrap this initialization in a JUnit TestSetup, as shown in listing 12.8.

Listing 12.8 Setting up the JNDI implementation in a JUnit TestSetup

```
package junitbook.ejb;
[...]
public class JNDITestSetup extends TestSetup
{
    private Mock mockContext;
    private Context context;

    public JNDITestSetup(Test test)
    {
        super(test);
        mockContext = new Mock(Context.class);
        context = (Context) mockContext.proxy();
    }

    public Mock getMockContext()
    {
        return this.mockContext;
    }

    protected void setUp() throws Exception
    {
```

```
NamingManager.setInitialContextFactoryBuilder(
    new InitialContextFactoryBuilder()
    {
        public InitialContextFactory
            createInitialContextFactory(
            Hashtable environment) throws NamingException
        {
            return new InitialContextFactory() {
                public Context getInitialContext(
                    Hashtable env) throws NamingException
                {
                    // Return the mock context here
                    return context;
                }
            };
        }
    }
);
}
}
```

Note that you can reuse this JNDITestSetup class as is and put it in your unit-testing toolbox. You're now ready to write the unit tests.

Writing the test case

The TestCase is shown in listing 12.9. Note that you factorize all mock setup in the JUnit setUp method. We did not do that right away when writing this example. As a practice, we begin by writing the first test and put all needed initialization in the first test method (testCreateOrderOk). However, once we started writing the second test (testCreateThrowsOrderException), we realized that there was lots of common setup code. So, we refactored the TestCase and moved the common bits into the setUp method.

> ### JUnit best practices: refactor test setups and teardowns
>
> As you write more tests in a given TestCase, always take time to refactor by factorizing out the common code needed to set up the tests (the same applies to tearDown methods). If you don't do this, you'll end up with complex tests that cannot be easily understood, will be very difficult to maintain, and, as a consequence, will break more often.

Listing 12.9   TestPetstoreEJB using the mock JNDI implementation strategy

```java
package junitbook.ejb.service;
[...]
public class TestPetstoreEJB extends TestCase
{
    private static JNDITestSetup jndiTestSetup;

    private PetstoreEJB petstore;

    private Mock mockOrderLocalHome;
    private OrderLocalHome orderLocalHome;
    private Mock mockOrderLocal;
    private Mock mockQueue;
    private Queue queue;
    private Mock mockQueueConnectionFactory;
    private QueueConnectionFactory queueConnectionFactory;
    private Mock mockQueueConnection;
    private QueueConnection queueConnection;
    private Mock mockQueueSession;
    private Mock mockQueueSender;
    private Mock mockObjectMessage;

    public static Test suite()                              ❶
    {
        TestSuite suite = new TestSuite();
        suite.addTestSuite(TestPetstoreEJB.class);
        jndiTestSetup = new JNDITestSetup(suite);
        return jndiTestSetup;
    }

    protected void setUp() throws Exception     ❷
    {
        petstore = new PetstoreEJB() {};

        jndiTestSetup.getMockContext().reset();      ❸

        setUpOrderMocks();
        setUpJMSMocks();
        setUpJNDILookups();

        jndiTestSetup.getMockContext().matchAndReturn("close",
            null);
    }

    public void setUpOrderMocks()     ❷
    {
        mockOrderLocalHome = new Mock(OrderLocalHome.class);
        orderLocalHome =
            (OrderLocalHome) mockOrderLocalHome.proxy();

        mockOrderLocal = new Mock(OrderLocal.class);
        OrderLocal orderLocal = (OrderLocal) mockOrderLocal.proxy();

        mockOrderLocalHome.matchAndReturn("create", C.ANY_ARGS,
```

```
        orderLocal);
    mockOrderLocalHome.matchAndReturn("findByPrimaryKey",
        new Integer(1234), orderLocal);
    mockOrderLocal.matchAndReturn("getOrderId",
        new Integer(1234));
}

public void setUpJMSMocks()        ❷
{
    mockQueue = new Mock(Queue.class);
    queue = (Queue) mockQueue.proxy();

    mockQueueConnectionFactory =
        new Mock(QueueConnectionFactory.class);
    queueConnectionFactory = (QueueConnectionFactory)
        mockQueueConnectionFactory.proxy();

    mockQueueConnection = new Mock(QueueConnection.class);
    queueConnection =
        (QueueConnection) mockQueueConnection.proxy();
    mockQueueConnection.matchAndReturn("close", null);

    mockObjectMessage = new Mock(ObjectMessage.class);
    ObjectMessage objectMessage =
        (ObjectMessage) mockObjectMessage.proxy();

    mockQueueSession = new Mock(QueueSession.class);
    QueueSession queueSession =
        (QueueSession) mockQueueSession.proxy();
    mockQueueSession.matchAndReturn("close", null);
    mockQueueSession.matchAndReturn("createObjectMessage",
        C.ANY_ARGS, objectMessage);

    mockQueueConnection.matchAndReturn("createQueueSession",
        C.ANY_ARGS, queueSession);

    mockQueueSender = new Mock(QueueSender.class);
    QueueSender queueSender =
        (QueueSender) mockQueueSender.proxy();
    mockQueueSender.matchAndReturn("close", null);
    mockQueueSender.matchAndReturn("send", C.ANY_ARGS, null);

    mockQueueSession.matchAndReturn("createSender",
        C.ANY_ARGS, queueSender);
}

public void setUpJNDILookups()        ❷
{
    jndiTestSetup.getMockContext().matchAndReturn(
        "lookup", JNDINames.ORDER_LOCALHOME, orderLocalHome);
    jndiTestSetup.getMockContext().matchAndReturn(
        "lookup", JNDINames.QUEUE_ORDER, queue);
    jndiTestSetup.getMockContext().matchAndReturn(
        "lookup", JNDINames.QUEUE_CONNECTION_FACTORY,
```

```
            queueConnectionFactory);
    }

    protected void tearDown()
    {
        jndiTestSetup.getMockContext().verify();
        mockOrderLocal.verify();
        mockOrderLocalHome.verify();
        mockQueue.verify();
        mockQueueConnection.verify();
        mockQueueConnectionFactory.verify();
        mockQueueSender.verify();
        mockQueueSession.verify();
        mockObjectMessage.verify();
    }

    public void testCreateOrderOk() throws Exception
    {
        mockQueueConnectionFactory.expectAndReturn(
            "createQueueConnection", queueConnection);

        int orderId = petstore.createOrder(new Date(), "item1");

        assertEquals(1234, orderId);
    }

    public void testCreateThrowsOrderException() throws Exception
    {
        mockQueueConnectionFactory.expectAndThrow(
            "createQueueConnection", new JMSException("error"));

        try
        {
            petstore.createOrder(new Date(), "item1");
            fail("Should have thrown an EJBException");
        }
        catch (EJBException expected)
        {
            assertEquals("error",
                expected.getCausedByException().getMessage());
        }
    }
}
```

❶ Use the JNDITestSetup class to set up the mock JNDI implementation only once.

❷ Create all the mocks and define their expected behaviors common for all tests (the behavior specific to a given test is in the test*XXX* method).

❸ This is the tricky part in this listing. The call to NamingManager.setInitial-ContextFactoryBuilder must happen only once per JVM (otherwise an Illegal-StateException is thrown). So, you need to share the MockContext mock across tests. Thus the jndiTestSetup variable is static so that jndiTestSetup.getMockContext always returns the same MockContext instance. The end consequence is that you need to reset the MockContext mock before each test so that it doesn't carry the expectations set on it from one test to another.

The rest of the code is straightforward; it looks the same as the code you saw in the previous section.

Extending the code for other tests

Here's an observation about the time it takes to write this test and to initialize all these mocks. Looking at the code's length, it seems this last strategy may be more costly than the previous ones. This isn't completely true. Indeed, in the factory method strategy and in the factory class strategy, you unit-test *only* the PetstoreEJB.createOrder method. However, in this JNDI implementation strategy, you unit-test not only the Petstore.createOrder method but also a good part of the OrderUtil.createOrder and JMSUtil.sendToJMSQueue methods. In addition, you also test the interactions between PetstoreEJB, OrderUtil, and JMSUtil; these weren't tested with the other strategies. Thus, with the other strategies you also need to write unit tests for OrderUtil and JMSUtil—and the combined length of the test code is either greater than or equivalent to the code you had to write in the mock JNDI implementation strategy.

Said another way, you have set up all the mock objects necessary for writing all unit tests revolving around PetstoreEJB, OrderUtil, JMSUtil, and OrderEJB. It's now very easy to write unit tests for any method of these objects. Indeed, at this stage, the refactoring you should perform is to move all the setup code in the setUp method to a CommonPetstoreTestCase class that can be extended by the different TestCases (see listing 12.10).

Listing 12.10 Common mock initialization for the simple Petstore application

```
package junitbook.ejb;
[...]
public class CommonPetstoreTestCase extends TestCase
{
    protected static JNDITestSetup jndiTestSetup;

    protected Mock mockOrderLocalHome;
    protected OrderLocalHome orderLocalHome;
    protected Mock mockOrderLocal;
    protected Mock mockQueue;
    protected Queue queue;
    protected Mock mockQueueConnectionFactory;
```

```java
    protected QueueConnectionFactory queueConnectionFactory;
    protected Mock mockQueueConnection;
    protected QueueConnection queueConnection;
    protected Mock mockQueueSession;
    protected Mock mockQueueSender;

    public static Test suite(Class testClass)
    {
        TestSuite suite = new TestSuite();
        suite.addTestSuite(testClass);
        jndiTestSetup = new JNDITestSetup(suite);
        return jndiTestSetup;
    }

    protected void setUp() throws Exception
    {
        jndiTestSetup.getMockContext().reset();

        setUpOrderMocks();
        setUpJMSMocks();
        setUpJNDILookups();

        jndiTestSetup.getMockContext().matchAndReturn("close",
            null);
    }

    public void setUpOrderMocks()
    {
        // same as in listing 12.9
        [...]
    }

    public void setUpJMSMocks()
    {
        // same as in listing 12.9
        [...]
    }

    public void setUpJNDILookups()
    {
        // same as in listing 12.9
        [...]
    }

    protected void tearDown()
    {
        // same as in listing 12.9
        [...]
    }
}
```

There are only two differences from listing 12.9. You make the class variables protected instead of private, so that they can accessed by subclasses. You also add a parameter to the static `suite` method so that suites can be easily created by subclasses.

To demonstrate the value of `CommonPetstoreTestCase`, let's write unit tests for `OrderUtil` as shown in listing 12.11 (see listing 12.2 for the `OrderUtil` sources).

Listing 12.11 Unit tests for OrderUtil using CommonPetstoreTestCase

```
package junitbook.ejb.domain;

import java.util.Date;
import javax.ejb.CreateException;
import com.mockobjects.dynamic.C;
import junit.framework.Test;
import junitbook.ejb.CommonPetstoreTestCase;

public class TestOrderUtil extends CommonPetstoreTestCase
{
    public static Test suite()
    {
        return suite(TestOrderUtil.class);
    }

    public void testGetOrderHomeOk() throws Exception
    {
        OrderLocalHome olh = OrderUtil.getOrderHome();
        assertNotNull(olh);
    }

    public void testGetOrderHomeFromCache() throws Exception
    {
        // First call to ensure the home is in the cache
        OrderUtil.getOrderHome();

        // Make sure the lookup method is NOT called thus proving
        // the object is served from the cache
        jndiTestSetup.getMockContext().expectNotCalled("lookup");      ❶
        OrderUtil.getOrderHome();
    }

    public void testCreateOrderThrowsCreateException()
        throws Exception
    {
        mockOrderLocalHome.expectAndThrow("create", C.ANY_ARGS,
            new CreateException("error"));

        try
        {
            OrderUtil.createOrder(new Date(), "item 1");
            fail("Should have thrown a RuntimeException here");
```

```
            }
            catch (RuntimeException expected)
            {
                assertEquals("Failed to create "
                    + "[junitbook.ejb.domain.OrderLocal]. Reason "
                    + "[error]", expected.getMessage());
            }
        }
    }
```

The tests are similar to those you've written so far. The only difference is in the `testGetOrderHomeFromCache` test, which verifies that the caching of the `Order` EJB home works. You test this by calling the `OrderUtil.getOrderHome` method twice, and you verify that the second time it's called, it isn't looking up the EJB home in JNDI (❶).

As you can see, you haven't had the burden of defining and setting up mocks again, because their definitions have been externalized in `CommonPetstoreTest-Case`. You have focused on writing the test logic, and the tests can be read easily. However, if you run this test case, it fails in the `testCreateOrderThrowsCreate-Exception` method.

Resolving the EJB home caching issue

Let's take the time to understand why the test fails, because it's a common issue in unit-testing EJB code. The reason for the `testCreateOrderThrowsCreateException` test failure lies in the caching of the EJB home in `OrderUtil`. You cache the home with the following code:

```
public class OrderUtil
{
    private static OrderLocalHome orderLocalHome;

    protected static OrderLocalHome getOrderHome()
    {
        if (orderLocalHome == null)
        {
            Object obj =
                JNDIUtil.lookup(JNDINames.ORDER_LOCALHOME);
            orderLocalHome =
                (OrderLocalHome) PortableRemoteObject.narrow(
                    obj, OrderLocalHome.class);
        }
        return orderLocalHome;
    }
[...]
```

The side effect is that the first test you run results in the `OrderLocalHome` mock being cached, along with the expectations set on it. Thus, the behavior of the `create` method defined in listing 12.11 (`mockOrderLocalHome.expectAndThrow("create", C.ANY_ARGS, new CreateException("error"))`) isn't used; instead, the behavior from the previous test is used (`mockOrderLocalHome.matchAndReturn("create", C.ANY_ARGS, orderLocal)`), leading to an error.

To fix this problem, you must reset the objects in their pristine states before each test. This is normally assured by the JUnit framework—except, of course, when you use static variables. One solution is to introduce an `OrderUtil.clearCache` method that you call in the `TestOrderUtil.setUp` method:

```
public class OrderUtil
{
    private static OrderLocalHome orderLocalHome;

    protected static void clearCache()
    {
        orderLocalHome = null;
    }

    protected static OrderLocalHome getOrderHome()
    {
        [...]
    }
[...]

public class TestOrderUtil extends CommonPetstoreTestCase
{
[...]
    protected void setUp() throws Exception
    {
        super.setUp();
        OrderUtil.clearCache();
    }
[...]
```

Running the tests now succeeds, as shown in figure 12.3.

12.5 *Using mock objects to test message-driven beans*

Unit-testing MDBs is easy when you use a mock-objects approach. The reason is that the JMS API is well designed: It uses a lot of interfaces and, in most cases, uses an IOC strategy by passing all the needed objects to method calls. Thus all the object instantiations are done in the client code, which makes it easier to control and mock. Let's see what this means on the simple Petstore application

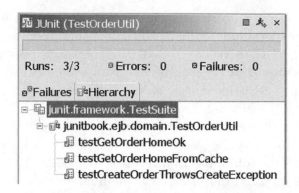

Figure 12.3 **Successful test after fixing the EJB home caching issue that prevented you from running the unit tests independently of one another**

by unit-testing the OrderProcessorMDB MDB (see figure 12.1). The method to unit test, onMessage, is shown in listing 12.12.

Listing 12.12 OrderProcessorMDB.java

```java
package junitbook.ejb.service;

import javax.ejb.EJBException;
import javax.ejb.MessageDrivenBean;
import javax.ejb.MessageDrivenContext;
import javax.jms.Message;
import javax.jms.MessageListener;
import javax.jms.ObjectMessage;

import junitbook.ejb.domain.OrderLocal;
import junitbook.ejb.domain.OrderUtil;

public class OrderProcessorMDB
    implements MessageDrivenBean, MessageListener
{
    public void onMessage(Message recvMsg)
    {
        ObjectMessage msg = (ObjectMessage) recvMsg;

        Integer orderId;
        try
        {
            orderId = (Integer) msg.getObject();
            OrderLocal order = OrderUtil.getOrder(orderId);
            proceedOrder(order);
        }
        catch (Exception e)
        {
            throw new EJBException("Error processing order...");
        }
    }

    private void proceedOrder(OrderLocal order) throws Exception
```

```
    {
        // Perform some business logic here and notify the customer
        // possibly by sending an email.
    }
    public void ejbCreate() {}
    public void setMessageDrivenContext(
        MessageDrivenContext context) {}
    public void ejbRemove() {}
}
```

This is similar to what you did in the previous sections when unit-testing session beans. Like session beans, MDBs can be unit-tested using several mock objects techniques: the factory method approach, the factory class strategy, or the mock JNDI implementation approach.

Let's use the mock JNDI implementation strategy and reuse the `CommonPet-storeTestCase` test case from listing 12.10. The resulting test case is shown in listing 12.13.

Listing 12.13   Unit test for OrderProcessorMDB.onMessage

```
package junitbook.ejb.service;

import javax.jms.ObjectMessage;

import com.mockobjects.dynamic.Mock;

import junit.framework.Test;
import junitbook.ejb.CommonPetstoreTestCase;
import junitbook.ejb.service.OrderProcessorMDB;

public class TestOrderProcessorMDB extends CommonPetstoreTestCase
{
    private OrderProcessorMDB orderProcessor;

    public static Test suite()                          ➊ Required to
    {                                                      initialize
        return suite(TestOrderProcessorMDB.class);         CommonPetstore-
    }                                                      TestCase

    protected void setUp() throws Exception
    {
        super.setUp();

        orderProcessor = new OrderProcessorMDB();
    }

    public void testOnMessageOk() throws Exception
    {
        Mock mockMessage = new Mock(ObjectMessage.class);
```

```
        ObjectMessage message =
            (ObjectMessage) mockMessage.proxy();

        mockMessage.expectAndReturn("getObject",
            new Integer(1234));

        orderProcessor.onMessage(message);

        mockMessage.verify();
    }
}
```

12.6   Using mock objects to test entity beans

Entity beans are the easiest to unit-test in isolation, especially if they are CMP entity beans. In that case, they are very much like standard Java beans. (For BMP entity beans, refer to chapter 11, "Unit-testing database applications," which shows how to unit-test JDBC code.)

Listing 12.14 shows the code for the OrderEJB CMP EB from the Petstore application (see figure 12.1).

Listing 12.14   OrderEJB.java

```java
package junitbook.ejb.domain;

import java.rmi.RemoteException;
import java.util.Date;

import javax.ejb.CreateException;
import javax.ejb.EJBException;
import javax.ejb.EntityBean;
import javax.ejb.EntityContext;
import javax.ejb.RemoveException;

public abstract class OrderEJB implements EntityBean
{
    public abstract Integer getOrderId();
    public abstract void setOrderId(Integer orderId);
    public abstract Date getOrderDate();
    public abstract void setOrderDate(Date orderDate);
    public abstract String getOrderItem();
    public abstract void setOrderItem(String item);

    public OrderLocal ejbCreate(Date orderDate, String orderItem)
        throws CreateException
    {
        int uid = 0;

        // Note: Would need a real counter here. This is a hack!
        uid = orderDate.hashCode() + orderItem.hashCode();

        setOrderId(new Integer(uid));
```

```
        setOrderDate(orderDate);
        setOrderItem(orderItem);

        return null;
    }
    public void ejbPostCreate(Date orderDate, String orderItem)
        throws CreateException {}
    public void ejbActivate()
        throws EJBException, RemoteException {}
    public void ejbLoad()
        throws EJBException, RemoteException {}
    public void ejbPassivate()
        throws EJBException, RemoteException {}
    public void ejbRemove()
        throws RemoveException, EJBException, RemoteException {}
    public void ejbStore()
        throws EJBException, RemoteException {}
    public void setEntityContext(EntityContext context)
        throws EJBException, RemoteException {}
    public void unsetEntityContext()
        throws EJBException, RemoteException {}
}
```

Let's unit-test the `ejbCreate` method. The only issue is that when you're using the EJB 2.0 specification, a CMP EB is an abstract class and the field getters and setters are not implemented. You need to create a class that extends `OrderEJB` and implements the getters and setters. (Note that doing so is very easy with a good IDE, because every good IDE has a "Generate Getters and Setters" feature.) Let's implement it as an inner class of the `TestCase` (see listing 12.15).

Listing 12.15   Unit-testing OrderEJB.ejbCreate

```
package junitbook.ejb.domain;

import java.util.Date;

import junit.framework.TestCase;

public class TestOrderEJB extends TestCase
{
    public class TestableOrderEJB extends OrderEJB          Make abstract EJB
    {                                                       testable
        private Integer orderId;
        private String item;
        private Date date;

        public Integer getOrderId()
            { return this.orderId; }
```

```
        public void setOrderId(Integer orderId)                    ↑  Make abstract EJB
            { this.orderId = orderId; }                               testable
        public Date getOrderDate()
            { return this.date; }
        public void setOrderDate(Date orderDate)
            { this.date = orderDate; }
        public String getOrderItem()
            { return this.item; }
        public void setOrderItem(String item)
            { this.item = item; }
    }

    public void testEjbCreateOk() throws Exception
    {
        TestableOrderEJB order = new TestableOrderEJB();

        Date date = new Date();
        String item = "item 1";

        order.ejbCreate(date, item);

        assertEquals(order.getOrderDate().hashCode()
            + order.getOrderItem().hashCode(),
            order.getOrderId().intValue());
        assertEquals(date, order.getOrderDate());
        assertEquals(item, order.getOrderItem());
    }
}
```

∎

> **NOTE** If the code that generates a unique ID was more complicated (which would be the case in a real-life application), you might need to mock it.

The attentive reader will have noticed that unit-testing an ejbCreate method using a mock-objects approach isn't fantastically interesting. Using mock objects to unit-test EB business logic is fine; but ejbCreate is called by the container, which returns a proxy that implements the abstract OrderEJB. Thus, it usually makes more sense to perform an integration unit test for testing ejbCreate, as you'll see in the next section.

12.7 *Choosing the right mock-objects strategy*

We have discussed three strategies. Choosing the right one for a given situation isn't always easy. Table 12.1 lists the pros and cons of each strategy, to help you make the correct choice.

Table 12.1 Pros and cons of the different mock-objects strategies for unit-testing EJBs

Strategy	Pros	Cons
Factory method refactoring	Makes unit tests quick to write	Needs to refactor the class under test. Unfortunately, the refactoring doesn't usually improve the code.
Factory class refactoring	Supposed to improve code flexibility and quality	Doesn't work too well with EJBs because the EJB model doesn't lend itself to user-provided factories (only the container is supposed to provide factory implementations). In addition, requires large amounts of code refactoring.
Mock JNDI implementation	Provides a good common fixture setup for all EJB unit tests and requires minimal (if any) code refactoring	Initial tests take more time to write because all domain objects used need to be mocked. This leads to lengthy setUp code.

12.8 Using integration unit tests

The best feature of a J2EE container is that it provides several services for the EJBs it hosts (persistence, life cycle, remote access, transactions, security, and so on). Thus developers are freed from coding these technical details. The flip side is that there are many deployment descriptors and container configuration files. So, in order to have confidence that the J2EE application is working, it's important to write unit tests not only for the Java code but also for the descriptors/configuration files. Testing these metadata could be delegated to functional testing, but then you face the same issues as when you don't have unit tests: It's harder to find the cause of bugs, bugs are found later in the development process, and not everything that could break is tested.

As a consequence, performing integration unit tests for an EJB application is very useful. If you start doing it early, you'll also be rewarded because you'll learn as you go to configure your container properly, you'll validate your database data set, and, more generally, you'll be able to deliver a working application at each development iteration.

There are two main solutions for writing integration unit tests for EJBs: pure JUnit test cases making remote calls, and Cactus.[1] We'll discuss these solutions in sections 12.9 and 12.10.

12.9 *Using JUnit and remote calls*

It's possible to use JUnit directly to unit-test EJBs, without the need for any other extension. However, this technique has several limitations:

- *Requires remote interfaces*—It only works with EJBs that present remote interfaces. Any EJB that only has a local interface can't be tested using pure JUnit,

- *Doesn't run from the production execution environment*—Very often, the production code that calls the EJBs is server-side code (servlets, JSPs, taglibs, or filters). This means that if you run the tests from a standard JUnit test case, your tests will run in a different execution environment than the production one. For example, you may write `new InitialContext` in server-side code to get access to the `InitialContext` (if the servlet and EJB containers are co-located), whereas you need to use the `new InitialContext(Properties)` form when writing client-side code, because you need to specify the address of the JNDI server and the credentials to access it.

- *Requires data setup and database startup*—Before you can call your JUnit tests, you need to set up data in your database and start your container. Possibly you'll want to automate this process as well.

- *Has limitations of functional tests*—Performing remote EJB calls is more like doing functional unit testing than unit testing. How do you test exception cases, for example? Imagine that you're testing `PetstoreEJB.createOrder` (see listing 12.1) and you want to verify the behavior when `OrderUtil.createOrder` throws a `RuntimeException`. This isn't possible with a pure JUnit solution calling a remote EJB.

Let's see how you can unit-test the Petstore application. You know that you won't be able to unit-test `OrderEJB` (see figure 12.1) because it's a local interface. However, luckily, both `OrderProcessorMDB` and `PetstoreEJB` have remote interfaces you can test. Let's test them, starting with the `PetstoreEJB` SLSB.

---

[1] There is also JUnitEE (http://www.junitee.org/), a JUnit test runner that executes JUnit test cases in the container. However, we won't discuss it, because most (if not all) of the JUnitEE features are also available in Cactus, which we use and describe in this chapter.

12.9.1 *Requirements for using JUnit directly*

Because you need a J2EE container and a database for executing these tests, you'll use JBoss and Hypersonic SQL for this example. (See chapter 11 for details on how to preset database data before the test using DBUnit.)

In addition to the source code, you need some configuration files to have a working application. The mock-objects solution shown at the beginning of this chapter only unit-tests the code, not the configuration file; thus you haven't had to write these files yet.

You need at least the application.xml file, which is the descriptor for packaging the application as an ear, and the ejb-jar.xml file, which is the descriptor for the Petstore EJB-jar. You also need some other files, but you'll discover these requirements as you progress through the examples.

Finally, you need to begin thinking about the project directory structure and decide where to put these files. You also need to think about the build system (which you use to build the ear, start the server, run the tests, and so on). Which build system will you use (Maven, Ant, Centipede)? It's good to ask all these questions as early as possible in the project life cycle, because it takes time to set everything up. This is the condition to have a working application! For the purpose of this exercise, you'll use Ant as the build tool.

Defining a directory structure

Let's use Ant to build the application and execute the JUnit tests. Figure 12.4 shows the directory structure.

Notice the conf/ directory where you put the configuration files: application.xml and ejb-jar.xml. You'll add other configuration files as you progress with the tests.

The src/ directory contains, as usual, the runtime sources and the test sources. The TestPetstoreEJB.java file contains the JUnit tests calling the PetstoreEJB EJB remotely. At the root are the usual Ant build.xml and build.properties files for building the project and running the tests automatically.

12.9.2 *Packaging the Petstore application in an ear file*

Let's start with the build file and see how to generate the application ear file. Listing 12.16 shows an Ant build script that has targets to compile the Petstore application source code, generate an EJB-jar, and wrap the whole thing in an ear file. Notice that to have a valid EJB-jar, you need to have an ejb-jar.xml deployment descriptor; and to have a valid ear, you need an application.xml descriptor.

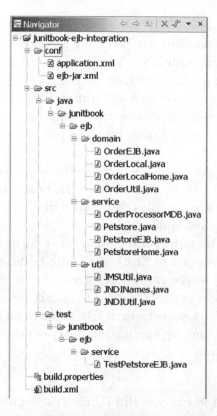

Figure 12.4
Full directory structure, including configuration files and Ant build files

---

Listing 12.16   Ant build.xml (targets to generate the Petstore ear file)

```xml
<?xml version="1.0"?>

<project name="Ejb" default="test" basedir=".">

  <property file="build.properties"/>

  <property name="conf.dir" location="conf"/>
  <property name="src.dir" location="src"/>
  <property name="src.java.dir" location="${src.dir}/java"/>

  <property name="target.dir" location="target"/>
  <property name="target.classes.java.dir"
    location="${target.dir}/classes"/>

  <target name="compile">    Compiles runtime classes
    <mkdir dir="${target.classes.java.dir}"/>
    <javac destdir="${target.classes.java.dir}"
      srcdir="${src.java.dir}">
    <classpath>
      <pathelement location="${j2ee.jar}"/>
    </classpath>
```

Generic Ant properties pointing to location on filesystem

```
        </javac>
    </target>

    <target name="ejbjar" depends="compile">          Generates EJB-jar
        <jar destfile="${target.dir}/ejb.jar">
            <metainf dir="${conf.dir}">
                <include name="ejb-jar.xml"/>
            </metainf>
            <fileset dir="${target.classes.java.dir}"/>
        </jar>
    </target>

    <target name="ear" depends="ejbjar">              Generates ear file
        <ear destfile="${target.dir}/ejb.ear"
            appxml="${conf.dir}/application.xml">
            <fileset dir="${target.dir}">
                <include name="ejb.jar"/>
            </fileset>
        </ear>
    </target>

</project>
```

The `build.properties` file contains Ant properties whose values depend on where you have put jars and where you have installed JBoss on your machine (see listing 12.17). (Installing JBoss is easy: Download it from http://jboss.org/ and unzip the zip file anywhere on your machine.)

Listing 12.17   build.properties (initial version)

```
jboss.home.dir = C:/Apps/jboss-3.2.1
jboss.server.dir = ${jboss.home.dir}/server/default
jboss.deploy.dir = ${jboss.server.dir}/deploy

j2ee.jar = ${jboss.server.dir}/lib/jboss-j2ee.jar
```

Listing 12.18 shows the ear `application.xml` deployment descriptor used by the ear Ant task in listing 12.16.

Listing 12.18   application.xml

```
<?xml version="1.0"?>

<!DOCTYPE application PUBLIC
    '-//Sun Microsystems, Inc.//DTD J2EE Application 1.2//EN'
    'http://java.sun.com/j2ee/dtds/application_1_2.dtd'>

<application>
```

```
<display-name>ejb</display-name>
<description>Sample Petstore Application</description>
<module>
   <ejb>ejb.jar</ejb>
</module>
</application>
```

Listing 12.19 shows the EJB deployment descriptor (`ejb-jar.xml`).[2]

Listing 12.19   ejb-jar.xml

```
<?xml version="1.0"?>

<!DOCTYPE ejb-jar PUBLIC
  '-//Sun Microsystems, Inc.//DTD Enterprise JavaBeans 2.0//EN'
  'http://java.sun.com/dtd/ejb-jar_2_0.dtd'>

<ejb-jar>
  <enterprise-beans>

   <session>
      <ejb-name>Petstore</ejb-name>
      <home>junitbook.ejb.service.PetstoreHome</home>
      <remote>junitbook.ejb.service.Petstore</remote>
      <ejb-class>junitbook.ejb.service.PetstoreEJB</ejb-class>
      <session-type>Stateless</session-type>
      <transaction-type>Container</transaction-type>
      <resource-env-ref>
        <resource-env-ref-name>
➜         jms/queue/petstore/Order</resource-env-ref-name>
        <resource-env-ref-type>
➜         javax.jms.Queue</resource-env-ref-type>
      </resource-env-ref>
   </session>

   <entity>
      <ejb-name>Order</ejb-name>
      <local-home>junitbook.ejb.domain.OrderLocalHome</local-home>
      <local>junitbook.ejb.domain.OrderLocal</local>
      <ejb-class>junitbook.ejb.domain.OrderEJB</ejb-class>
      <persistence-type>Container</persistence-type>
      <prim-key-class>java.lang.Integer</prim-key-class>
      <reentrant>False</reentrant>
      <cmp-version>2.x</cmp-version>
```

---

[2] The deployment descriptors can also be automatically generated by XDoclet (http://xdoclet.sourceforge.net/). XDoclet is a wonderful tool that makes EJB development easier by generating most of the needed files. For more information on XDoclet, see *XDoclet in Action* by Craig Walls and Norman Richards (Greenwich, CT: Manning, 2003).

```
        <abstract-schema-name>Order</abstract-schema-name>
        <cmp-field>
          <field-name>orderId</field-name>
        </cmp-field>
        <cmp-field>
          <field-name>orderDate</field-name>
        </cmp-field>
        <cmp-field>
          <field-name>orderItem</field-name>
        </cmp-field>
        <primkey-field>orderId</primkey-field>
    </entity>

    <message-driven>
      <ejb-name>OrderProcessor</ejb-name>
      <ejb-class>junitbook.ejb.service.OrderProcessorMDB</ejb-class>
      <transaction-type>Container</transaction-type>
      <message-driven-destination>
        <destination-type>javax.jms.Queue</destination-type>
      </message-driven-destination>
    </message-driven>

  </enterprise-beans>
  <assembly-descriptor/>
</ejb-jar>
```

Executing ant ear generates the application ear, ready to be deployed in JBoss.

12.9.3 *Performing automatic deployment and execution of tests*

Let's now modify build.xml (see listing 12.20) to include a deployment target and targets for starting and stopping JBoss.

> **Listing 12.20   Additional targets in build.xml to deploy the ear and start and stop JBoss**

```
<?xml version="1.0"?>

<project name="Ejb" default="test" basedir=".">

  [...]
  <property name="src.test.dir" location="${src.dir}/test"/>

  [...]
  <property name="target.classes.test.dir"
      location="${target.dir}/classes-test"/>

  [...]
  <target name="compile.test" depends="compile">
    <mkdir dir="${target.classes.test.dir}"/>
    <javac destdir="${target.classes.test.dir}"
        srcdir="${src.test.dir}">
```

```
      <classpath>
        <pathelement location="${j2ee.jar}"/>
        <pathelement location="${junit.jar}"/>
        <pathelement location="${target.classes.java.dir}"/>
      </classpath>
    </javac>
  </target>

  [...]
  <target name="deploy" depends="ear">
    <copy todir="${jboss.deploy.dir}"
        file="${target.dir}/ejb.ear"/>
  </target>

  <target name="start" depends="deploy">
    <java classname="org.jboss.Main" fork="yes">
      <jvmarg
          value="-Dprogram.name=${jboss.home.dir}/bin/run.bat"/>
      <arg line="-c default"/>
      <classpath>
        <pathelement location="${jboss.home.dir}/bin/run.jar"/>
        <pathelement path="${java.home}/../lib/tools.jar"/>
      </classpath>
    </java>
  </target>

  <target name="stop">
    <java classname="org.jboss.Shutdown" fork="yes">
      <arg line="-s localhost"/>
      <classpath>
        <pathelement
            location="${jboss.home.dir}/bin/shutdown.jar"/>
        <pathelement path="${java.home}/../lib/tools.jar"/>
      </classpath>
    </java>
    <sleep seconds="15"/>
  </target>

</project>
```

The deployment is simple and consists of dropping the ear file into the correct
JBoss `deploy` directory. The `compile.test` target compiles the test classes. You start
and stop JBoss by starting a JVM and calling the correct JBoss Java class (JBoss is a
Java application).

This code is fine, but you still need a `test` target that performs the orchestra-
tion of all these individual targets.

Creating a test target

In the test target, you need to deploy the ear, call the start target in a separate thread (so you can continue executing build commands), wait for the server to be started, run the tests, and stop JBoss. Fortunately, Ant 1.5+ has a nice parallel task that runs build commands on a separate thread, as shown in listing 12.21. (Note that this code can be further improved using the Ant http and socket tags from the condition task, but doing so is outside the scope of the example.)

Listing 12.21   Adding a test target to build.xml

```xml
<target name="test" depends="compile.test">
  <parallel>
    <antcall target="start"/>
    <sequential>
      <sleep seconds="30"/>
      <antcall target="run"/>
    </sequential>
  </parallel>
</target>

<target name="runtest">
  <junit printsummary="yes" fork="yes" errorproperty="test.error"        ❶
      failureproperty="test.failure">
    <formatter type="plain" usefile="false"/>
    <test name="junitbook.ejb.service.TestPetstoreEJB"/>
    <classpath>
      <pathelement location="${target.classes.java.dir}"/>
      <pathelement location="${target.classes.test.dir}"/>
      <fileset dir="${jboss.home.dir}/client">
        <include name="*.jar"/>
      </fileset>
    </classpath>
  </junit>
</target>

<target name="checktestfailures" if="test.failure">        ❶
  <fail>There were test failures</fail>
</target>

<target name="checktesterrors" if="test.error">        ❶
  <fail>There were test errors</fail>
</target>

<target name="run"
    depends="runtest,stop,checktesterrors,checktestfailures">        ❶
</target>
```

Note that you use the errorproperty and failureproperty attributes of the junit Ant task (❶). You use these attributes instead of the more familiar haltonfailure and haltonerror attributes because you want the stop target to be called whatever the outcome of the test, in order to cleanly stop the container.

Verifying deployment

To verify that the application deploys correctly, type **ant test** and relax. The output is shown in figure 12.5.

> **NOTE**   Before you run JBoss 3.2.1 for the first time, you need to edit the server/default/conf/jboss-service.xml file (located in the directory where you installed JBoss) and change the line
>
> ```
> <attribute name="RecursiveSearch">False</attribute>
> ```
>
> to
>
> ```
> <attribute name="RecursiveSearch">True</attribute>
> ```
>
> The reason is that JBoss 3.2.1 was shipped with an incorrect value that prevents the JMS services from being deployed correctly. If you don't make this change, you'll get a *DefaultJMSProvider not bound* error when JBoss tries to deploy the OrderProcessorMDB MDB.

```
C:\WINDOWS\System32\cmd.exe                                           _  □

    [java] 22:55:27.671 INFO  [MainDeployer] Starting deployment of package: file:/C:/App
s/jboss-3.2.1/server/default/deploy/ejb.ear
    [java] 22:55:27.671 INFO  [EARDeployer] Init J2EE application: file:/C:/Apps/jboss-3.
2.1/server/default/deploy/ejb.ear
    [java] 22:55:28.433 WARN  [verifier] EJB spec violation:
    [java] Bean   : Order
    [java] Method : public OrderLocal ejbCreate(Date, String) throws CreateException
    [java] Section: 10.6.4
    [java] Warning: The return type of an ejbCreate(...) method must be the entity bean's
 primary key type.

    [java] 22:55:28.433 WARN  [verifier] EJB spec violation:
    [java] Bean   : Petstore
    [java] Section: 7.10.3
    [java] Warning: A Session bean must define at least one ejbCreate method.

    [java] 22:55:28.433 WARN  [verifier] EJB spec violation:
    [java] Bean   : Petstore
    [java] Section: 7.10.2
    [java] Warning: Session bean class must not be abstract.

    [java] 22:55:28.463 ERROR [MainDeployer] could not create deployment: file:/C:/Apps/j
boss-3.2.1/server/default/tmp/deploy/server/default/deploy/ejb.ear/29.ejb.ear-contents/ejb
.jar
    [java] org.jboss.deployment.DeploymentException: Verification of Enterprise Beans fai
led, see above for error messages.
```

Figure 12.5   Boss deployment errors when running the Ant test target

Argh! And you thought the application was working! It doesn't even deploy! The output shows that you have at least three errors. We say "at least" because errors are like trains—one error can hide another. In practice, there are seven errors, as shown in table 12.2. Note that we purposely didn't include these errors; they are genuine errors we made when coding the EJB sample. We started by writing the mock-object tests and they ran fine. Then we moved to the integration unit tests and discovered all these errors…. This is a clear demonstration that unit testing in isolation is not enough and needs to be supplemented by either integration unit tests or functional tests.

Table 12.2   Deployment errors uncovered by the integration unit test

Error description	Fix

OrderEJB implementation of `ejbCreate` must return the primary key (`Integer`) and not the bean interface (`OrderLocal`).	Replace
	
	    public OrderLocal ejbCreate[...]
	
	with
	
	    public Integer ejbCreate[...]

OrderEJB implementation of `ejbCreate` was returning null. It must return the primary key.	Replace
	
	    return null;
	
	with
	
	    return new Integer(uid);

CMP EB fields cannot be primitive types; they must be Java objects. One method of the `OrderLocal` interface was using a primitive type.	Replace
	
	    void setOrderId(int orderUId);
	
	with
	
	    void setOrderId(Integer orderUId);

The `createOrder` method of the `Petstore` interface wasn't throwing a `RemoteException`. This is required for remote methods.	Replace
	
	    int createOrder([...]);
	
	with
	
	    int createOrder([...])
	        throws RemoteException;

The `PetstoreEJB` session bean was wrongly declared `abstract`. Only CMP EB classes can be declared `abstract`.	Replace
	
	    public abstract class PetstoreEJB
	        implements SessionBean
	
	with
	
	    public class PetstoreEJB
	        implements SessionBean

continued on next page

Table 12.2 Deployment errors uncovered by the integration unit test *(continued)*

Error description	Fix
The `PetstoreEJB` class was missing the implementation of `ejbCreate`. This is required for a session bean.	Add ``` public void ejbCreate() throws CreateException, RemoteException {} ```

The `create` method of the `PetstoreHome` interface wasn't throwing a `RemoteException`. This is required for remote methods.	Replace
	
	``
	Petstore create() throws
	    CreateException;
	``
	with
	
	``
	Petstore create() throws
	    CreateException, RemoteException;
	``

Once all these errors are fixed, you will still stumble across another error, which is difficult to diagnose (see figure 12.6).

```
[java] org.jboss.deployment.DeploymentException: Error while creating table: - nested
throwable: (java.sql.SQLException: Unexpected token: ORDER in statement [CREATE TABLE ORD
ER (orderId INTEGER NOT NULL, orderDate TIMESTAMP, orderItem VARCHAR(256), CONSTRAINT PK_O
RDER PRIMARY KEY (orderId))])
```

Figure 12.6   This error is difficult to diagnose.

What happens is that JBoss automatically creates database tables for your CMP entity beans. However, because the CMP EB is named `Order`, JBoss generated the following SQL code:

```
[CREATE TABLE ORDER (orderId INTEGER NOT NULL, orderDate TIMESTAMP,
orderItem VARCHAR(256), CONSTRAINT PK_ORDER PRIMARY KEY (orderId))]
```

That tripped Hypersonic SQL (the default database used by JBoss) because `ORDER` is a reserved SQL keyword. We had to introduce a `jbosscmp-jdbc.xml` JBoss-specific file to solve this problem (we mapped the `Order` bean to the `Orders` table):

```
<?xml version="1.0" encoding="UTF-8"?>

<!DOCTYPE jbosscmp-jdbc PUBLIC "-//JBoss//DTD JBOSSCMP-JDBC 3.0//EN"
  "http://www.jboss.org/j2ee/dtd/jbosscmp-jdbc_3_0.dtd">

<jbosscmp-jdbc>
  <enterprise-beans>
    <entity>
      <ejb-name>Order</ejb-name>
      <table-name>Orders</table-name>
    </entity>
```

```
    </enterprise-beans>
  </jbosscmp-jdbc>
```

These are the kind of errors you have to solve when you perform real integration unit testing.

Let's now imagine that you have fixed all the deployment errors. It's high time to write the TestPetstoreEJB test class.

12.9.4 Writing a remote JUnit test for PetstoreEJB

The principle is simple: The test is a client of the remote Petstore EJB. Listing 12.22 demonstrates how to write such a test.

Listing 12.22   TestPetstoreEJB.java

```java
package junitbook.ejb.service;

import java.util.Date;

import javax.naming.InitialContext;
import javax.rmi.PortableRemoteObject;

import junit.framework.TestCase;
import junitbook.ejb.util.JNDINames;

public class TestPetstoreEJB extends TestCase
{
    public void testCreateOrderOk() throws Exception
    {
        Properties props = new Properties();                        ❶
        props.put(Context.INITIAL_CONTEXT_FACTORY,
            "org.jnp.interfaces.NamingContextFactory");
        props.put(Context.PROVIDER_URL, "localhost:1099");
        props.put(Context.URL_PKG_PREFIXES,
            "org.jboss.naming:org.jnp.interfaces");
        InitialContext context = new InitialContext(props);

        Object obj = context.lookup(JNDINames.PETSTORE_HOME);       ❷
        PetstoreHome petstoreHome =
            (PetstoreHome) PortableRemoteObject.narrow(
                obj, PetstoreHome.class);

        Petstore petstore = petstoreHome.create();
        Date date = new Date();
        String item = "item 1";

        int orderId = petstore.createOrder(date, item);
        assertEquals(date.hashCode() + item.hashCode(), orderId);
    }
}
```

1 You're making an out-of-JVM call to the container, so you need to specify the JNDI properties.

2 Perform a JNDI lookup to retrieve the `PetstoreEJB` home instance.

At this stage, you have the deployment working and the test case written. If you try running the tests by typing **ant test**, you'll discover that it still fails. You still need to adjust the JNDI names: You must match the JNDI names you use to look up objects with the JNDI names under which JBoss publishes the objects.

12.9.5 *Fixing JNDI names*

The JNDI names used in the application are defined in `JNDINames.java`, as shown in listing 12.23.

Listing 12.23 JNDI names used to look up the J2EE objects

```java
package junitbook.ejb.util;

public abstract class JNDINames
{
    public static final String QUEUE_CONNECTION_FACTORY =
        "ConnectionFactory";
    public static final String QUEUE_ORDER =
        "queue/petstore/Order";
    public static final String ORDER_LOCALHOME =
        "ejb/petstore/Order";
    public static final String PETSTORE_HOME =
        "ejb/petstore/Petstore";
}
```

In order to publish the objects under these names, you need to define a JBoss-specific `jboss.xml` file (see listing 12.24) that matches the JNDI names defined in `JNDINames.java`.

Listing 12.24 jboss.xml with JNDI names matching JNDINames.java

```xml
<jboss>
  <enterprise-beans>

    <session>
      <ejb-name>Petstore</ejb-name>
      <jndi-name>ejb/petstore/Petstore</jndi-name>
      <resource-env-ref>
        <resource-env-ref-name>
    →      jms/queue/petstore/Order</resource-env-ref-name>
        <jndi-name>queue/petstore/Order</jndi-name>
      </resource-env-ref>
```

```
      </session>

      <entity>
        <ejb-name>Order</ejb-name>
        <local-jndi-name>ejb/petstore/Order</local-jndi-name>
      </entity>

      <message-driven>
        <ejb-name>OrderProcessor</ejb-name>
        <destination-jndi-name>
    →      queue/petstore/Order</destination-jndi-name>
      </message-driven>

    </enterprise-beans>
  </jboss>
```

You must also modify the `ejbjar` Ant target so that it picks the new JBoss-specific files you have added (changes are in bold):

```
<target name="ejbjar" depends="compile">
  <jar destfile="${target.dir}/ejb.jar">
    <metainf dir="${conf.dir}">
      <include name="ejb-jar.xml"/>
      <include name="jbosscmp-jdbc.xml"/>
      <include name="jboss.xml"/>
    </metainf>
    <fileset dir="${target.classes.java.dir}"/>
  </jar>
</target>
```

12.9.6 *Running the tests*

At last, you're ready to run the tests. They should now execute fine. Typing **ant test** generates the results shown in figure 12.7.

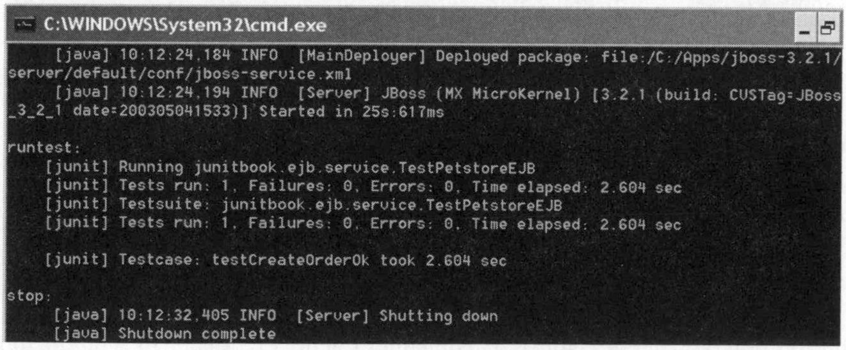

Figure 12.7 Successful execution of pure JUnit tests calling the running container remotely

12.10 *Using Cactus*

Let's now use Cactus to run some EJB unit tests. Cactus has several advantages over a pure JUnit solution:

- Cactus lets you unit-test Enterprise Beans using local interfaces, because Cactus tests run inside the container. For example, you have not been able to perform integration unit tests for the Order CMP entity bean (which uses a local interface). We'll demonstrate how to do this using Cactus.

- The Ant scripts were a bit complex because you had to script the container's start and stop (JBoss, in this case). Cactus provides an Ant integration that simplifies this operation. In addition, this Cactus Ant task supports several containers out of the box (JBoss, Tomcat, Resin, Orion, WebLogic, and so on), making it easy to run the tests on any container.

At this time of this writing, Cactus doesn't yet provide EJB Redirectors you can use to directly write tests against EJBs as you have done for servlets, taglibs, and filters in previous chapters.[3] Thus, you can't yet perform fine-grained integration tests, such as testing exceptions cases.

12.10.1 *Writing an EJB unit test with Cactus*

The current Cactus solution consists of transparently using the Cactus servlet Redirector so that the tests are executed within the context of the web container. For the pure JUnit solution, the tests perform a lookup on the EJB to unit-test and call its method to test. The difference is that this lookup is performed from the web container context and thus also works for local interfaces.

Let's demonstrate this on the OrderEJB CMP entity bean (listing 12.25).

> **Listing 12.25   OrderEJB unit test as a Cactus ServletTestCase**

```
package junitbook.ejb.domain;

import java.util.Date;

import javax.naming.InitialContext;

import junit.framework.TestCase;
import junitbook.ejb.util.JNDINames;

public class TestOrderEJB extends ServletTestCase
```

---

[3] The addition of EJB redirectors is scheduled for Cactus 1.6 or later (it is on the todo list: http://jakarta.apache.org/cactus/participating/todo.html).

```
{
    public void testEjbCreateOk() throws Exception
    {
        OrderLocalHome orderHome =
            (OrderLocalHome) new InitialContext().lookup(
                JNDINames.ORDER_LOCALHOME);

        Date date = new Date();
        String item = "item 1";

        OrderLocal order = orderHome.create(date, item);

        assertEquals(date, order.getOrderDate());
        assertEquals(item, order.getOrderItem());
        assertEquals(new Integer(date.hashCode()
            + item.hashCode()), order.getOrderId());
    }
}
```

❶ Lookup executed from inside container

Compared to listing 12.22, you don't need to set up JNDI properties before calling new InitialContext() (**❶**) because the test runs inside the container.

Let's now run this test using Ant.

12.10.2 *Project directory structure*

Figure 12.8 defines the directory structure for the Cactus tests. Compared to the directory structure from figure 12.4, you add the conf/cactus/ directory, which contains configuration files for running Cactus tests, and the src/test-cactus/ directory, which contains the Cactus unit tests. You also add an Ant build-cactus.xml buildfile that contains the Ant targets to automatically execute the Cactus tests using the Cactus/Ant integration. (For more details on the Cactus/Ant integration, refer to section 11.5.2 from chapter 11.)

You'll use the same Ant script introduced in listing 12.16 to package the application as an ear file. However, you need to add some targets to package the Cactus tests and execute them.

12.10.3 *Packaging the Cactus tests*

Because the Cactus tests execute in the web container, you need to package them in a war inside the ear. Fortunately, Cactus provides a cactifywar Ant task that makes the creation of this war easy:

```
<cactifywar version="2.3" destfile="${target.dir}/cactus.war"
    mergewebxml="${conf.dir}/cactus/web.xml">
  <classes dir="${target.classes.cactus.dir}"/>
</cactifywar>
```

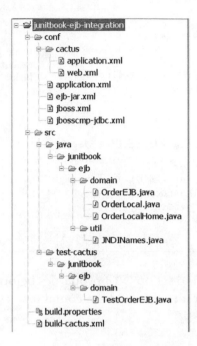

Figure 12.8
Full directory structure, including
configuration files and Ant build files
for Cactus tests

The version attribute specifies that you build a war for the Servlet API 2.3. Notice
the mergewebxml attribute. This is needed because TestOrderEJB is called from a
web context and is calling an EJB. Thus, as the J2EE specification mandates, you
need an <ejb-local-ref> in the war web.xml file, as shown in listing 12.26.

Listing 12.26   conf/cactus/web.xml containing ejb-local-ref entry to call OrderEJB

```
<?xml version="1.0" encoding="ISO-8859-1"?>
<!DOCTYPE web-app
    PUBLIC "-//Sun Microsystems, Inc.//DTD Web Application 2.3//EN"
    "http://java.sun.com/dtd/web-app_2_3.dtd">
<web-app>
   <ejb-local-ref>
     <ejb-ref-name>Order</ejb-ref-name>
     <ejb-ref-type>Entity</ejb-ref-type>
     <local-home>junitbook.ejb.domain.OrderLocalHome</local-home>
     <local>junitbook.ejb.domain.OrderLocal</local>
     <ejb-link>Order</ejb-link>
   </ejb-local-ref>
</web-app>
```

The last packaging step is to package the war in the ear:

```
<ear update="true" destfile="${target.dir}/ejb.ear"
    appxml="${conf.dir}/cactus/application.xml">
  <fileset dir="${target.dir}">
    <include name="cactus.war"/>
  </fileset>
</ear>
```

You update the application ear by overwriting the `application.xml` deployment descriptor with the special Cactus one. This step is necessary in order to add the Cactus war in `application.xml`, as shown in listing 12.27. This step is required only because your production ear doesn't container any war. Had it contained one, you could have reused this war by cactifying it. In that case, you wouldn't have needed to provide an additional `application.xml` file containing Cactus-specific definitions.

Listing 12.27   Special application.xml file containing the Cactus war definition

```
<?xml version="1.0"?>
<!DOCTYPE application PUBLIC
  '-//Sun Microsystems, Inc.//DTD J2EE Application 1.2//EN'
  'http://java.sun.com/j2ee/dtds/application_1_2.dtd'>
<application>
  <display-name>ejb</display-name>
  <description>EJB Chapter Sample Application</description>
  <module>
    <ejb>ejb.jar</ejb>
  </module>
  <module>
    <web>
      <web-uri>cactus.war</web-uri>
      <context-root>test</context-root>
    </web>
  </module>
</application>
```

The full Ant script is shown in listing 12.28.

Listing 12.28   Cactification of the application ear

```xml
<?xml version="1.0"?>

<project name="Ejb" default="test" basedir=".">
[...]
  <property name="src.cactus.dir"
      location="${src.dir}/test-cactus"/>
[...]
  <property name="target.classes.cactus.dir"
      location="${target.dir}/classes-test-cactus"/>
[...]
  <target name="compile.cactus" depends="compile">
    <mkdir dir="${target.classes.cactus.dir}"/>
    <javac destdir="${target.classes.cactus.dir}"
        srcdir="${src.cactus.dir}">
      <classpath>
        <pathelement location="${target.classes.java.dir}"/>
        <pathelement location="${cactus.jar}"/>
        <pathelement location="${j2ee.jar}"/>
      </classpath>
    </javac>
  </target>

  <target name="ear.cactify" depends="compile.cactus,ear">

    <taskdef resource="cactus.tasks">
      <classpath>
        <pathelement location="${cactus.ant.jar}"/>
        <pathelement location="${cactus.jar}"/>
        <pathelement location="${logging.jar}"/>
        <pathelement location="${aspectjrt.jar}"/>
        <pathelement location="${httpclient.jar}"/>
      </classpath>
    </taskdef>

    <cactifywar version="2.3" destfile="${target.dir}/cactus.war"
        mergewebxml="${conf.dir}/cactus/web.xml">
      <classes dir="${target.classes.cactus.dir}"/>
    </cactifywar>

    <ear update="true" destfile="${target.dir}/ejb.ear"
    appxml="${conf.dir}/cactus/application.xml">
      <fileset dir="${target.dir}">
        <include name="cactus.war"/>
      </fileset>
    </ear>

  </target>

</project>
```

12.10.4 *Executing the Cactus tests*

You execute the Cactus tests using the Cactus-provided `cactus` task. This is the nice part, compared to the pure JUnit approach from section 12.9, because the `cactus` task does everything for you: It deploys the ear, starts the container, executes the tests, and stops the container. The `cactus` task extends the `junit` JUnit Ant task and thus inherits from all its features. Listing 12.29 demonstrates how to use the `cactus` task to run the `TestOrderEJB` test.

Listing 12.29   Running Cactus tests automatically with the cactus task

```xml
<?xml version="1.0"?>

<project name="Ejb" default="test" basedir=".">
[...]
  <target name="test" depends="ear.cactify">

    <cactus earfile="${target.dir}/ejb.ear" fork="yes"
        printsummary="yes" haltonerror="true"
        haltonfailure="true">
      <containerset>
        <jboss3x dir="${cactus.home.jboss3x}"          Run Cactus tests in
            output="jbossresult.txt"/>                  JBoss container
      </containerset>
      <formatter type="brief" usefile="false"/>
      <test name="junitbook.ejb.domain.TestOrderEJB"/>
      <classpath>
        <pathelement location="${target.classes.java.dir}"/>
        <pathelement location="${target.classes.cactus.dir}"/>
      </classpath>
    </cactus>

  </target>

</project>
```

Executing the tests by typing `ant -f build-cactus.xml test` yields the result shown in figure 12.9.

```
C:\WINDOWS\System32\cmd.exe

C:\junitbook\ejb\integration>ant -f build-cactus.xml test
Buildfile: build-cactus.xml

compile:
    [mkdir] Created dir: C:\junitbook\ejb\integration\target\classes
    [javac] Compiling 11 source files to C:\junitbook\ejb\integration\target\classes

compile.cactus:
    [mkdir] Created dir: C:\junitbook\ejb\integration\target\classes-test-cactus
    [javac] Compiling 1 source file to C:\junitbook\ejb\integration\target\classes-test-cactus

ejbjar:
    [jar] Building jar: C:\junitbook\ejb\integration\target\ejb.jar

ear:
    [ear] Building ear: C:\junitbook\ejb\integration\target\ejb.ear

ear.cactify:
[cactifywar] Building war: C:\junitbook\ejb\integration\target\cactus.war
    [ear] Updating ear: C:\junitbook\ejb\integration\target\ejb.ear

test:
    [cactus] ----------------------------------------------------------------
    [cactus] Running tests against JBoss 3.2
    [cactus] ----------------------------------------------------------------
    [cactus] Running junitbook.ejb.domain.TestOrderEJB
    [cactus] Tests run: 1, Failures: 0, Errors: 0, Time elapsed: 0.741 sec
    [cactus] Testsuite: junitbook.ejb.domain.TestOrderEJB
    [cactus] Tests run: 1, Failures: 0, Errors: 0, Time elapsed: 0.741 sec

    [cactus] Shutdown complete

BUILD SUCCESSFUL
Total time: 31 seconds
C:\junitbook\ejb\integration>
```

Figure 12.9   Result of executing Cactus EJB tests with the Cactus/Ant integration

12.11 *Summary*

EJBs are complex and powerful beasts. Unit-testing doesn't have to be difficult. This chapter has demonstrated several techniques for handling EJB unit tests: mock objects for out-of-the-container testing of any kind of EJBs (session beans, entity beans, message-driven beans) and integration unit testing for testing Enterprise Beans when they run inside the container. We demonstrated integration unit testing with two tools: pure JUnit tests that call the EJBs remotely; and Cactus, which runs the tests from inside the container and lets you unit-test local interfaces.

When you're performing integration unit tests, writing the tests isn't even half the story. The hard part, which isn't specifically related to unit testing, is about automating the packaging of the application, its deployment and test execution, and the start/stop of containers. We've demonstrated several techniques using Ant, including using some Cactus custom-made Ant tasks that have helped in this endeavor.

The source code

A

This appendix covers

- Installing the book source code
- Software versions required
- Directory structure conventions

This appendix gives an overview of the book's source code, where to find it, how to install it, and how to run it. When we were writing, we decided to donate all of the book's source code to the Apache Software Foundation because we've used a lot of frameworks from there in the making of this book. Thus we have made our source code available as open source on Sourceforge at http://junitbook.sourceforge.net/.

We're also committed to maintaining this source code and fixing it if bugs are found, as a standard open source project. In addition, a Sourceforge forum has been set up for discussing the code at http://sourceforge.net/forum/forum.php?forum_id=291665.

A.1 Getting the source code

There are two possibilities for getting the source code on your local machine:

- Download a released version from http://sourceforge.net/project/show-files.php?group_id=68011 and unzip it somewhere on your hard drive.

- Use a CVS client and get the source from CVS HEAD. Getting the source from CVS is explained at http://sourceforge.net/cvs/?group_id=68011.

Either way, place the source code in a local directory named junitbook/ (for example c:\junitbook on Windows or /opt/junitbook on UNIX).

A.2 Source code overview

Once you put the source code in the junitbook/ directory, you should have the directory structure shown in figure A.1. Each directory represents the source code for a chapter of the book (except the repository/ directory, which contains external jars required by the chapter projects). The mapping between chapter names and directory names is listed in table A.1.

Each directory maps directly to a project. A project is a way to regroup Java sources, test sources, configurations files, and so on under a single location. A project also has a build, which lets you perform various actions such as compiling the code, running the tests, and generating the Javadoc. We have used different build tools (Ant and Maven) for the different projects, as explained in the chapter matching each project.

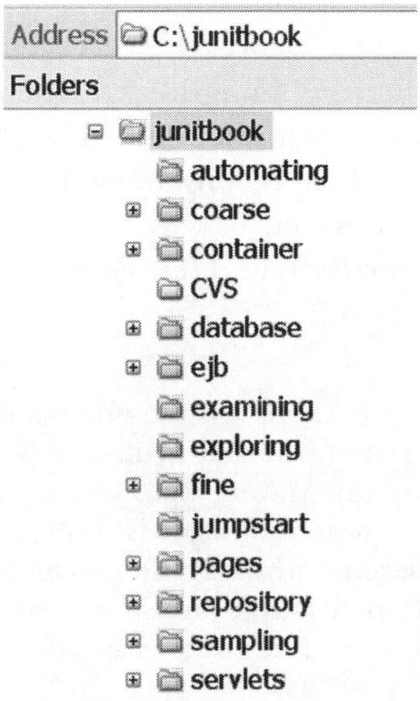

Address 🗀 C:\junitbook

Folders

- 🗀 junitbook
  - 🗀 automating
  - 🗀 coarse
  - 🗀 container
  - 🗀 CVS
  - 🗀 database
  - 🗀 ejb
  - 🗀 examining
  - 🗀 exploring
  - 🗀 fine
  - 🗀 jumpstart
  - 🗀 pages
  - 🗀 repository
  - 🗀 sampling
  - 🗀 servlets

Figure A.1
Directory structure for the source code, shown here in Windows Explorer. (Note that the directories are colored by the TortoiseCVS CVS client.)

Table A.1   Mappings between chapter names and source directory names

Chapter name	Directory name
Chapter 1: JUnit jumpstart	`junitbook/jumpstart/`
Chapter 2: Exploring JUnit	`junitbook/exploring/`
Chapter 3: Sampling JUnit	`junitbook/sampling/`
Chapter 4: Examining software tests	`junitbook/examining/`
Chapter 5: Automating JUnit	`junitbook/automating/`
Chapter 6: Coarse-grained testing with stubs	`junitbook/coarse/`
Chapter 7: Testing in isolation with mock objects	`junitbook/fine/`
Chapter 8: In-container testing with Cactus	`junitbook/container/`
Chapter 9: Unit-testing servlets and filters	`junitbook/servlets/`
Chapter 10: Unit-testing JSPs and taglibs	`junitbook/pages/`
Chapter 11: Unit-testing database applications	`junitbook/database/`
Chapter 12: Unit-testing EJBs	`junitbook/ejb/`

A.3 *External libraries*

You may have noticed a directory named `repository/` in figure A.1. It contains the different external libraries (jars) that all the other projects need in order to compile and run. As a convenience, we're making them readily available to you to prevent you from having to fish for them all over the Net.

The directory structure of `repository/` is of the format `<library name>/jars/ <library name>-<version>.jar`, as shown in figure A.2.

NOTE We have chosen this directory layout because it is the one needed to make the `repository/` project a remote Maven artifact repository (see chapter 5 for a presentation of the Maven repositories). When you install Maven the first time, its remote repository is configured to point to http://www.ibiblio.org/maven/, which is the official Maven repository containing hundreds of open source jars. Maven supports having several remote repositories, so adding yours is as easy as adding the following in your `build.properties`.

On Windows:

```
maven.repo.remote =
➜ http://www.ibiblio.org/maven/,file://c:/junitbook
➜ repository/
```

On UNIX:

```
maven.repo.remote =
➜ http://www.ibiblio.org/maven/,file:///opt/junitbook
➜ repository/
```

With this configuration, Maven will look for any dependency on `ibiblio` first and then in the `junitbook` repository in your filesystem.

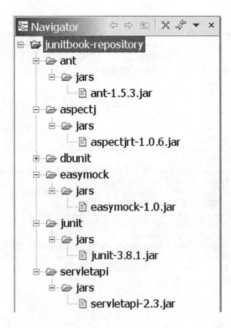

Figure A.2
Some jars from the `repository/`
directory, shown in the Eclipse
navigator view

A.4 *Jar versions*

Table A.2 lists the versions of all external jars and applications used in the projects. We recommend using these versions when you try the book examples.

Table A.2   External jar/application versions (sorted in alphabetical order)

External project name	Version	Project URL
Ant	1.5.3	http://ant.apache.org/
AspectJ	1.0.6	http://eclipse.org/aspectj/
Cactus	1.5	http://jakarta.apache.org/cactus/
Commons BeanUtils	1.6.1	http://jakarta.apache.org/commons/beanutils.html
Commons Collections	2.1	http://jakarta.apache.org/commons/collections.html
Commons HttpClient	2.0	http://jakarta.apache.org/commons/httpclient/
Commons Logging	1.0.3	http://jakarta.apache.org/commons/logging.html
DbUnit	1.5.5	http://dbunit.sourceforge.net/
EasyMock	1.0	http://easymock.org/
Eclipse	2.1	http://eclipse.org/

continued on next page

Table A.2   External jar/application versions (sorted in alphabetical order) *(continued)*

External project name	Version	Project URL
HttpUnit	1.5.3	http://httpunit.sourceforge.net/
Jakarta Taglibs / JSTL	1.0.2	http://jakarta.apache.org/taglibs/
JBoss	3.2.1	http://jboss.org/
Jetty	4.2.11	http://jetty.mortbay.org/
JUnit	3.8.1	http://junit.org/
Maven	1.0 beta 10	http://maven.apache.org/
MockObjects	0.09	http://www.mockobjects.com/
MockMaker plugin for Eclipse	1.12.0	http://www.mockmaker.org/
Servlet API	2.3	http://www.ibiblio.org/maven/servletapi/jars/
Tomcat	4.1.24	http://jakarta.apache.org/tomcat/

A.5   *Directory structure conventions*

For each project, we have followed the directory conventions listed in table A.3.

Table A.3   Directory structure conventions

Directory name	Explanation
<project name>/src/java	Java runtime sources.
<project name>/src/test	Java test sources.
<project name>/src/test-cactus	Java Cactus test sources.
<project name>/src/webapp	Web app resources (JSPs, web.xml, taglibs, and so on).
<project name>/conf	Configuration files (if any).
<project name>/target	Directory created by the build process (Ant or Maven) to store generated files and temporary files. It can be safely deleted, because it's re-created by the build.

Eclipse quick start

This appendix covers

- Installing Eclipse
- Setting up the book source code in Eclipse
- Running JUnit tests in Eclipse

In this appendix, you will learn how to install Eclipse (http://eclipse.org/) and how to run the book's source code from within the IDE. This appendix is meant as a quick start to get you up and running quickly with Eclipse and with the integrated JUnit.

B.1 Installing Eclipse

Installing Eclipse is very simple; the process consists of downloading Eclipse from http://eclipse.org/ and then unzipping it to somewhere on your hard drive. We recommend downloading Eclipse 2.1 or greater. In the remainder of this appendix, we'll assume Eclipse is installed in [ECLIPSE_HOME] (for example, c:\eclipse-2.1).

B.2 Setting up Eclipse projects from the sources

The good news is that it's extremely easy to set up an Eclipse project, because we have provided the Eclipse project files with the book's source code distribution. Please refer to appendix A ("The source code") for directory structure organization and project names.

The first Eclipse project to import corresponds to the junitbook/repository/ directory. It contains all the external libraries (jars) required by all the other projects. All the other Eclipse projects for this book depend upon this repository project for their classpath, which is why you need to import it first.

To import this project, select File→Import and then select Existing Project into Workspace. Point the Project Content to the junitbook/repository/ directory on your hard disk, as shown in figure B.1.

Repeat the same process for all the projects you wish to see in your Eclipse workspace. If you import all the projects, you should end up with the workspace shown in figure B.2.

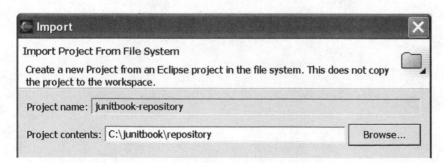

Figure B.1 Importing the junitbook-repository **project into Eclipse**

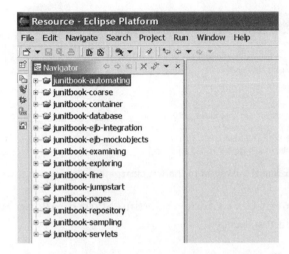

Figure B.2
Eclipse workspace when all the book projects have been imported

B.3 *Running JUnit tests from Eclipse*

To run a JUnit test in Eclipse, select the Java perspective ( ), click on the test class to execute, click the Run As icon arrow ( ), and select JUnit Test. Figure B.3 shows what you'll get if you run the TestAccount test case found in the junit-book-examining Eclipse project from chapter 4.

For full details on how to run JUnit tests from Eclipse, please see the integrated Eclipse Help: Click Help→Help Contents. Then, in the Help browser, select the

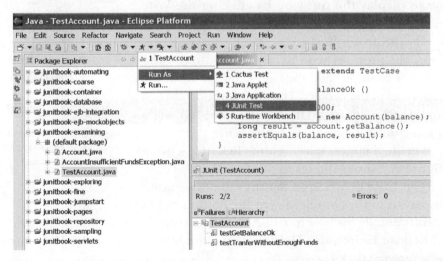

Figure B.3   Running the TestAccount test case in Eclipse using the built-in JUnit plugin

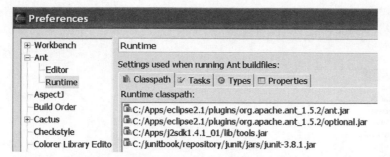

Figure B.4   Adding the JDK `tools.jar` and the JUnit jar to the Ant classpath in Eclipse

following topic: Java Development User Guide→Getting Started→Basic Tutorial→Writing and Running JUnit tests.

B.4   *Running Ant scripts from Eclipse*

Before running Ant scripts, make sure you've added the JDK `tools.jar` library to your Ant classpath (it's needed by the Ant `javac` task). In addition, you also need to add the JUnit jar to the Ant classpath. To do so, select Window→Preferences, choose Ant→Runtime in the Preferences dialog box, and add the jars as shown in figure B.4.

Figure B.5
Eclipse displays the Ant view.

To execute a target from an Ant buildfile, first tell Eclipse to display the Ant view by clicking the Window→Show View menu entry and selecting Ant. Figure B.5 shows the result.

Then, click the 🔧 icon to add a buildfile to the Ant view. For example, add the `build.xml` file from the `junitbook-sampling` project. The Ant view now lists all the Ant targets it has found in the `build.xml` file, highlighting the default target (see figure B.6).

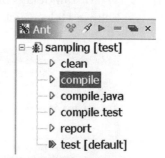

Figure B.6   The Ant view displays all the Ant targets found in `build.xml`.

To execute a target, select it and click the ▶ button. Figure B.7 shows the result of executing the compile target. Note that Eclipse captures the Ant output and displays it in the console view at the bottom right of the figure.

For full details on how to run Ant scripts from Eclipse, please see the integrated Eclipse Help: Click Help→Help Contents. Then, in the Help browser,

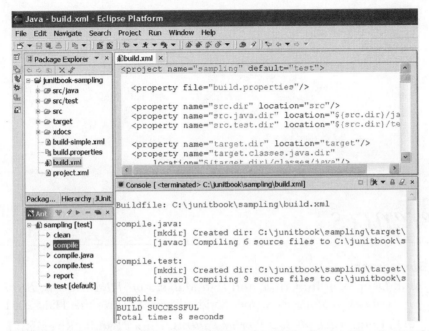

Figure B.7   Result of executing the `compile` Ant target for the `junitbook-sampling` project

select the following topic: Workbench User Guide→Getting Started→Ant & External Tools Tutorial→Eclipse Ant Basics.

B.5 *Running Cactus tests from Eclipse*

Executing a Cactus test involves several steps: packaging the application to run as a war file, deploying it to the container, starting the container, and launching the tests using a JUnit runner. Launching a JUnit runner is easy, as demonstrated by the previous section. However, the other steps are harder to perform. The Cactus project provides two solutions to help:

- A Jetty integration, which can be run from any IDE (including Eclipse). This integration is described in detail in chapter 8 ("In-container testing with Cactus").

- A Cactus plugin for Eclipse, which lets you run Cactus tests within several containers (Resin, WebLogic, Tomcat, Orion, and so on). However, this plugin is still experimental (at the time of this writing). Full information about using the Eclipse plugin is available on the Cactus web site at http://jakarta.apache.org/cactus/integration/eclipse/index.html.

references

Bibliography

Alur, Deepak, John Crupi, and Dan Malks. *Core J2EE Patterns: Best Practices and Design Strategies.* Upper Saddle River, NJ: Prentice Hall, 2001.

Beck, Kent. *Smalltalk Best Practice Patterns.* Upper Saddle River, NJ: Prentice Hall, 1996.

———. *Extreme Programming Explained: Embrace Change.* Reading, MA: Addison-Wesley, 1999.

———. *Test Driven Development: By Example.* Boston: Addison-Wesley, 2003.

Earles, John. "Frameworks! Make Room for Another Silver Bullet." http://www.cbd-hq.com/PDFs/cbdhq_000301je_frameworks.pdf.

Fowler, Martin. "The New Methodology." http://www.martinfowler.com/articles/newMethodology.html.

———. *Patterns of Enterprise Application Architecture.* Boston: Addison-Wesley, 2003.

———. *Refactoring: Improving the Design of Existing Code.* Reading, MA: Addison-Wesley, 1999.

Fowler, Martin, and Kendall Scott. *UML Distilled: A Brief Guide to the Standard Object Modeling Language.* Reading, MA: Addison-Wesley, 2000.

Gamma, Erich, et al. *Design Patterns: Elements of Reusable Object-Oriented Software.* Reading, MA: Addison-Wesley, 1995.

Hatcher, Erik, and Steve Loughran. *Java Development with Ant.* Greenwich, CT: Manning, 2003. http://www.manning.com/hatcher/.

Jeffries, Ron. On the TestDrivenDevelopment mailing list: http://groups.yahoo.com/group/testdrivendevelopment/message/3914.

Johnson, Ralph, and Brian Foote. "Designing Reusable Classes." *Journal of Object-Oriented Programming* 1.5 (June/July 1988): 22–35. http://www.laputan.org/drc/drc.html.

Marick, Brian. "How Many Bugs Do Regression Tests Find?" http://www.testingcraft.com/regression-test-bugs.html.

Potapov, Roman. "The Origin of Murphy's Law." http://www.geocities.com/murphylawsite/.

Rainsberger, J. B. "Refactoring: Replace Subclasses with Collaborators." http://www.diasparsoftware.com/articles/refactorings/replaceSubclassWithCollaborator.html.

Sisson, Derek. "Types of Tests." http://www.philosophe.com/testing/tests.html.

Walls, Craig, and Norman Richards. *XDoclet in Action.* Greenwich, CT: Manning, 2003. http://books.manning.com/walls/.

Software directory

The software packages listed here are covered by the main text. Appendix A also provides a detailed list of the software packages and versions used by the book's source code.

Table R.1 Software directory

Name	Web site	Quick description
Ant	http://ant.apache.org/	Build tool
AspectJ	http://eclipse.org/aspectj/	AOP framework
Cactus	http://jakarta.apache.org/cactus/	J2EE unit-testing framework
Clover	http://www.thecortex.net/clover/	Test coverage tool
Commons BeanUtils	http://jakarta.apache.org/commons/beanutils/	Reflection and introspection utilities for working on JavaBeans

continued on next page

Table R.1 Software directory *(continued)*

Name	Web site	Quick description
Commons Collections	http://jakarta.apache.org/commons/collections.html	Complements the Java Collections API with other powerful data structures
Commons Httpclient	http://jakarta.apache.org/commons/httpclient/	HTTP client
Commons Logging	http://jakarta.apache.org/commons/logging.html	Logging façade to other logging systems
DbUnit	http://www.dbunit.org/	Database unit-testing framework
EasyMock	http://easymock.org/	Mock objects generation framework
Eclipse	http://www.eclipse.org/	Tools platform and Java IDE
HttpUnit	http://httpunit.sourceforge.net/	JUnit extension for testing web applications
JBoss	http://www.jboss.org/	J2EE container
Jester	http://jester.sourceforge.net/	Tool to verify quality of unit tests
Jetty	http://jetty.mortbay.org/	Servlet/JSP container
JMeter	http://jakarta.apache.org/jmeter/	Load-testing tool
JSTL	http://java.sun.com/products/jsp/jstl/	Standard JSP tag libraries
JUnit	http://junit.org/	Unit-testing framework
JUnitBook	http://sourceforge.net/projects/junitbook/	Source code for *JUnit in Action*
JUnitPerf	http://www.clarkware.com/software/JUnitPerf.html	JUnit extension for measuring performance and scalability
Maven	http://maven.apache.org/	Project comprehension build tool
MockObjects	http://www.mockobjects.com/	Mock-objects framework

continued on next page

Table R.1   Software directory *(continued)*

Name	Web site	Quick description
MockMaker plugin for Eclipse	http://www.mockmaker.org/	Static mock-objects generation framework
Taglibs	http://jakarta.apache.org/taglibs/	Jakarta's implementation of JSTL
Tomcat	http://jakarta.apache.org/tomcat/	Servlet/JSP container
xPetstore	http://xpetstore.sf.net/	Sample Petstore application

Software licenses

- The source code created for this book is provided under the Apache Software License (http://apache.org/LICENSE).

- JUnit is provided under the Common Public License (http://oss.software.ibm.com/developerworks/oss/license-cpl.html).

index

Numerics

302 response code (redirect) 73

A

abstract classes, testing 311
AbstractHttpHandler method
    (Jetty) 128
AbstractHttpListener class
    (Jetty) 128
acceptance testing 6, 71, 75–76
Account class 82, 141–145
account transfer testing 141
AccountManager interface
    141–143
AccountService.transfer
    method 141, 143–146
add method 7–8
addAccount method 144
addHandler method 42, 50,
    60, 128
addTest method 23
addTestSuite method 24
Administration
    application 188–189, 216,
    240, 261
administrators 188
AdminServlet
    Administration application
        and 216
    DataAccessManager and
        244–247
    refactoring 243–244
    testing with Cactus 189–192

agile methodologies 68
Algol 68
alternate path of execution *See*
    failures
Ant
    book 93
    build process management
        with 92
    build system choice with 315
    build.properties file 94, 317
    buildfiles 91, 93–94, 98,
        101–102
    cactification 266
    cactifywar task 266–271, 329
    cactus task 333
    cactus testing with 265–274
    Cactus/Ant integration
        module 265–274, 329
    configuration of 91
    database integration testing
        and 261
    ear task 317
    fileset element 100
    installing 91–92, 98
    Java application building
        tool 91–92
    javac task 94–96
    JDBC query invoking with 91
    junit jar 98
    junit task 96–98, 100–101,
        272, 322, 333
    junitreport task 98–100
    parallel task 321
    project XML tag and 93
    properties of 94
    property elements 93

property task 94
    retaining test results with 27
    SQL task 266
    targets 93, 101–102
    taskdef element 273
    tasks 93
    WAR task 266
    web site 91
AOP (Aspect-Oriented
    Programming) 173
Apache test server 124
APIs (Application Programming
    Interface)
    contract defined 6
    methods 81
    testing of public 72, 78
    verifying behavior of 171
application.xml file 315, 317–
    318, 331
architecture patterns 41
Aspect Oriented Programming
    (AOP) 173
AspectJ jar 177
aspectjrt.jar 270
assertEquals method 14, 31,
    131, 134, 153, 219, 250
AssertionException 256
AssertionFailedError 159
assertSame 54
Avalon framework 149

B

BaseTestRunner class 21
BasicDynaClass class 219–220

batchtest element 272
beanutils.RowSetDynaClass 247
Beck, Kent 5, 40, 70, 164,
    166, 240
beginIsAuthenticatedNoSession
    method 181
best practices
    business logics and
        mocks 144
    Cactus tests, location of 176
    code improvement with
        testing 60, 62
    continuous regression
        testing 86
    exception test readability 62
    failure explanation in assert
        calls 51
    packaging and directory loca-
        tions of test classes 64
    refactor long setups when
        using mock objects 254
    refactor test setups and
        teardowns 299
    refactoring and agile
        methodologies 68
    test method naming 50
    throw an exception for meth-
        ods that aren't
        implemented 204
    unit test one object at a
        time 48
    unit tests and testMethods 53
    use TDD to implement The
        Simplest Thing That
        Could Possibly Work 197
    verification of test failure 192
    what to test 56, 145
black box testing 78, 81
body tag 228
BodyContent class 230
BodyTagSupport class 229
bottlenecks, finding with
    profilers 74
branches, conditional 78
Brunner, John 89
build cactus.xml buildfile 329
build.properties file 111, 317
buildfiles (Ant) 91, 93–94, 97–
    98, 101–102
Bureau of Extreme
    Programming 45

business logic unit tests 144, 280
ByteArrayISO8859Writer class
    (Jetty) 128

C

C2 Wiki 163
cactification 192, 267, 270–
    271, 331
Cactus
    Ant integration 266–267, 328
    DbUnit integration 271–273
    defined 173, 267
    directory structure for
        tests 329
    EJB unit tests 328
    FileRedirector 212
    front ends 179
    in-container testing with 166,
        173–183
    integration with Jetty 175–178
    jars 177
    JSP testing 217–218, 238,
        331, 333
    mock objects compared
        to 213, 216, 237, 278
    running tests 174–175
    setInitParameter method 211
    task 273
    taskdef 270
    test runners 174–178
    testing filters 208–213
    testing life cycles 179–180,
        230–233
    testing taglibs 224–233, 237
    testing under Jetty with
        Eclipse 177
    testing under Maven 196
    web sites 166, 267, 274
    when to use 213–214, 216,
        237, 278
    XML and 329–331
cactus.jar 270
Cactus/Ant integration
    module 266–267
cactus-ant integration jar 267
Calculator class 6–7
CalculatorTest program 8–10
callView method 189, 198, 200–
    201, 242
Carroll, Lewis 282

Centipede 315
class factory refactoring 156
classloaders 10, 12
classpath 94, 97–98, 177, 270,
    272
classpath element 96
clean build 92
CLEAN INSERT strategy 264
clean target 101
clearCache method 307
close calls 258
close method 159
Clover 79–80
coarse-grained testing 121
code issues 146
codesmell 62
collaboration tags, testing
    of 233
collecting parameters 25–27
Common Public License 5
CommonMockStatement 251
CommonPetstoreTestCase 305–
    306, 309
Commons-HttpClient jar 177
Commons-Logging jar 177
compile targets 95–96, 268
compile.cactustest target 269
compile.test target 319
condition task 321
conditional branches 78
Connection object 248–249, 258
ConnectionFactory class
    156–157
Container Managed Persistence
    (CMP) 282–283
container-related code
    testing 167
continuous integration 179,
    279–280
controller component 40–45
Controller interface 41–42
controller object 50
Controller project 116
countTestCases method 30
Craig, Philip 140
create method 307
createCommandResult
    method 201
createdb target 267–268
createOrder method 283, 286–
    287, 290, 293, 297, 303, 314

createOrderHelper
    method 290, 293
cron job 99
Cunningham, Ward 75
custom taglibs 216
customer
    always right 62

D

data access unit tests
    types of 241
data.sql file 266
data.xml 263–264, 270
DataAccessManager class 262
DataAccessManager
    interface 243, 247
database
    access layer interface
        implementation 243
    access unit tests 241, 278
    connection pooling 241
    connectivity 29, 258, 260,
        263–264
    constraints 260
    features 242, 260
    in-memory 278
    integration testing 260–264,
        279–280
    queries 261
    referential integrity 260
    schema 266–267
    triggers 260
    unit-testing 240–242, 260–274
DatabaseTestSetup 275–276
DataSource
    implementation 262
DbUnit
    adding jar 273
    Cactus integration 272
    database data presetting
        with 263
    database testing and 242,
        260–261
    web site 260
dbunit.jar 270
DefaultAccountManager
    class 147–149
DefaultController 43, 45, 48,
    79, 91
DefaultJMSUtil class 294

DefaultOrderUtil class 294
definitions
    acceptance tests 6
    API contract 6
    component 167
    container 167
    domain object 47
    expectation 159
    fixture 29
    framework 5
    integration tests 6
    mock object 141
    refactor 52
    regression tests 90
    stub 121
    Test-Driven Development 81
    unit of work 5
    unit test 6
dependency in software
    development 120
deployment
    automatic 319
    descriptors 173, 238, 313,
        318, 331
    ears 333
    targets 319
Design by Contract website 6
design patterns
    collecting parameters 27
    command pattern 25
    composite pattern 25
    Factory 134
    Interfaces 164
    Inversion of Control 42, 149,
        155, 164
    MVC Model 2 199
    observer 28
development cycle 82
diagnostic tests 55
directory structure 63, 105, 111,
    315, 329
dist target 101
doAfterBody method 229, 231
document root 125–126
doEndTag method 226, 228
doGet method 201–204, 206,
    242, 246
domain object 47–48
doStartTag method 226–228
doubles 7
duplication eliminating 83

dyna beans 218–220
DynaBean class 199
DynaBeans 219, 225–226
dynamic proxies 167
Dynamic Proxy 204, 233, 238
DynaMock
    EasyMock compared to 204
    testing session beans with 284
    writing mocks with 246
DynaPropertiesTag class 225

E

ear files 315–317, 319–321, 329,
    331, 333
EasyMock 167–170, 204
Eclipse
    adding jars 177
    Cactus testing under Jetty
        with 177
    plug-ins 175, 234
    projects 113, 115, 175–177
    Quick Fixes 191
    test results retention with 27
    TestDefaultController, run-
        ning with 114
    web site 112
EJB
    defining sample
        applications 282
    façade strategies 283–284
    home caching issue 306
    limitations of JUnit with 314
    local interfaces 328, 334
    Redirectors 328
    remote interface testing 314
    remote interfaces 314
    unit test writing with
        Cactus 328
    unit testing with Cactus 329
ejbCreate method 311–312
EJBException class 293
ejb-jar.xml file 315
ejb-local-ref element 330
Electric XML 271
eliminating duplication 83
Emacs 112
embedded servers 124
endCallView method 221
entity beans 282, 310
EntityBean class 310

error conditions 56, 152
error handling 26, 56, 152
errorproperty attributes 322
ErrorResponse class 44, 79
Example TimedTest class 75
exceptions 42, 55–56, 60
execute method 248–250, 257–258, 261
executeCommand method 189, 198, 201, 242
executeQuery method 251
exml.jar 271
expectAndReturn method 293
expectAndThrow method 307
expectations 159, 163, 256
Extreme Programming 5, 197

F

fail statements 61
failureproperty attributes 322
failures 51, 56–57, 132–133, 258
field getters/setters and absolute
    classes 311
fileset element 101
filesystem 126
FilterChain 209–210, 212
FilterConfig 209, 212
filters 188, 208, 314
FilterTestCase 182
findAccountForUser
    method 142–144, 147, 149
findAncestorWithClass
    method 233
fit framework
    web site 75
Fixtures 50
    controller object created by
        default 58
    defined 29
    de-initializing with
        tearDown 32
    long and complex 254
    test case sharing of 53–54
    TestSetup 129, 134, 145, 275–276, 297–298
fork attribute 97
formatter element 272
Fowler, Martin 4
framework 4–5
Freeman, Steve 140

G

Galileo 120
Gamma, Erich 112
Gang of Four 5
Generate Getters and Setters
    feature 311
getBalance method 82
getColumnCount method 254–255
getCommand method 189–191, 197–198, 242–243
getConnection method 249, 258
getContent method
    (WebClient) 122
getHandler method 44, 47, 60, 79
getInputStream method 136–137, 153
getMetaData method 254–255
getName method 55
getOrder method 287
getOrderHome method 287, 306
getOrderId method 292–293
getParameter method 206
getParent method 233
getRequest method 50
getRequestDispatcher
    method 220
Giraudoux, Jean 140
green-bar tests 21

H

haltonerror attribute 97, 272
haltonfailure attribute 96–97, 272
Handler class (Jetty) 127–128
Hashtable 144
Heisenberg Uncertainty
    Principle 155
Hollywood Principle 42
hsqldb.jar 268
HTML DOM 222

HTTP
clients 40
connection mock objects 150
connections 122–123, 150–151, 181
cookies 181–182
elements 40
headers 40, 181–182, 222
parameters 40, 216, 225
protocols 157
HTTP requests
    AdminServlet
        requirements 189
    doGet method entry point
        for 242
    functional unit tests using 73
    HTTPContext processing
        of 126
    HTTP-related parameters
        in 181
    interception by the security
        filter 216
    receipt by application 188
    using Cactus to add SQL com-
        mand to 210
    web controller acceptance 40
HTTP response 128, 182, 210, 212, 222, 225, 230
HTTP sessions 40, 181, 225
httpclient.jar 270
HttpConnectionFactory class
    157
HttpContext 126
HttpContext class 125–126, 129, 132–133
HttpRequest class 128–129
HttpResponse class 127, 133
HttpServer class 125, 129–130, 132
HttpServer class (Jetty) 125
HttpServlet class 166, 168, 242, 245
HttpServletRequest class 166, 168–170, 181, 205
HttpServletResponse class 181, 220
HttpSession class 166, 168–170, 181
HttpSocketListener class
    (Jetty) 129

HttpUnit class 167, 217, 221, 225
HttpURLConnection class 123, 133–134, 136–138, 153, 157
HttpURLConnection interface 123
Hypersonic SQL 260, 278, 315, 324

I

IDE (integrated development environments) 56, 112
IEEE 5
IllegalStateException 298
incomplete mock object test 251
in-container testing 166, 173, 178
InitialContext class 285, 297–298, 314
inner classes 48
InputStream class 159
integrated development environments (IDE) 56, 112
integration testing 6, 71–72, 133–134, 283
integration unit testing
    comparison with logic and functional unit testing 76, 172
    database testing with 242, 260–264, 279–280
    defined 76, 172–173
    EJBs and 313
    errors in 323–325
    execution time 179
    J2EE testing with 166
    mock objects approach compared to 179–180
    with Cactus and JUnit 334
interactions between objects 81
introspect method 253
invalid URLs 132–133
Inversion of Control (IOC) 148–149
isAuthenticated method 166, 168–169, 173
isolation testing 134, 140, 150, 164, 217
It Works! return 127–128, 130

J

J2EE
    component unit testing 166–167
    containers 260, 315
    integration issues, costs of 279
jar proliferation 109
Java Complier (javac) 94–96
Java IDE's 112
Java Messaging Service (JMS) 283–284
Java Naming and Directory Interface (JNDI) 284–285, 297–307, 314
Java Server Pages (JSP) 188–189, 216–233
Java Virtual Machine (JVM) 96, 320
JAVA_HOME 92
JavaBean 56
javac (Java Compiler) 94–96
Javadocs 14, 23, 30, 92, 102
JBoss
    development 320
    Hypersonic SQL and 260, 315, 324
    installing 317
    JNDI and 326
    version 3.2.1 273
    website 317
jboss.xml file 326
jboss3x element 273
jbossresult.txt file 273
JDBC 91, 120, 141, 145–147, 284
JdbcDataAccessManager class 243–244, 247, 249–250, 261–262
JEdit 112
Jeffries, Ron 148
Jester 80
Jetty
    benefits of 124–125, 138, 175
    Cactus testing under, with Eclipse 177
    embedded server used as 125
    handler that returns 127
    Handlers 127–128
    JettySample class 125
    modularity 125

NotFoundHandler 132
opening a URL 125
pros 125
setting up stubs with 124–125
starting and stopping 129
starting from code 125–127
website 124
Jetty classes
    AbstractHttpHandler 127–129, 133
    ByteArrayISO8859Writer 128
    Handler 128–129
    HttpContext 125, 129
    HttpServer 125
    HttpServer class 129
    JettySample 125
    SocketListener 125, 129
Jetty methods
    addHandler 128
    handle 128
    setContextPath 126
    setResourceBase 126
    setUpandtearDown 127
JMeter 73
JMS (Java Messaging Service 283–284
JMSException class 293
JMSUtil class 287, 294–295, 303
JMSUtil interface 295, 297
JNDI (Java Naming and Directory Interface) 284–285, 297–307, 314
JNDI API 188
jndi.properties file 297
JNDINames class 326
JNDITestSetup 298
Joyce, James 18
JspRedirector class 224
JSPs (JavaServer Pages) 216
JspTagLifecycle class 228, 230
JspTestCase class 182, 224–225, 227, 230
JSTL 219, 226
JUnit
    Assert interface 30
    core classes 19–20
    core members 19
    design goals 15, 24, 30
    FAQ 56
    features 13
    IDEs and 112

JUnit *(continued)*
life cycle 37–38
motto 20
overview 5
Test interface 23
JUnit classes
BaseTestRunner class 20, 22
TestCase class 13, 18, 25, 28, 31
TestFailure class 25
TestListener interface 27
TestResults class 25
TestRunner class 18, 20, 180
TestSuite class 18, 21–23, 131
JUnit methods
assertEquals method 13–14, 30, 126
JUnit TestClass constructors
version 3.8.1 and later 15
junit.jar file 98
JUnitEE website 314
JUnitPerf website 74
JUnitReport 99
JVM (Java Virtual Machine) 32, 96, 320

K

Kawasaki, Guy 66

L

Log interface 147
Log object 146
Log4j 109
LoggerFactory class 146
logging.jar 270
logic unit tests 76, 172, 241
lookup method 287

M

Mackinnon, Tim 140
Marick, Brian 216
matchAndReturn method 293, 307
Maven
artifacts 109
cactification 192
compared to Ant and Eclipse 90, 112

configuring 103–105
dependency handling 108–109
directory structure 193, 212
goal seeking 102, 109
handling dependent jars 109
HTML reports 196
ID element 105
IDEs and 112
installing 103
JUnit test with 109
JUnit testing with 109
maven-linkcheck-plugin 106
PATH 103
plugins 102–103, 105–106, 109, 192, 196
portability 103
project configuration files 222
project description 104
Project Object Module (POM) 104–108
project.xml 108–109, 196
reports element 108
repositories 109
running Cactus tests 192–193, 212–213
url element 105
version element 105
website 102
website generation with 105–108
welcome page 106–107
workflow 109
maven site 109
MAVEN_HOME 103
maven-changelog-report 106
MavenLJUnit test with 109
mergewebxml attribute 330
Message Driven Beans (MDB) 282–283, 307–310
metadata 173, 218, 238, 313
Method Factory refactoring 155
Mock DataAccessManager 246
mock objects
as probes 159
as Trojan horses 159
benefits of 140
best practices 254
Cactus compared to 213, 216, 237, 278

defined 141
entity beans, testing with 310–312
finding methods to mock 250
HTTP connection and 150–159
in-container testing with 166
indirect calls, discovery of 253
JNDI implementation stragegy 297, 303, 309
making generic 144
making mocks generic 144
message-driven bean testing 308
mocking at a different level 254
practical example 150
pros and cons 144, 170–171
real objects compared to 163
servlet testing with 167–170
session beans 284–285
standard JDK APIs 163
stubs compared to 120, 141, 144
web site 163
when to use 121, 138, 163, 213–214
white box tests and 78, 81
MockAccountManager class 143–144
MockConfiguration class 149
MockConnectionFactory class 157, 160
MockHttpURLConnection class 153
MockInputStream class 159
MockLog class 149
MockMaker 234, 237–238
MockMultiRowResultSet class 252
MockObject JDBC package 247
MockObjects
framework SQL package 280
jar 112
project web site 163
MockSingleRowResultSet class 252
MockURL class 150, 153
monumental methodologies 197
Murphy's Law 56

MVC Model 2 199

N

name property 42
Newton 25

O

objective standards 77
openConnection method 134
optional.jar file 98
Oracle 278
OrderEJB class 310–312
OrderFactory class 295
OrderProcessMDB 314
OrderProcessorMDB class 286
OrderUtil class 286, 303,
    306–307
OrderUtil interfaces 294
Orion 171, 273

P

PageContext class 224, 234, 238
Pascal 68
performance testing 74
Petstore application 314–315
Petstore OrderEJB class 314
PetstoreEJB class 285, 289–291,
    295, 303, 314
play-testing 4
POJO (Plain Old Java
    Object) 212, 283
POM (project object
    model) 104–108
pre-test state 50
printsummary attribute 97, 272
process method 42, 49
processRequest method 42, 44,
    51, 57, 79
production environments, draw-
    backs in testing 124
profilers 73
project directory structure 265
project object model
    (POM) 104–108
project.xml file 104
PropertyResourceBundle
    class 147
ProtocolException 136

proxy redirector 180
pushBody method 230

Q

QA teams 75

R

read-only data, factoring 275
red-bar tests 21, 58
redirect 302 response code 73
refactoring 244
    best practice 60
    class factory, used for 155–159
    courage for 68
    defined 52
    easy method technique
        for 152–155
    extract hierarchy 62
    extract method 62
    making code unit-testable
        with 69, 283
    Method Factory 155
    mock objects used as tech-
        nique for 146–149
    natural solution 245
    PetstoreEJB 294
    renaming 294
    sample 58–59
    setDataAccessManager 245
    suite of unit tests, benefits
        for 140
    TDD two-step 83
referential integrity 260
reflection and introspection 10
regression testing 86, 90–91
report target 100
Request 209, 212
Request interface 41, 58
RequestDispatcher 208
RequestHandler class 42, 47,
    49–50
RequestHandler interface 41
Resin 273
Response 209, 212
response code (302) redirect 73
Response interface 41, 44
results.jsp 218
ResultSet interface 248, 251
RowSetDynaClass 247

run method 30
RuntimeException class 44, 58,
    60, 314

S

Sample servlet 166
Sampling project buildfiles
    93, 96
scriptlets 189
Security error page 211
security filter 216
SecurityFilter class 208
SecurityFilter Filter 208
SELECT queries 216
SELECT statement 206, 208,
    250
sendToJMSQueue method
    286, 303
sendToJMSQueueHelper
    method 290
sequence diagrams 33
Service Level Agreement
    (SLA) 188
Servlet class 180
ServletConfig 181
ServletRedirector 179, 181
ServletRedirector class 180
ServletRequest 208
ServletResponse 208
servlets
    API 188
    containers 125, 189, 223, 273
    Pet Store sample 283
    remote web resources as 122
    sample method for unit
        testing 166
    server side code that calls
        EJBs 314
    testing a method 166
    unit testing 188
    writing tests for using
        Cactus 189
ServletTestCase class
    Cactus and 180, 182, 217
    extending with
        TestAdminServlet 190,
        200
    presetting database data
        with 261–262
ServletUnit 167

SessionBean class 290, 295
setConnection method 250
setContextPath method 125
setDataAccessManager
    method 245–246
setDoInput method 136
setExpectedCloseCalls
    method 256
setExpectedQueryString 256
setInitialContextFactoryBuilder
    method 297–298
setJMSUtil method 293, 297
setOrderFactory method 297
setOrderUtil method 293
setPageContext method 224,
    227
setParent method 227, 233
setResourceBase method 125
setUp methods 126–128, 130
setURLStreamHandlerFactory
    method 134
simulations, using tests to
    create 57, 133, 150
SLA (Service Level
    Agreement) 188
SocketListener class 125, 133
software accidents 72
software, testing 71
sortHTMLTable tag 228
SortHtmlTableTag class 228
SQL
    commands 210
    queries 189, 208–211
    statements 208
standard output 8
start target 319
stateless session beans 283
Statement class 248
static modifier 294
stepwise refinement 68
stop target 319
stored procedures 242
strategies/techniques for testing
    adjusting build failure
        criteria 79
    Cactus in-container 167,
        213–214
    choosing an appropriate
        260–264
    creating a component
        class 249

creating a wrapper class 249
database access layer 244
exploring alternative 58
façade 283–284
factory class 285, 293,
    303, 312
factory method 285, 289, 303,
    309, 312
mock 297
mock JNDI 285, 297–307,
    309, 312
mock object 140–141, 151,
    213, 313
stubbing 120–121, 124, 138
stress/load testing 71–75, 261
Strong, William 188
Struts 40, 77, 199, 219
StubHttpURLConnection
    class 136
StubHttpURLStreamHandler
    class 134
stubs
    choosing 124–125
    compared to mock
        objects 120, 138,
        141, 144
    creating sophisticated tests
        with 64
    how to use 121
    overview 120–121
    pros and cons 121
    replacing real code with 122
    sample use of 121–124
    stubbing connections
        134–138
    stubbing web server's
        resources 126–134
    when to use 121, 138
    white box testing and 81
StubStreamHandlerFactory
    class 134
subclasses, replacing with
    collaborators 156
suite method 34
Swing applications 283

T

tag life cycle testing
    method 227–228, 230–233
taglibs (tag libraries) 188, 216

Body tag container life
    cycle 230
EJB calling with 314
unit testing with Cactus
    224–233
unit testing with mock
    objects 233–237
TagSupport class 225
TDD (Test Driven Develop-
    ment)
    automatic documentation 69
    avoiding interface overdesign
        with 44
    best practice principle
        using 60
    core tenets 83
    defined 81
    design process 82
    effective adjustment to con-
        ventional development
        cycle 82
    elimination of refactoring
        code in unit testing
        enabling with 164
    initial step of 89
    reference book about 164
    Test First 189
    writing tests before writing
        code 189
teams, working with 120, 140
tearDown method 126–130
terrific trio 18–19
Test class, writing the 131
Test Driven Development
    (TDD) See TDD (Test
    Driven Development)
test runners 11–12, 21, 26–27,
    277
TestableJdbcDataAccessMan-
    ager class 249
TestableOrderEJB 311
TestablePetstoreEJB class 291–
    292
TestableWebClient class 154
TestAccount 82
TestAccount class 82
TestAccountService 144
TestAccountService class 144
testAddHandler method 52
TestAdminServlet 190, 200

TestAdminServlet class 192, 196, 199, 219
TestAdminServletDynaMock 246
TestAdminServletMO class 205
TestAll class 24
TestCalculator class 13, 34
TestCalculator program 18, 22, 25
TestCalculator walk-through 33
TestCallView 201
TestCase class 61
TestCases 131
  collecting results from 25
  defined 20
  extending from JUnit 13
  extracting from JUnit 13
  fixtures and 29
  for PetStoreEJB 295
  grouping for
    performance 277
  how to group 22
  objects, adding to Test
    Suites 18, 25
  requirements for 29
  running several at once 18
  test interface and 23
  TestSampleServletIntegration 180
  typical 29
  working with 28–32
  writing the 299–303
TestClass constructors version 3.8.1 16, 22
testCreateOrderOk method 299
testCreateOrderThrowsCreate-Exception method 306
testCreateOrderThrowsException method 306
testCreateThrowsOrderException method 299
TestCustomerAll 277
TestCustomerAll class 277
TestDefaultController class 46, 49–57, 101, 114
Test-Driven Development (TDD)
  failures and 192
TestDynaPropertiesMO 234
TestDynaPropertiesTag class 227

TestExceptionHandler class 57
testExecuteCloseConnectionOn Exception 258
testExecuteOk method 256
TestFailure class 25
testGetBalanceOk method 82
testGetContentOk class 153
testGetContentOk method 154, 158, 161–162
TestGetContentOkHandler class 127, 129
testGetOrderHomeFromCache method 306
test-infected programs 4, 45, 70
testing
  as first customer 62
  challenges 120
  components 167
  database access 241
  database logic 241
  effectiveness 102
  fine-grained 164, 173
  in isolation 129, 150, 164
  inside the container 167
  live database 260
  outside the container 167
  performance turning 275
  prime objective 214
  strategies 121
TestJdbcDataAccessManagerIC 261
TestJdbcDataAccessManagerIC2 276
TestJdbcDataAccess-ManagerMO1 class 250
TestJdbcDataAccess-ManagerMO3 255
TestOrderEJB 311, 328
TestOrderProcessorMDB 309
TestOrderUtil class 305
TestPetStoreEJB 299
TestPetstoreEJB class 292, 295, 325
TestPetstoreEJB.java file 315
testProcessRequest method 52, 54
TestRequest class 57–58
  constructor 59
TestRequestHandler 57
TestResponse class 49, 51, 54
TestResult 25, 27

TestRunner class 18, 20, 180
TestRunners
  Cactus and 174, 180
  combining with a TestSuite 24
  defined 19
  defining 21
  failures and 25–26
  launching tests with 20–21
  read-only database data
    and 277
  running graphical and text 11
  selecting 20
tests
  comparison of 172
  composit and command patterns and 25
  coverage 67, 79–80
  fine-grained 164
  folders 64
  simulation cases 293
  targets 93, 96, 101, 273, 321
  types of 71–77, 172
TestSampleServlet 168
TestSampleServletIntegration class 173, 180
TestSetup 128–131, 134, 145, 275–276, 297–299
TestSetup class 129
TestSortHtmlTableTag 230
testSubtract method 23
TestSuite class 18, 21–23, 131
TestSuites
  composing tests with 21–25
  customizing 23–25
  defined 19–20
  TestCustomerAll 277
  TestJdbcDataAccessManager 276
  TestSetup and 128
TestWebClient1 131
TestWebClient class 134, 137, 150, 158
TestWebClient test case 122
TestWebClient1 class 131
TestWebClientSetup1 class 129, 131
TestWebClientSkeleton class 126
TestWebSetup1 class 132
TextPad 112
Tomcat 171, 192, 273

too simple to break 7, 228
tools for analysis and
    reporting 79
transfer method 144
transparency 123
trap doors 148, 151
trial and error 250
triggers 242
try/catch block 10, 61
try/finally block 258

U

UML 33
unit of work 5, 7
unit testing
    application life cycle 76
    as first-class users 146
    co-dependent tests, problems
        with 32
    core tenet of 7
    defined 6
    description of a typical 6
    drawbacks of 166
    flavors 76
    functional 76–77
    integration 76
    interaction 76
    logic 76
    need for 66–69

old school 146
    running 20
UNIX 91, 103
updateAccount method 144
URL interface unavailability 153
URLConnection interface 123
URLStreamHandler class 134
URLStreamHandlerFactory
    class 134

V

verify method 256
version attribute 330

W

War plugin 222
war target 268
wars, creating 268
web application 222
web servers 124
WebClass methods
    getContent 150
WebClient
    refactored using
        ConnectionFactory 156
    refactored using
        MockConnectionFactory
        158

testing for failure
    conditions 132–133
verification for failure
    conditions 126
WebClient methods
    getContent 122, 150, 158
    getHttpConnection 154
    setHttpURLConnection 154
WebLogic 273
WebRequest class 224
WebResponse class 219, 224,
    232
white box testing 76, 78, 81
Windows 91, 103
Wirth, Nikolas 68
writing a failing test 83

X

XDoclet 282, 318
XP2000 140
xPetstore application
    web site 282
XSL stylesheet 99
xUnit 5

Y

YAGNI 68